G000113854

To Duncan,

Glad you got to meet the speum

in my life who "tamed me!"

Cheers, Tony

A Rising Son
In The Land of
NINE DRAGONS

*A Eurasian Boy's coming of age
during Hong Kong's Lost Era of the '50s
and '60s*

Anthony G. Tebbutt

ISBN: 0615766056
ISBN-13: 9780615766058

Cover photo of HK Harbor 1966
courtesy of Tom Briggs

Dedication

This body of work is dedicated to my children, Jason and Heather. I love you both so much and I am so proud of the young adults you have become. I hope you enjoy stories from my youth as much as I have enjoyed watching your stories unfold over the years. If others read this book and find it entertaining, well, that is an added bonus.

I also want to thank my wife Karen for all the years she kept me balanced and not too serious and analytical about life, as is my tendency.

To my Dad "Sonny," I thank him for the abundance of love I received growing up and to my brother Steve. I miss them both greatly.

Finally, many thanks to my mother, Edyth, to whom I owe so much, especially the competitive edge I wield in every aspect of my life.

Acknowledgements

There are several persons without whose encouragement and assistance, my foray into story-telling would never have come to pass. Early in the process, Linda and Skip Sweeney read my rough draft and urged me to continue. Without their enthusiasm I would have abandoned the project in its infancy. My stepfather Gus Figueiredo was also instrumental in keeping the fire burning in the early days. Later I received similar encouragement and feedback from Bunny Loftman and Ron Reemsnyder that gave me the courage to continue. My daughter Heather is such a talent and her edits and comments were invaluable, especially as she knows me so well that she can read my thoughts behind the words. Finally my editor and coach throughout the final stages of the process, thank you, Alice Eachus.

Introduction

There were a few instances that prompted writing tales describing my wild and often crazy years growing up in the fascinating city of Hong Kong.

The first event that pushed me to tell my story occurred at midnight on June 30, 1997. That was the day Hong Kong reverted back to China after one hundred and fifty years of British colonial rule.

It struck me the door had been closed to a way of life that had influenced me substantially, and that door would never again be opened for future generations to enter. I felt it would be interesting to write about a time when Oriental and Occidental lifestyles were entwined in ways never to be seen or experienced again.

I watched the transfer ceremonies on TV; they took place in pouring rain and somehow I thought it was fitting that the heavens were crying. A soul had been lost, a soul whose light had shined the brightest and strongest in Asia.

I switched off the tube and was enveloped by the darkness of the room. I was truly concerned for my homeland and for the many people I knew who had chosen to stay. The uncertainty as to what the future would hold was troubling and I wiped a tear from my eye.

As it turned out, I greatly underestimated the resiliency of the *fragrant harbor* and of the hard-working inhabitants. Under different governance, Hong Kong has successfully maintained its status as the leading commercial center in Asia.

The second event occurred a few years ago when it suddenly struck me that I had become a sexagenarian. My God! I am now greater than a half-century old and have morphed into what I used to think of as ancient. *I am an old fart!*

Like many old farts before me, I sense my visit on this earth is fading and at best my soundtrack would be playing somewhere on the "B side" of a one-hit record. With my passing, what would I leave behind? My cherished offspring would be my greatest legacy, but other than my kids, what would I leave with permanence?

Sure, there would be photographs and fond memories shared among friends and family, but I realized there would be nothing that was a testament to the spirit of my being on this earth. Nothing to document the life I had so gloriously enjoyed. Artists leave a tangible legacy with their hands, but I am not an artist. What was there that I could do to perpetuate myself beyond my mortal inheritance?

I came to the conclusion that I could write a book. But what would I write about?

How to be successful in business? No. I'm not successful enough to do that, even though by some standards I have done well. Could I write about my sports career? No! Although I am gifted with athletic prowess, I have never excelled to the degree that anybody would pay to see me play any sport, not by a long shot.

I am not blessed with the ability of the Bard or Hemingway, but I have the great fortune to carry memories founded in a fantastic childhood vastly different from what the average kid experiences. I could write about the mischievous antics of my youth! People seemed to be captivated when I shared my youthful escapades, all happening during a wonderful period in Hong Kong's history.

As you read my pages you will learn about an adolescent living in a fascinating Oriental city during a very special period in its history. My story is a mélange of my own life experiences, interwoven with imagination of what might have been. Or then again, did it all really happen? After all, I am over sixty and my memory is starting to fade.

I only hope that whoever reads my story will get a taste of the rich experience that embraced my youth. By that, I would gain a legacy beyond mere mortal existence.

And the title of this book, how did it come to be named? I grew up on the Kowloon side of the Hong Kong harbor and Kowloon translates from Cantonese to be "nine dragons." The Far East is often referred to as the "Land of the Rising Sun" and I was a "rising son" in this special place at a very special time.

CHAPTER ONE
"Boys"
DIXON AND FARRELL

I walked onto the formidable stage and sat in the chair clearly marked #1. There were fifty chairs clustered on the platform, five rows of ten, each with a nametag attached to the back. Chairs were arranged in alphabetical order by name.

Normally when names are in alphabetical order, a person's last name is used, but for some obscure reason, this day event organizers elected to sort contestants by first names. With my given name Anthony, I was designated to occupy the leadoff spot. This designation really didn't bother me; I felt sure and confident as I marched to my seat. I would just as soon go first and make the other forty-nine contestants keep up with me. That is, if they could!

The place was the Princess Theater on Nathan Road in Kowloon, Hong Kong. The year was 1960 and the occasion was the Russell Yo-Yo Championship of Hong Kong and Macau.

Hong Kong was the foremost thriving British Crown Colony and a shopper's paradise, while Macau was a small Portuguese colony about four hours away by ferry. The Princess was a grand movie theater decorated in traditional ornamental style. It was located in Kowloon, just across the road from the Miramar Hotel.

An upstairs balcony divided the theater into Loge and Dress Circle seats, very British and most fitting for a British colony. Lower level seats were generally regarded as the cheap seats and not so desirable, although the view was no better or worse than what was experienced in the upper level seating. It was a status thing, so often found in the colonies.

The movie screen was fronted by a wooden stage draped with massive velvet maroon curtains. The ceiling was painted gold and decorated with figures and ornate cones resembling beehives.

I had been to the Princess many times with my parents to watch movies and I particularly remember enjoying Tony Curtis and Burt Lancaster in *Trapeze* and Victor Mature starring in *The Robe.* The latter scared the crap out of me and I had to cover my ears because the music was shattering when the centurion cruelly pierced Christ's side with a spear.

I looked forward to going to the Princess on Saturday mornings for special viewings of cartoons. Of all the cartoons that flashed on the screen, my all-time favorite was "Lambert, the Sheepish Lion," the story of a timid and often teased lion that was raised by sheep. The storyline evolved with the birthing stork on his way to deliver Lambert to a lioness, but somehow made the mistake of delivering Lambert to a lonely, childless ewe. Once Mama Ewe had Lambert in the cradle, she refused to give him back when the mistake was discovered. Lambert loved to play with the baby lambs, but they bullied him because he was different. This caused the little lion to grow up timid and shy.

Lambert only recognized his noble lineage after a fierce sheep-eating wolf threatened his mother's life. His mother had run to the edge of a cliff to escape the wolf's ravages but the wolf was closing in to gobble her up. The terrified ewe had nowhere to go. Things looked grim, but in the nick of time, something snapped in Lambert's mind when he saw his mother's life was in serious jeopardy.

Lambert finally realized he wasn't a sheep; he was a lion, the King of All Animals!

As a cub Lambert butted heads while playing with his adopted brothers and usually ended up with a sore noggin as the result. But he was now a thousand pounds heavier and odds had shifted in his favor. Lambert let out a terrifying roar before he used a lion-sized head butt to propel the evil wolf off the edge of the cliff. Lambert came through as a hero and every time, every single time, the kids in the theater would hoot and holler when Lambert victoriously conquered the wolf.

As a kid sitting in that dark theater I would ask myself questions. *Would I come through like Lambert did when it counted? Would I be so brave?* These were serious issues for a little kid to ponder!

I was a quiet youth, a little shy, and certainly not one to seek attention. However, inside my chest I knew a courageous heart was beating and I knew I had a competitive spirit that soared. I had the ability to win, now could I channel my skills to make it happen.

As I sat on the stage at the Princess the day of the prestigious yo-yo championship, thoughts of Lambert raced through my head.

The theater was packed, but those filling the seats were not there to see a movie or cartoon that day. They were there for the grand championship yo-yo finals. After months of preliminary events held at parks and locations throughout the British Colony, this was the big event.

A huge amount was at stake for the young contestants. First prize was the unbelievable amount of seven thousand five hundred Hong Kong dollars, a whole lot of money for a kid, trust me. One US dollar was worth about six Hong Kong dollars, still this sum was more than I could imagine, especially in a place like Hong Kong.

In addition to the whopping first prize check, soccer balls, wristwatches, and a year's supply of Coca-Cola, the event's sponsor, filled the podium of prizes.

I felt good and was confident I would do well. I loved the pressure that competition brought, even at this very early age.

Charlie Corano was the reigning World Champion and had traveled from New Jersey to serve as Master of Ceremonies for our prestigious competition. Charlie confided I was his top pick to win, which made me feel good and his admission boosted my confidence. Charlie had befriended me early in the preliminary competitions and taught me tricks requiring a higher level of skill. He was now giving me moral support to bolster my assurance as the anticipated show-down was about to begin.

The only hint of my hidden anxiety was I would not let my parents come to the theater to watch me compete. They had to stay at home and wait for my phone call to give the results.

Unlike today's major happenings, the event was not televised so my parents had to wait it out. Much later Mum and Dad told me they paced like expectant parents anxiously awaiting a telephone call. Their young son was on the verge of becoming a minor celebrity in the Colony and was poised to win a significant amount of money for schooling in later years.

Finally the contestants were all seated and ready to go. The heavy velvet curtains slowly parted to reveal fifty kids filling the alphabetized chairs. Music was blaring as Charlie and the other yo-yo professionals performed tricks using both hands simultaneously in sync with the music. It was awesome to see them perform their elaborate tricks, known as two-handed loops. Yo-yos were flying everywhere to the beat of "Sweet Georgia Brown." The pros executed unbelievable maneuvers with the simple wooden toys as each would try to outdo the others by introducing variations of the trick, usually accompanied with a twist of humor. A rivalry existed among the pros as one after another they tried to one-up the others with a more spectacular trick. These talented ringers were certainly setting the stage for what was to come. Let the competition begin!

I was a young and innocent thirteen-year-old excited at the prospect of winning something big . . . something *really* big in my city of Hong Kong.

The music finally quieted. Yo-yos were shuffled into pockets and the event started with Charlie being introduced along with the other yo-yo professionals from the States. The pros were all "East Coast guys" hailing from New Jersey and New York neighborhoods. Most would be considered young Turks, all dressed in shiny silk suits accented with thin ties. These guys knew they were celebrities as they basked in glory before their Hong Kong fans. A couple weeks earlier, the visiting pros gave a special performance at my high school. They ranged in age from young twenty-twos to an old guy about forty. Barney was the name of the "old man" in the group.

On cue, Charlie put his yo-yo in his pocket, took the microphone, welcomed everybody, and laid out the contest rules. Each contestant had to perform a series of mandatory tricks without making a mistake; those with perfect scores would move on to a play-off in which they had to perform as many loop-the-loops as possible. The grand prize winner would be the boy (yo-yos were obviously a man's sport) who had a perfect score in the compulsories, followed by completing the highest number of loops.

Before the final tournament, the word on the street whispered it would take over four hundred loops to win the contest. I knew I could easily hit that number and was sure I could exceed five hundred, providing I encountered no unforeseen incident like an unexpected twisting of the string.

There were several compulsory tricks with names probably familiar to many people from that era. Tricks included The Sleeper, Walk the Dog, Around the Corner, Three-leaf Clover, Rock the Baby, Over the Falls, Flying Saucer, and Around the World. These tricks are fairly standard and easily performed by the boys who reached this stage of competition. The tricky part was to handle the mental pressure that the competitive setting and cheering audience brought to the contest. The more difficult string tricks, such the daunting Roller Coaster and Man on a Trapeze, were not part of this competition as only a few top amateurs could perform these more complicated maneuvers.

A bit of history here: The yo-yo is thought to have been around for over twenty-five hundred years and is sometimes considered the second-oldest toy in history, the oldest being the doll. Some believe ancient Greeks played with this toy and decorated the halves with drawings of their gods.

The word "yo-yo" is said to come from Tagolog, the native language of the Philippines, and means "come back." A much larger version of the yo-yo was reportedly used in the Philippines. That yo-yo had sharp edges and was used as a weapon, not a toy. I suspect that tale was nothing but folklore. Realistically, if there was a choice between using a fighting yo-yo and a big knife to save your life, which would you choose?

On one occasion my own yo-yo came close to being a weapon. My friend Rigo was hanging out at my house one day after school. I was practicing throwing my yo-yo down and away from me as hard as I could. I wanted it to spin for a long time so I could do multiple tricks. Rigo was sitting across the room reading a comic book, happily minding his own business. I threw my yo-yo down with a little extra zip and suddenly, *Snap! Whap! Ow!*

My yo-yo string had snapped. The yo-yo flew across the room and hit Rigo smack on the forehead with such speed and force that the impact almost knocked him out. I'll never forget the sound. It was like two wooden blocks crashing together like blunt cymbals.

Rigo was stunned. He stood up and staggered wildly, holding his hands to his forehead as a huge egg was laid on his head. I felt terrible and ran through the apartment to get my mum who administered first aid to the hapless victim of my attack. Fortunately my friend recovered with nothing more to show than a bruise tattooing his forehead.

Pedro Flores, a Filipino immigrant, is credited with starting a yo-yo manufacturing business, registering a patent in 1928. An entrepreneur by the name of D.F. Duncan Sr., the inventor of the Eskimo Pie, originator of the Good Humor ice cream truck, and the successful marketer of the first parking meter, saw the toy's potential and bought Flores' company.

Shortly thereafter, a major contribution to yo-yo technology followed - the looped slip string consisting of a sliding loop around the axle instead of the usual tied knot. With this improvement the yo-yo was able to spin or "sleep" when thrown out to the full length of the string. Many tricks evolved soon after.

The yo-yos we used in the Hong Kong championship tournament were made of wood and manufactured by Russell Yo-Yos. They were virtually identical to the Duncan Imperial yo-yo.

I quietly sat on my front row chair on the stage at the Princess, along with the other forty-nine contestants. I was nervous, but it was a good feeling, just like I often experienced before an important soccer or cricket match. Some boys were in bad shape and looked ready to wet their pants. I quickly dismissed them as serious competitors. Others were gazing around the stage, looking at the ceiling, or staring into space as kids often do. I mentally eliminated these air cadets as well. The kids who looked focused, alert, and a little antsy were the ones to watch out for, and fortunately I did not see too many in my field of competitors. There was one kid taller than the rest, looked older, and I had never seen him at any of the qualifying competitions. Something about his manner told me he could be a threat. The guy looked like he had a purpose in mind.

In a sudden death competition like this, who really has the advantage? The first contestant or the last? In any case, I had no choice, thanks to the first name alphabetical order prescribed. I was the leadoff contestant destined to set the standard, or quickly fall to earth.

The first trick prescribed to perform was a simple sleeper - just throw the yo-yo down and let it spin at the end of the length of string. Charlie introduced me to the audience and motioned me to the front of the stage. The audience politely clapped as I started to feel a twinge of excitement mixed with a touch of nervousness. I stood up, walked to meet the audience and completed a few practice spins.

The audience saw a nondescript kid on the small side with short, dark brown hair wearing a white cotton short-sleeve shirt bottomed with khaki shorts, white socks, and penny loafers.

My hands were not sweaty and I was feeling pretty good. I motioned I was ready to perform the trick. With a flourish, I threw the yo-yo down, let it sleep for three seconds and then retrieved it into my hand without allowing more than three inches of loose string to hang. I had started the championship competition with a perfect execution. The audience clapped and I returned to my seat to watch what the other competitors could do. If I had bobbled the trick, dropped the yo-yo, or in any way did not execute perfectly, I would have been eliminated from the competition. It was sudden death elimination in every sense. This process was repeated for each of the eight compulsory tricks.

The mandatory tricks were not really difficult to execute, but the mental pressure was excruciating. Contestant #2 had no problems with his first trick; similarly Contestant #3 breezed through his routine. The next kid wasn't so lucky. He gave the OK sign and threw his yo-yo down. The top was supposed to sleep, but something went terribly wrong and the disk shot back into his hand. The poor kid was shocked; he had probably done this trick a thousand times but messed up when it counted, leading to his elimination.

Great disappointment covered his face and as he was led behind the curtain, I could see tears streaming from his eyes.

For what seemed eternity, contestants showed their stuff, one by one and trick by trick. The pressure continued to build but I was unbothered. One after another contestant walked to the front of the stage and attempted to remain in the contest. The elimination process took well over an hour and by the time all contestants completed the last trick, the starting group had been cut to twenty-five. We entered the final stage of the championship; it was time to do consecutive loop-the-loops to see who could register the highest number and determine the winner. A loop-the-loop happens when the yo-yo is thrown out in front, returns to the body, and with a flick of the wrist is thrown out in front again, without the yo-yo touching the contestant's hand. The process is repeated so loops are continuous. This was a relatively easy trick to perform, but not when hundreds of eyes were watching, huge prizes were at stake, and prestige was on the line.

When the yo-yo craze first hit Hong Kong, I remember my parents complaining I was wasting my money and time with such a worthless pastime.

As event sponsor, Coca-Cola made sure advertising filled the local media. Advertisements first spread the word about the qualifying events held throughout Hong Kong and Kowloon, and heavier publicity followed announcing the quarter and semi-final events. Every week I anxiously looked in the newspaper for the locations of the qualifying events and showed up to participate; there was no limit the number of times a kid could participate in the early events. As time went by, I won a number of prizes - yo-yo equipment, soccer balls, and piles of Coca-Cola paraphernalia. The prizes became more valuable as the challenges progressed. I won countless fountain pens and watches and it was funny how my parents' interest revved when they realized that young Tony might just have the talent to win the big cash scholarship awarded to the Grand Prize winner.

My dad deserves a lot of credit for helping me become a skilled player.

It was Dad who realized that all yo-yos were not alike. He drove me all over the Colony to find what he considered to be superior equipment. We visited dozens of little shops scattered throughout Kowloon to find exactly the right yo-yos and string.

Most people wouldn't think that one wooden yo-yo could possibly be superior to another, but not my father. Together we determined which yo-yos had better balance, and then smoothed them with sandpaper to reduce friction, thereby preventing the string from becoming frayed and breaking prematurely.

Dad recognized that when doing loops, the length of the string was the major determining factor because eventually loops would twist the string until it became too tight to continue. He determined the longer the string, the better the chance to make more loop-the-loops. But there was a limit to just how long a string could be before too much twisting resulted in loss of control. Since yo-yo strings were specially made, we searched through plenty of toy store inventories to find the best ones.

Dad also discovered that the spindles in the center of the wooden yo-yo would eventually develop a groove due to the friction of the spinning toy. A creased spindle would negatively affect the number of loops that could be thrown. We made sure for the championship I had new, well-balanced yo-yos with smooth spindles.

The cost of a new yo-yo ran a couple Hong Kong dollars and strings cost thirty cents for a package of three. All yo-yos used in the tournament were Coca-Cola red and bore the famous logo on each side. Today yo-yos are making a cyclical comeback. New technology uses space-age plastic and alloy materials that are mind-boggling. Now a top-of-the-line yo-yo can cost one hundred and fifty US dollars!

The transition to plastics was a technical achievement that came at a price because with technology, an art form was lost. Charlie and many other champions were accomplished wood carvers. At the end of each demonstration, instead of giving autographs, the pros would pull out a pocketknife and carve their names into our wooden yo-yos. Charlie was particularly skilled and gifted me with yo-yos bearing not only his name, but intricately carved ornate patterns.

I have never been artistically gifted, and when I tried to carve the wood, all I did was slice big chunks of skin from my fingers. At my very best I could carve a vague representation of my name. There were definite limitations to my yo-yo prowess.

The eliminations were over. I now stood at the front of the stage ready to make my bid to win this event. I was a pretty small kid, about sixty-five pounds soaking wet, and one of the youngest in the competition. By all appearances I was not the likely winner.

Before throwing loops it is important to tighten the string as during the trick the string will unwind, and then rewind in the other direction, thus establishing a physical limit to the number of loops possible. To tighten the string I made my yo-yo do Flying Saucers, a trick that accomplishes the objective. After several repetitions I had a good tight string. There was nothing else to do but go for it. I signaled Charlie I was ready to begin. It would be up to me to set the target for the others.

I was really excited, but felt I was in control and focused on what I had to do. The audience seemed to grow with enthusiasm as I began to move my fingers. Soon they would have a winner. Over the roar I heard cheering and the occasional shout, "Tony!" I got the go sign from Charlie and started my loops. Charlie counted out loud, "One, two, three..."

I was focused big time and my yo-yo was spinning in top form. Once I got past the first ten loops I *knew* I was in control, everything was working like clockwork. My nervousness disappeared and months and months of rote practice took over.

One hundred loops, two hundred, three hundred! This little boy was proving to be one cool customer! I realized I was feeding off the excitement and pressure of the competition. By the time I reached four hundred loops the audience was going wild, cheering and hollering like I had never heard before. Charlie was leading the count, but the entire theater chanted with him. The number of loops I was throwing was astounding.

I can't tell you what a thrill it was to have so many people featured in my "fifteen minutes of fame." For comic relief, Charlie goofed around and plopped down on the stage, elbow resting on the floor pretending to look bored and sleepy because of the excessive time it took me to set the mark. I glanced in his direction, careful not to disrupt my rhythm and he winked. Charlie was pleased to see his protégée live up to his expectations.

"Five hundred nineteen, twenty, twenty-one, twenty-two, twenty-three, twenty-four, twenty-five…!" Finally, the yo-yo loops became erratic and the little disk jerked out of control. I was finished. My string was completely twisted; it was impossible to continue. I set the pace at a mind-blowing five hundred and twenty-five loops. I had been doing loops for almost half an hour and the crowd was still cheering wildly. Pandemonium filled the theater, nobody expected to see that many loops, especially from the very first contestant. Following procedure, the professional judges checked my equipment to make sure nothing was amiss. Somebody suddenly cried, "Uh, oh! There's a knot in the string!"

There was a hush followed by murmurs rippling through the crowd. I was horrified. I could not believe what I was hearing and almost started to cry. The rules state a knot cannot be tied at the end of the string to make it easier to do loops. There was now some question about my performance. For what seemed like hours, I stood alone and felt terrible because I knew I had not cheated. I could not understand what had happened.

The yo-yo was no longer in my hand. The professionals were huddled together carefully inspecting my toy. Finally Charlie took the microphone. He was ready to make an announcement as I was standing on my toes in nervous anticipation. Would I be disqualified?

"Ladies and gentlemen," he began. "The judges have examined the yo-yo and the string carefully and we determined the knot was caused by the tightening of the string as it wound around. There is no evidence that a knot was tied before the competition began, so the five hundred and twenty-five loops will stand."

There was a tremendous roar and cheer from the crowd and an even bigger sigh of relief from yours truly. The pros figured out what I already knew, the knot was not there when I started my first spin. I had not broken the rules. *Whew!*

I sat down and began to shake with excitement and anxiety; my heart was beating a hundred miles an hour. Now with this harrowing episode behind me, I had to wait it out while the twenty-four remaining contestants took their turn to try to beat me. Five hundred and twenty-five was an awesome number, but perhaps some other kid was up to the challenge?

For a young boy of thirteen, the next couple hours were agonizing. One by one the others threw their yo-yos to the cadence of counts. One by one they failed to match my target. Some boys were so nervous they blew it soon after starting. Others reached the hundreds before they too folded.

My biggest challenge would come from the champion of Macau. The Portuguese champion was sixteen years old and was much bigger than I was. He was also the favorite of the few professionals who had bet against me. I watched him like a hawk as he went through his routine. The young man had completed the mandatory tricks flawlessly. Now he had reached three hundred loops and still counting, the closest to my record so far. As he reached the four hundred mark, I noticed his string was rapidly tightening. This was a good sign for me as it meant it was only a matter of time before it would be impossible for him to continue. He obviously did not know what Dad had taught me about equipment; his string was probably slightly shorter than the one I had used. He continued for a short time before his yo-yo spun out of control.

On that one day in time I was just too good. The runner-up managed four hundred and twenty loops, not even close to my five-twenty-five.

I won! I was the champion! Ecstatic, I walked to the front of the stage with the judges raising my arms like a champion prizefighter. Charlie officially declared me the Yo-yo Champion of Hong Kong and Macau. The crowd cheered wildly; I wanted my glory day to go on and on. But, as all good things, it had to end and finally the curtain closed over the stage.

A reception was going on across the way at the Miramar Hotel where we were all celebrated. The first thing I did was to find a telephone so I could call my parents and tell them the good news. Needless to say, they were thrilled, but sad they missed my moment in the sun.

Mum and Dad arrived at the reception soon after to mingle with celebrities from the Colony. Both English and Chinese press covered the event; I was interviewed in English and had my photograph taken with the Managing Director of Coca-Cola when he presented me with the check for seven thousand five hundred dollars. Microphones surrounded me as reporters asked about my school, favorite subjects, teachers, pastimes, and especially what I wanted to be when I grew up.

It was fun being the center of such attention. I basked in the adulation, but my shyness enveloped me as I answered questions. It would be the first time my name and picture appeared in newspapers. It felt good and I thought to myself that I would really like to repeat this celebrity experience. Today those pictures have a place of honor in my scrapbook and my parents wisely invested the winnings for me in IBM stock, which led to a nice nest egg later in my life. For weeks I was a minor celebrity and was asked to show my yo-yo tricks wherever I went. At school the teachers recognized my accomplishment in front of the entire class. Even adults asked for a demonstration of my skills and I always complied.

I felt pretty good about myself. The event boosted my self-esteem and self-confidence, something that would serve me well in my formative years. The yo-yo championship was my first major achievement and started me on a lifelong track that led me to accept no less than my very best at anything I tried. I had a taste of winning big and it encouraged me to believe in myself. From that point on, I was fitted with a personal barometer to measure how my life was going…I would be either winning or losing.

Life at thirteen was fabulous!

CHAPTER TWO
"Do You Want To Know A Secret?"
JOHN LENNON AND PAUL MCCARTNEY

I was born Anthony Gordon Tebbutt in Hong Kong on September 14, 1947 to Sonny and Edie.

Four years later my brother Steven Graham arrived to complete our family circle. Like most brothers do, we fought. Steve and I had very different interests, but we were also very close. I was the jock and Steve was the rock musician in our family. We were both darn good in our chosen areas of interest.

Dad and Mum were both born and raised in Shanghai, which in the 1920s was a cosmopolitan trading center similar to what Hong Kong eventually became. It was a vibrant commercial port for China and the Far East. Dad's father was born to English parents in Taiwan and his mother was born in Shanghai of mixed Asian and American descent. Mum's dad was an English riverboat captain who met his Japanese wife on a voyage to Nagasaki and whisked her off to Shanghai.

Sadly, I realize I don't really know much about my grandparents. I know little about their youth, where they grew up, what was special to them, what their talents were, or what they were like as individuals.

Both grandfathers died before I was born and my grandmothers lived in Japan and Canada, quite far away from our home in Hong Kong. There were no diaries or memoirs to read and few photographs to study. I know virtually nothing of my grandparents' youth and not much more about their adulthood. I feel somewhat cheated by this absence.

Today when asked my background, I usually say "Heinz 57" because there's a lot of variety in my gene pool - English, Japanese, Chinese, and Canadian.

My parents attended high school in Shanghai, but never had the opportunity to go to college. However, they worked hard and long to provide our family with a solid middle-class way of life. People of mixed heritage, such as my parents, were often referred to as "Eurasian."

Dad's real name was Claude, but everyone knew him as Sonny. He didn't complete high school because he had to go to work following the death of his father. Just before his senior year, Dad left school to find work at the British American Tobacco Company in Shanghai. He began as a lowly clerk, but through hard work eventually became the purchasing manager for the cigarette factory in Hong Kong.

At the time I thought a purchasing manager was surely one of the company's top executives and I wanted to be just like my famous father. In my eyes my dad was a giant among men. I loved going to his office located in a big red building on the waterfront in Wanchai. I'd sit in his chair pretending to be Mr. Big before accompanying my dad to meet his colleagues and see the cigarette machinery in action. The smell of tobacco hung heavy in the air; I never did enjoy the smell and thus have never been a smoker. Tobacco was a provider for our family in those early years, but a "taker" in the long run because it brought my dad to a premature death from heart disease at the young age of 52.

Dad was a gentle, kind man who was incredibly patient and understanding. From him I learned that there are always two sides to a coin. Once I had an argument with a girlfriend and told my dad about it, expecting his support for my cause. I became extremely frustrated with him because he seemed to take my girlfriend's side against mine. What he did was teach me to see things from another person's perspective, a skill I've retained to this day and has served me well in business dealings.

Dad would frequently taxi my friends and me to soccer games but was a relatively silent cheerleader when I played sports. It wasn't his style to shout and cheer madly like the other parents did, but when I performed well on the field, I knew he was beaming on the sidelines. My friends all liked my dad. I was extremely proud of him and we had a wonderful father-son relationship.

My mother Edyth was, and still is, a beautiful, intelligent woman, even today at 92 years of age. She was the parent from whom I inherited my drive, ambition, and high standards. Because of my mother's relentless pursuit of perfection, I honestly don't think I can ever be fully satisfied with any achievement; I always wonder if there is room for improvement. Obviously such expectations to achieve perfection have positive and negative components, as I was to discover in my life's journey.

When I was young, Mum gave me a framed copy of Kipling's poem "If" and I displayed it by my bedside. That poem strongly influenced my thinking; the words truly set standards for me to reach. My mother was clearly the driving force for me to attain the best education possible. Mum never had the opportunity to attend college, but I am convinced she would have excelled if given the chance. She wanted me to have what she did not and pushed me to achieve academically.

Mine was a working mum, possibly the most successful executive assistant in Hong Kong. Her casual title was "Girl Friday" and she was the right hand to one of the wealthiest and most influential industrialists in the Colony. Her office was located in a corner of the St. George's Building, adjacent to her employer Lord Kadoorie. Mum's office had a spectacular view of the Hong Kong harbor. How many executive assistants have you known who were chauffeured to work in a Bentley? Mum certainly didn't have a routine or boring job. No son could ask for two more loving and understanding parents, and I often murmur a quick thank you to the man upstairs for such a wonderful gift.

During WW II my parents were interned in a Japanese civilian camp outside Shanghai. Several years ago, Steven Spielberg made a movie based on J.D. Ballard's memoir *Empire of the Sun*. Ballard's work gives a good presentation of the situation non-Chinese civilians faced in Shanghai during the war. My parents' camp internment was under the authority of the Japanese Consular Corps, and was heavy with restrictions placed on those living in the camp. Although not unduly severe like a military POW camp, internment was definitely not a pleasant experience. Occupants were not mistreated, but it was made clear if they tried to escape they would be shot. Fortunately no one met this end as far as I could determine.

Early every morning a camp roll call sounded and occupants had a strict 9:00 p.m. curfew. Duties were assigned for cooking, laundry, hospital, and other chores. Occupants had enough food, but the variety was limited to variations of pork stew. Occasionally there were reports of contaminants in the food, such as weevils or mouse droppings.

While in camp my father was the chief cook and baker, a responsibility he enjoyed. Fortunately he passed his culinary talents on to me. Give me a glass of wine and a well-stocked kitchen and I guarantee I'll whip up a meal to make your taste buds sizzle.

I was surprised to learn inmates were allowed to enjoy Saturday night dances. My dad played the clarinet in the ragtag band.

There were 750 civilian prisoners kept in "Camp Yangchow C" for 30 months from March 1943 until the war's end in August 1945. Other family members were interned, including my paternal grandmother Cecile, and my dad's sisters Maud, Edie, and Babs.

After the war ended, the communist wave swept over China and my family knew they had to leave Shanghai. Fortunately the British American Tobacco Company transferred Dad to Hong Kong where he ultimately remained for the rest of his career. Most people left Shanghai with only minimal belongings; anything of value was confiscated by the communists at departure. There were stories of people melting gold and casting the precious metal into buttons sewed onto cardigans and smuggled out of the country. There had to be a wide range of unique methods used to smuggle treasures out of Communist China in those days.

I love and respect my parents greatly and I am so very, very grateful to be their son. They raised me in liberal ways, but still managed to instill strong values and an unwavering sense of right and wrong. I enjoyed considerable freedom growing up in Hong Kong, but that was not atypical of local-born children. Most of my friends from middle-class families experienced wide space and freedom in their youth. In a spicy, active city like Hong Kong, we were given more leeway than the average teenager growing up in the States or England. We took full advantage of that!

Growing up in Hong Kong in the '60s was a blast. There was so much to explore, so much to taste in this city of tantalizing delights! Many parents would be horrified at the freedom I enjoyed as a teenager, probably thinking I had an immoral upbringing. Nothing was further from the truth! We certainly had liberal nurturing, but we were strongly guided by our parents' value systems that clearly distinguished mischievous from bad behavior.

I was also heavily influenced by Catholicism featuring a practice which required incredible penance in the form of catechism classes taught by the Maryknoll nuns twice a week. The "black and whites" scared me silly and I was convinced that if Hell wasn't a reality, I would surely end up in Purgatory at best. A favorite ploy was to ask sister how children were conceived and watch her face go bright red. My pragmatic side often led me to amass an inventory of Days of Forgiveness by reciting hundreds of Our Fathers and Hail Marys. I wasn't taking any chances! At confession I'd spill my guts about naughty thoughts starring my third grade PE teacher. In my mind, every little fib would grow into a huge evil, grievous lie if I didn't admit to it weekly. Those Franciscan priests and Maryknoll nuns scarred me for life!

.

CHAPTER THREE
"There's a Place"
JOHN LENNON AND PAUL McCARTNEY

I did not feel good about myself during my pre-teen years. I struggled with my identity growing up in Hong Kong because it was "cool" to be from abroad, especially if you could say you were from England or the USA. I was just a local boy with few distinguishing characteristics.

Prejudice exists in every society, and Hong Kong was no exception. Prejudice just took a slightly different twist from what existed in Great Britain or the United States. Living in a British Crown Colony, the nation with which we most closely identified was England.

The Governor of Hong Kong was appointed by Her Majesty the Queen, and all senior civil servants were also from the British Isles. Many business leaders were American expatriates.

Since we lived in a British Colony, it was no surprise that my childhood idols were English sports stars. The Michael Jordans of my time were English cricketers - Ted Dexter and Freddy Trueman and soccer players like Jimmy Greaves and Bobby Charlton. During this period in my life, I'd spend hours staring in the mirror growing upset because I saw mixed-Asian features looking back at me. I was not from the Motherland they taught about in school. Many boys I played with were from England, and occasionally one would let me know I was just a local, and by inference was different, perhaps not quite their equal.

Due to youthful ignorance, I didn't recognize the benefits that would come to me years later because I was able to move across cultures easily. I was neither Asian nor European. I was Eurasian and exposed to the benefits of both cultures. Today I am secure in my thoughts and representations of "self" and realize that instead of being cursed as a descendent of mixed heritage, I am unbelievably blessed. But, if you had asked me how I felt about myself in those early days, I'd have told you I wished I was born in England with blue eyes and blond hair.

Hong Kong was adapted from a Chinese word, and translated means "Fragrant Harbor." When one spoke of Hong Kong it usually meant the collective areas comprised of Hong Kong Island, Kowloon peninsula, and the New Territories, which shared borders with China. The combined area equals 426 square miles, 90 percent of which encompassed the New Territories.

The population of the Colony was 95 percent Chinese and five percent other ethnic origins. That five percent included Europeans, Americans, Australians, and an assortment of expatriates. Also included in that grouping were East Indians and Pakistanis, of which there was a large community living in Hong Kong at the time. The population was concentrated in Hong Kong and Kowloon.

Also within the five percent was my small group which was positioned somewhere in between. Neither Chinese nor expatriate, we were the "locals" born in Hong Kong and of diverse ethnic backgrounds.

Like most locals, I spoke Cantonese fluently, but never formally studied the language and thus never learned to read or write it. I attended a British school and English was the mother tongue we spoke in my home. Cantonese was the dialect spoken in the province of Canton in the South of China. Mandarin was the official language of the Peking government and was spoken by the more educated Chinese.

I learned to speak Cantonese from the maids who raised me. They were my *amahs,* but I couldn't understand one word of Mandarin and neither could they. Almost every family had several *amahs* to raise the children and do the housework; many became very integrated into the family. Cultural barriers did not allow the development of familial ties frequently seen with Western nannies, however I grew fond of Ah Tsun who was the poor soul who had to wake me up throughout my high school years. She did not speak a word of English, which in turn helped to develop my fluency in Cantonese.

One of our *amahs* named Ah Sum raised my dad in Shanghai and after the war left Shanghai to rejoin our family in Hong Kong. Ah Sum never liked me very much and showed obvious favoritism to Steve which caused occasional problems. Our cook's name was Ah Woo. He was quite a character, exceptionally talented in his preparation of meals from multiple countries, but also thought he knew everything there was to know about cooking and would drive my dad crazy with his inability to explain the monthly food expenditures.

In the West we think of maids as only for the wealthy, but in the Far East having household help was the way of life for almost every family except the very poor. Because I had a working mum, we had two *amahs* and a cook and they lived with us in maids' quarters in the back of our apartment. Their rooms were tiny, just big enough for a bed and perhaps a few shelves, but all seemed happy, especially because they were able to save money to help their extended families.

Their families lived in small apartments in another part of town and our *amahs* would frequently travel to visit them. Almost everybody lived in apartments; living in a house was a tremendous luxury enjoyed only by the very wealthy and a few expatriates. We were lucky our apartment was located in the affluent neighborhood of Kadoorie Avenue and was larger than most, probably three thousand square feet boasting four bedrooms and three bathrooms. This compared handsomely to the average apartment consisting of eight to twelve hundred square feet most families occupied.

Our home was in the Kowloon district, which translates as Nine Dragons. It was said the nine dragons represented nine prominent hills, although I never figured out just where they all were located. Our luxury apartment was one compensation perk my mother earned working for a very special family – the Kadoories.

Hong Kong was a wonderful place to grow up in the 1950s and 1960s. We were exceptionally cosmopolitan and very aware of everything going on in the rest of the world. We knew all about the Beatles and Disneyland, while growing up in a British colonial setting that still held vestiges of "old China." It was the best of both worlds. With the ability to speak Cantonese and with looks that were neither pure Chinese nor pure European, I grew up playing with friends from all walks of life, from the wealthiest golden boys to the poorest street urchins.

I clearly remember the street merchants of the late 1950s. On any given day, I might hear a bell ringing and the singsong call of a Chinese knife sharpener walking through neighborhoods in search of a few cents to be earned by sharpening kitchen knives. If he was lucky enough to find a cook who needed his services, he would proudly produce his special sharpening stone, pour water on it, and repeatedly slide the blade until he was satisfied the job was done well.

We also had entertainment provided by the "monkey man," the Chinese version of an organ grinder. The monkey man would walk through neighborhoods with his little furry friend until enough people gathered for him to start his show. He would hold a tall pole upright and swing the monkey round and round at the end of a long piece of rope, faster and faster. The little simian would ride a miniature bicycle, pickpocket his master, and have the children and their *amahs* squealing with laughter. At the end of the performance, the monkey would take off his little hat and hold it out for us to deposit a few coins or the occasional dollar bill.

Our early exposure to R- rated entertainment involved an old man carrying a big black suitcase. Out of his mysterious suitcase would appear beautifully colored clay figures of Chinese opera players impaled on sticks. The vivid hues of yellow and red were particularly brilliant and I always wondered what clay concoction the old man used to make his little people so vibrant. It certainly wasn't typical modeling clay commonly known as plasticine. The old man's clay had a distinctive pungent smell signaling it was homemade, perhaps with ingredients including flour and rice. The clay had a short lifespan as it had a tendency to dry and become brittle.

Deeper in the black bag were models of men and women in compromising positions that would draw giggles from kids who, even at an early age, were well aware of sex. I don't think our parents ever knew we inspected these naughty clay figurines so carefully. For a few coins I purchased several coupling models and hid them in my bedroom closet. I would take them out when alone, absolutely fascinated how the bodies fit together. It looked so gross and I could not believe my parents would ever do *anything* like that.

Not only did we have street entertainment, we had street goodies to eat. Often food merchants would come through our neighborhood peddling their wares, offering everything from roasted chestnuts and deep-fried bean curd to Chinese *tucks*. A *tuck* was the nickname given to Chinese snacks like *wa muis* which are very salty dried plums. *Wa muis* are light brown in color, wrinkled, and have a hard pip in the center. They are covered with salt, enough to make saliva glands go orgasmic.

We also enjoyed sweet sticky plums called *chum ping muis* and dried orange peels. The deep-fried bean curd the merchants peddled had an obnoxious smell, but if you could get by the stench, the curd tasted delicious, especially with a dab of red chili slathered on it. The Chinese translation for bean curd was *smelly to-fu*.

Another dish peddled in the neighborhood was *chee cheung fun* which is a wide, flat rice noodle about six inches long and folded to contain shrimp or pork. Traditionally the noodle would be served with soy sauce and a dash of sesame oil. Both tofu and *chee cheung fun* would be paraded through neighborhoods on bamboo poles carried on a food merchant's shoulders with cookers and supplies balancing on each end. This was a scene often portrayed as very stereotypically Chinese.

During my early childhood, playing marbles was a popular pastime. It was a game that could be played on any sandy patch. Sadly, playing marbles has long been replaced by video games.

A game of marbles was an excellent way to make friends because anybody could join a local game provided they had a few marbles they could afford to lose. It wasn't unusual for several of my English friends and I to be playing on the street and have Chinese boys join the game, always thinking they would take us for a ride. Needless to say, many were sorely mistaken as I was a crack shot and easily collected a sack of marbles from challengers. If it was a competitive game requiring physical skill, I was good at it. Often the best players were the poorest

Chinese boys who could ill afford to lose their precious agates. Over games I befriended a few of them. That was how I first met Chow Chai.

I was ten years old and city workmen had just finished building Nairn House, a British Government Housing apartment complex where many expatriates lived. Most worked for the Public Works Department, or PWD as it was more commonly known.

Before we moved to the apartment on Kadoorie Avenue, we lived in the apartments next to the China Light & Power Company offices on Argyle Street. Nairn House was directly across the road at the junction of Argyle Street and Waterloo Road. Roger Poynton lived at Nairn House; he was the son of a British bureaucrat. Roger and I became good friends because we were both athletic and loved to play soccer and cricket. We were also good at marbles.

One afternoon we were cleaning up by whipping all-comers, especially a bespectacled, redheaded boy by the name of Michael Bell. It was almost cruel to play with Michael because he was such a rotten shot and literally lost hundreds of marbles to Roger and me.

Play was taking place on a sandy piece of land that was destined to become a sidewalk, but for now served as the "Marble Stadium of Kowloon." As we played, I noticed a street urchin watching us shoot. His eyes were transfixed on the bounty of pretty agates.

One of the British kids yelled at him. "Oy, chink, what the hell do you want? Bugger off."

"Wait," I said. "He's not hurting anyone and it looks like he just wants to play with us. We shouldn't mind if he wants to lose marbles, his are as good as yours."

I turned to the kid in bare feet standing close by. He wore tattered shorts that at one time had presumably been khaki, but were now muddy brown; he wore no shirt.

The kid was scruffy and dirty, but there was something in his eyes that caught my attention, a fire that was difficult to describe. I spoke to him in Cantonese, "Do you want to risk your marbles by playing with us? You are sure to lose!"

He responded by moving his head, nodding yes. "What is your name?" I asked.

"I am called Chow Chai. And what is your name?" I was surprised by his casual response; he did not seem at all intimidated by the non-Chinese surrounding him. Chow Chai was a nickname that translated meant Son of Chow.

"My name is Tony," I said with a smile and then introduced Chow Chai to the others who didn't seem keen to meet him, except Roger who nodded a friendly greeting. Chow Chai tried to say my name many times, but the best he could do was mutter *Tong-nay* but I felt that was close enough.

With introductions over, we proceeded to play a serious game of marbles. Four of us were in the game and the rules were quite simple. Each player put ten marbles into the circle. We would "lag throw" our shooting marble to a line about ten feet away. The closest to the line would be the first to shoot, and the order of shooters would follow.

Throwing our shooters from the line back at the circle, we would start knocking marbles out of the circle without the shooter marble entering into the circle's perimeter.

Beginning this game, I was closest to the line, followed by Chow Chai. Between the two of us, we cleared almost the entire circle before the other players had a chance to shoot. This went on for another half dozen games, the pattern repeating itself, except Chow Chai and I would alternate between shooting first and shooting second.

Before long we cleaned up and there were no more marbles to be won. I won so many marbles that day that I had to carry them in a small bag. Chow Chai had his pockets crammed with his newly won treasures. Game over, I smiled at my new friend and congratulated him on playing well, to which he responded with a huge toothy grin as he stood to leave.

"Where the hell do you think you're going?" screamed John as he grabbed Chow Chai by the arm. John was the group bully so this was no surprise.

"Give over those marbles, *chink*, I want them, and I want them now!" Chow Chai did not know what to do. He didn't understand English, but he was smart enough to figure out what was going on. He looked terrified.

"Leave him alone!" I ordered. "He won those marbles fair and square, just because you aren't good enough to win, you shouldn't take them away from him."

Alone I didn't have much chance against John, but Roger stood tight beside me and like most bullies, John backed off when the odds weren't in his favor. Chow Chai looked at me with his deep dark eyes and without uttering a word, I knew he was saying thank you. I made a new friend that day. Chow Chai turned and ran down the road, dropping a few marbles from his pockets as he escaped. I thought he probably lived in one of the squatter settlements on Homantin Hill.

From that day on I saw Chow Chai quite often. He would watch us play marbles, but only as a spectator. I think he knew it was better that he not cross into the world of the *gwai-los,* the Chinese term for foreigners that literally translates as "foreign devils."

One afternoon after we finished playing, we visited the ice cream man stationed across the street to buy Popsicles. I could tell from the way Chow Chai was eyeing us that this was a luxury he could not afford. I dipped into my pocket and paid ten cents for another iced treat which I gave to him. The smile crossing his face was priceless and one I will always remember. My newest friend enjoyed that Popsicle as if it was the most special treat in his life, ever.

We played marbles close to Homantin, a community boasting a Chinese food market and several typical Chinese shops. Homantin Hill also had a commune of squatters and I learned this was where Chow Chai lived.

Chow Chai and I would frequently walk to Homantin and wander through the village, then climb to the hillside housing the community of squatters. The very poor lived amid squalor in shacks we called "squatter huts." The huts were built on barren hillsides and were usually not much more than lean-tos with corrugated iron roofs. Water was fetched from a spout somewhere at the bottom of the hill so conditions were far from hygienic. There were no sewers, only ditches overloaded with trash and human waste. Dogs would be forever roaming these ramshackle habitats looking for whatever they could scavenge.

Hong Kong faced constant illegal immigration of refugees from China, which became Communist in 1949. Despite border patrols on land and on sea, hundreds of thousands would find their refuge in the Colony. Many illegals had no money or a place to stay, so they congregated in crowded squatter communities. Every so often, terrible fires destroyed squatter homes and hundreds of inhabitants died. Occasionally, fires were deliberately set by desperately poor people who knew the destruction of their hovels would force the government to relocate victims to subsidized tenement apartments.

Every squatter community was a fireman's nightmare due to the cardboard and plywood building materials used for construction. Once a fire started, a whole village could be razed in a matter of minutes with many lives lost.

Another threat the poor faced were devastating typhoons (translated as big winds), known as hurricanes in the West. These storms could wipe out entire settlements in a matter of hours. When I was growing up, typhoons were graded for intensity by a signal rating of 1 to10; today they are rated on the Saffir-Simpson scale from 1 to 5.

I have vivid memories of standing safely on our apartment verandah during a howling Signal #8 storm with winds approaching 150 mph and watching the horizontal rain carry advertising signs through the air as if they were made of Styrofoam. Standing safe on my veranda in a solid brick building, I found it exhilarating to watch nature's full fury pounding the streets below. The passing of the eye of the storm fascinated me when relative calm settled serenely before the vicious return of wind and rain.

As dangerous as I knew it could be, I often walked around the streets viewing devastation to the landscape, sometimes basking in an eerie light when the sun poked through holes in the clouds. But for thousands of people, typhoons were not so intriguing; they would bring heartache, devastation, and all too often, death.

Chow Chai was a small gutsy boy who obviously had to fight for everything in life. Once he invited me to the squatter hut where he lived with his parents and two younger brothers. It was a typical shack built of plywood and topped with a corrugated iron roof. The hut contained a single room with thin quilt bedding covering the floor.

In one corner a small kerosene stove stood, an accident just waiting to happen. No running water or toilet in this shack, just a bucket of water that had to be carried from the community tap at the bottom of the hill.

Chow Chai admitted he had an older sister, but she had run away from home and was working in a bar in Wanchai. Wanchai was famous for its bars and brothels - an unfortunate place where many uneducated, jobless, and homeless girls found a place to ply their ancient trade.

One day we were climbing a sprawling tree on Homantin Hill. As Chow Chai put his hand on a branch to pull himself up, I noticed a very distinctive scar on the back of his right hand. It was circular and very deep. Looking at it from a certain angle, the scar resembled a shining sun. I asked my friend how he got the scar and he told me older boys in his village often bullied the younger ones. The bullies asked him to steal items from a store and he refused.

For his refusal, they punished him by inflicting a cigarette burn on the back of his hand. Hearing this story was beyond my comprehension; I came from a middle-class background and was raised in beautiful surroundings and showered with love. Later that night when I was in bed, I told my father about what I had seen and heard that day. I started to cry because I felt so bad for Chow Chai and the life he suffered. Dad explained that there were people in this world who were not very nice and warned I should avoid them. From that night on, I always had one eye open for mean-looking people with cigarettes dangling from their fingers.

Almost everybody loves Chinese food and Hong Kong has some of the best in the world. When I think of the stuff I casually bought from street vendors, I now realize I must have developed a tremendous resistance to local bacteria, the effect of which would make Mexico's Montezuma's Revenge look like child's play.

I loved to buy large rocks of raw sugar crystal from a merchant in Homantin Village and suck it like candy. The crystal was the size of a baseball and was streaked with veins of white and yellow.

Adjacent to the official market were several street stalls serving tasty noodles in boiling soup broth; this went on 24 hours a day. Hanging from scaffolding were selections of fowl and animals, often with their necks cut so they could bleed out before being cooked or roasted. This scene would be the worst nightmare for anyone overly concerned with hygiene or the humane treatment of animals.

Of course Chinese food is known throughout the world for its wonderful variety and exquisite, sometimes unusual, taste. Walking into my favorite Kowloon Restaurant on Nathan Road near the Shamrock Hotel, the smell of garlic, onions, soy, and ginger would almost knock me over. Shark fin soup was a delicious way to start a meal, followed by an assortment of meats and vegetables cooked to perfection. Cantonese, Hakka, Shanghainese, Szechuan, and many more Chinese provinces were represented, each with its own unique style of cooking. Strange, but as a child I did not particularly care for Chinese food even though I love it today.

Throughout my life, people I met often assumed I was raised in a Hong Kong household eating traditional Chinese meals every day. This was not the case; in fact we would have a traditional Chinese meal only once a week, usually on Sunday for lunch. The rest of the time I wanted to eat Western foods like spaghetti and roast beef. I was convinced I didn't like Chinese food as much as I did Western cuisine, perhaps due to my insecurity about being an ordinary local boy.

People also assumed my family was fluent in Chinese, but again this was not the case. My dad and I spoke Cantonese (a dialect of Southern China) fluently, while my brother Steve spoke only a few phrases and my mother spoke none. Yes, we were living in Asia, but as a very typical British family.

In my later years when I came upon someone who demonstrated immense ignorance about Asia, Hong Kong in particular, I might weave a tale of how I was raised on a sampan fishing boat. I told of being tied to the anchor chain and existing on a diet of fish heads and rice. Another favorite tale reserved for those who thought Hong Kong was located smack in the middle of Japan - my patience strained - I would whisper I was of Mongolian descent.

Visiting the open Chinese food market in Tsim Sha Tsui was an assault on all the senses, particularly the olfactory. It was not a place to go if you had a queasy stomach. Every type of fish and meat was displayed for sale on wooden tables that stood on cement floors. The market was a multi-story, brick building that had no windows, thank goodness. If there had been windows confining all the different odors, the effect would have been nauseating, especially in Hong Kong's hot and humid summer months.

Exotic game, reptiles, and assorted sea creatures were on display throughout the market. Contrary to what is often believed, dog meat was illegal and could only be found at underground establishments frequently raided by the police. Most of these unsavory establishments were located in the New Territories; the town of Shatin seemed to be particularly notorious.

For reasons I never understood, black Chow dogs were preferred by those who had a taste for dog meat. A market like Tsim Sha Tsui would never pass today's Western health inspection standards, but it was a fascinating place to shop for food, provided you could stand the smell and gory sight.

Next to the Tsim Sha Tsui market, one of the best-known herbalists in Kowloon kept a shop. If you have never visited a Chinese herbalist establishment, it is a fascinating experience. From floor to ceiling dozens and dozens of little wooden drawers are stacked, housing ingredients ranging from roots and leaves to more exotic fare like Rhino tusk, tiger penis, and bear paw. There was something to treat every conceivable ailment from the common cold to lack of sexual drive. All prescriptions could be found in an herbalist's lair. Concoctions for a cold usually took the form of leaves and twigs to be boiled in water and then taken like a tea.

Body parts of larger animals were often associated with remedies for sexual complaints . . . the original Viagra!

My paternal grandma lived with us on Argyle Street for a few years during my early childhood before moving to Toronto, Canada. She was born in Shanghai and would frequently drink herbal potions after complaining she had *yeet heh* which means "hot blood." Hot blood would be the explanation for all physical problems from pimples to generally feeling poorly. A good potion would "cool the blood" and make one feel better.

Growing up we consulted English doctors usually trained in London, but there was a time I remember going with Grandma to the herbalist because I had *yeet heh,* taking the form of a festering boil on my leg. I don't think Grandma told my parents she was taking me to the other side of town, but I'm not really sure they would have objected to her mission.

My grandmother dragged me into the Tsim Sha Tsui herbalist's store and spoke in Cantonese to the man sequestered behind the glass display case. Grandma instructed me to show him the boil on my leg and I complied. He examined the hot-looking enormous pimple mounding on my thigh and reached into one of the many drawers behind him to extract his choice of ingredients.

We went home and Grandma boiled the prescribed herbal mixture in water and let it cool for a few minutes. I remember drinking a vile steaming drink as Grandma unwrapped another rolled paper package and applied an ungodly-looking hot paste poultice on my thigh to draw the crud from my carbuncle. After a few hours the boil came to a pus-filled head and when Grandma squeezed the offending lump with a warm towel, it erupted like a mini-Vesuvius.

Today scientists are discovering many ancient cures used by herbalists contain the same active ingredients used in modern-day drugs. Start-up drug companies have been formed to explore these opportunities. Most exotic animal parts once used are now banned (or at least not publicly available) due to the threat of extinction of many species.

Not all our tasty treats were Chinese; we were also crazy about world-wide childhood pleasures like ice cream and chocolate. My primary source for the latter was a great man by the name of Lam Ming.

Lam Ming was an ice cream vendor for the Dairy Farm Company. He rode a specially equipped bicycle with an ice cream freezer built onto the front of the frame. Lam Ming would park his bike everyday in the same spot on my route home from school, a shady space leading to the driveway for Nairn House where many of my school chums lived.

In addition to ice cream, Lam Ming sold chocolate and candies. To this day, my all time favorite candy is Cadbury's Milk Flake, which unfortunately is only available in England and her former colonies. My friends and I would stop and spend our money with this friendly man and if we were short, credit would be extended. Pretty unusual, an ice-cream vendor giving credit to ten year-olds, but he was never cheated, not once! Lam Ming was an institution when I was growing up; he was a very kind man and a friend who seemed very happy with his simple life riding his bicycle around the streets of Kowloon. Ice cream sellers were often darkly tanned and had knotted calves from riding their bicycles for many years, but today they exist only in our memories.

Kids today must wonder what we used to do in the olden days before the advent of X-Box, computers, amusement parks, and malls. When I was eight or nine, a typical pastime I enjoyed with my friends was climbing the hills across the street from our apartment. There was always something to find in those hills and one of our favorite spots to explore was a tunnel we discovered during our exploration of the hillside. The tunnel was about thirty or so yards from one end to another.

The tunnel appeared to be relatively safe from collapse and we were able to crouch and walk through to the other side. The far end overlooked a vegetable field that had been cultivated by a peasant farmer, measuring roughly 40x80 yards. Mostly carrots filled the field.

One day my friend Roger and I hid inside the tunnel and plotted a bit of mischief. When the farmer wasn't looking, we jumped out of the tunnel, ran down to the carrot patch, grabbed a handful of the golden spikes, and quickly ducked back into the cover of the tunnel.

Safe from discovery, we'd slip our Cub Scout pocketknives from our pockets, shave the skin off the carrots, and munch on them like Bugs Bunny. It wasn't that the carrots tasted particularly good, it was the thrill of the hunt that captured our imaginations.

This great adventure was repeated several times, until the day we discovered how the Chinese peasant farmer fertilized his field.

Let me tell you, the fertilizer he spread was a far cry from the Monsanto agri-chemicals that come in nice shiny printed bags. On that day of rude awakening we noticed the farmer used a bucket to scoop something from a large wooden tub located at the far end of the field. He mixed the bucket holdings with water and poured the concoction into two smaller watering cans. In the classic stereotypical pose of Asian farmers, he carried both cans, one on each side, hung on a stick over his shoulders as he walked through the fields pouring the dark mixture onto his crops.

Our curiosity piqued, Roger and I *had* to see what was in the mysterious wooden tub. We patiently waited inside the tunnel for the right opportunity when the farmer wandered off to tend to another matter. We jumped out of our hiding place, scrambled along the edge of the field, and made our way to the wooden tub. A heavy wooden plank covered the tub and we quickly lifted it, only to be greeted with an ungodly sight and smell.

Crawling inside the vat were thousands of maggots gorging themselves on feces lining the bottom of the vessel. It was nauseating. Roger and I almost threw up on the spot, but were so mesmerized by the hideous dancing brew that we almost didn't see the farmer running toward us. He was yelling a torrent of Chinese swear words.

"Dew nei lo mo," the man screamed as we raced for our tunnel sanctuary. We reached the mouth of the tunnel and quickly made our way to the safety of the other side as we knew the farmer would not abandon his field to chase us. To this day my appetite for carrots has never equaled that of other garden vegetables.

Oh yes, the hill across the street offered a world of adventure and occasionally an interesting discovery! As kids are wont to do, we poked around searching for secret caves and mysterious artifacts. One day we were rewarded with a small earthen pot snuggled in a crevice deep in the hillside. Not knowing what to expect, we emptied the contents of the pot and discovered a collection of interesting items.

Inside the vessel were old Chinese coins and a strange earthy chalk mixture. We had discovered a burial pot containing ashes and bone fragments of a Chinese peasant, most likely a farmer. Along with his remains, a few coins were put in the pot to provide the departed one with currency for the afterlife. Such burial pots were normally used only by the very poor; there was no headstone to mark the burial spot, it was just placed in a hillside crevice. Generally a relative or close friend would conduct a simple burial ceremony as a final farewell, and that was that.

Recognizing we had disturbed something sacred, we returned the contents to the pot and put it back into its subdued resting spot, hopefully not to be discovered by other curious youths. We never knew how long that pot had been there. Ten years? Twenty years? A hundred years?

Occasionally a nomadic group of men appeared in the hills surrounding Hong Kong and spent a couple weeks plying their trade of weaving ropes from twine. After carrying bales of twine to the flat empty spaces on the hilltops they used for a workshop, the men offered the products of their mobile cottage industry to the community.

Using age-old technology and generational skills, the craftsmen wove the twine together using a manual contraption that integrated the twine to create a coarse heavy rope. Whenever the rope makers staked claim to the hills, we all had a great time jumping from one bale of twine to another, laughing and shrieking until eventually the men chased us away.

Fun times were had by all until I discovered one unfortunate drawback of playing near the rope men. They did not carry portable toilets with them, such as those usually seen on construction sites today. The men would simply dig holes in the ground and void when nobody was watching. The problem was the men did not clearly mark their tiny toilet holes so the hilly terrain was scattered with a multitude of land mines.

On one hilltop visit, I had the unpleasant experience of jumping from a bale of twine and upon hitting the ground, had one foot land smack dab into a gooey surprise. Unfortunately, it was a multi-use hole that had been a drop for many workers over a period of months. My foot went down, down, down, and I found myself knee deep in human excrement. "Yuuch!" I moaned, over and over again.

I had a twenty minute walk down the hill to get home, and all the way people stared at my colorful mustard yellow leg nestled in a very wet shoe. Noses wrinkled at the vile smell I was emanating. I cried as I made my way home - I was so uncomfortable and embarrassed at my pitiful situation.

No, we didn't have video games or high tech entertainment, but things were never dull playing on our neighborhood hills.

Fishing is a popular pastime in the States. Tales of Huck Finn and paintings brushed by Norman Rockwell portray a young boy dressed in overalls wearing a straw hat decorated with bunches of hayseed to keep the sun from his eyes. Always barefoot, the boy is depicted holding a pole over a pond in the countryside.

Where I grew up, fishing garb was much different. We headed to Hong Kong's fishing holes dressed in shorts, t-shirts, and penny loafers, but we liked to fish just as much as Twain's kid from Mississippi did.

The first time I caught a fish with my rod and reel I was with my parents at a local beach. I reeled in a grouper about six inches long, but my mother was so upset by the thought of the fish dying that she made me throw it back. Being a good son I obeyed her, but I was really disappointed and decided I needed to find another spot where I could fish undisturbed, a place where a fish would end up in my bucket, not back in the water.

I found a fishing hole I loved, but it was not the usual country stream or river so often described. This spot was right in the middle of the city with thousands of people streaming by every day. Different? Definitely yes!

The Island of Hong Kong was separated from the Mainland of Kowloon and the New Territories by one of the best natural harbors in the world. For many years the only way to cross the harbor was by boat, and the most popular commuter transport was the Star Ferry. This highly efficient commuter system transported thousands of people each day; the crossing took only ten minutes. Back and forth the green and white ferries motored, from early morning until very late at night. In typical English fashion, a First Class section was located upstairs on the top deck and was outfitted with comfortable bench seats and an enclosed section in case of inclement weather.

Second Class seating was located on the lower deck of the ferry. It casted a more Spartan seating arrangement with exposure to the roar and fumes emitting from the ferry engine. First-class tickets cost twenty cents and second-class fares were ten cents. The Star Ferry was one of the best bargains going, not only as transportation, but for the expansive views of Hong Kong and Kowloon presented from the middle of the harbor.

The Star Ferry dock provided kids with a great local fishing grotto. We situated ourselves at the ferry terminal exit and dropped our lines into the harbor water while thousands of people passed us by. The harbor water was filthy and occasionally blobs of sewage floated by, so none of the fish caught was fit for human consumption. Any fish I reeled in were fed to our pet cats.

Our fishing methods were not exactly the most sporting, but were certainly highly effective. We used "spider hooks." A spider hook looks much like its name suggests - a leggy spider. A central weight formed the spider's body and attached to it were eight large, firm hooks. A piece of *yau za kwei*, deep-fried Shanghainese bread, was used as bait and tied just above the weight. When a fish nibbled at the bread, we would jerk the line and the fish would be snagged on the hooks. Like I said, this was not exactly a traditional fishing method; in fact, it was pretty gory.

Mostly we caught sticklebacks, a six-inch fish with spiky spines marching down its back. If not handled properly, the small fish would give a mighty sting. Other fish we frequently landed were puffer fish that would enlarge themselves like a balloon once they were out of water. These fish were considered poisonous so we would usually throw them back into the harbor. There you have it, fishing Hong Kong-style at the Star Ferry dock, just another great pastime I loved as a kid.

In the United States we celebrate the Fourth of July with firework displays that are mammoth productions often organized by local municipalities. The English celebrate Guy Fawkes Day much the same way.

In Hong Kong, the Chinese New Year is celebrated almost exclusively with firecrackers.

There were very few New Year fireworks displays; all the excitement came from the personal thrill of lighting crackers to make explosive bangs intense enough to make ears ring for days.

The Chinese New Year does not fall on the same day every year; it is based on a lunar calendar, most often falling sometime in January or February. When the big day arrived, my friends and I would uncover our cache of firecrackers of every size imaginable and light them using a "joss stick" that would glow for several hours. Joss sticks are incense sticks Buddhists light when they pray. The sticks have no perfumed scent and will burn for several hours, enough time for us to get the celebratory job done. Some firecrackers we had in our stash were awesomely powerful and could cause a nasty wound if they exploded too close to the body - they were the equivalent to what are referred to as M-80s in the States.

Despite knowing the power of the explosions, we foolishly took pride in lighting the fuse and throwing the sticks high in the air. It was considered wimpy to light firecrackers safely placed on the ground. Nine times out of ten, the fuse would burn at a consistent rate and two or three seconds would elapse before the gunpowder exploded. As always, some fuses were not properly made and would flash instantly, giving no time to throw them into the air. This always ended in painful screams.

Over the years I came close to injury and suffered limited damage to my throwing hand, but nothing serious ever occurred. After every holiday local newspapers would report incidences of people suffering severe hand or eye injuries, sometimes tragic and fatal occurrences.

One of the more stupid things we did with firecrackers was to throw double bangers into the sky and cautiously watch their random propulsion, followed shortly by an ear-popping explosion. A double banger cracker is a cylinder about six inches long and three-quarters of an inch in diameter. The firecracker is marked with an arrow along its length and after ignition, a sound like *whoompff* would be heard before the firework shot forty feet into the air in the direction the arrow pointed. A tremendous explosion followed within seconds, hence the name double banger. When throwing one of these double whammies end-over-end into the air, you never knew in which direction it would *whoompff*. It wasn't uncommon for us to stand on top of a hill, light a double banger, throw it into the air, only to scramble for cover when it *whoompffed* back in our direction exploding in a fury right next to us.

Another tradition that was really neat during the Chinese New Year was the practice of giving "lucky money." The Chinese name for money was *lycee* and traditionally at Chinese New Year, the custom was to give friends and relatives paper money in a small red paper packet with gold

Chinese characters written on both sides. What a great way for kids to get a little extra pocket money to buy more firecrackers! It seemed especially nice when the money came as brand new, crisp bills, which was also part of the tradition.

There were other occasions when firecracker explosions filled the air. One was the opening of a new shop when it was customary to have 30-50 feet of string loaded with red firecrackers hang down from an upper floor of the store building. Lighting the string of explosives welcomed ten minutes of ear-splitting noise aimed at warding off evil spirits that might threaten the new proprietor. Those celebratory firecrackers would always be red in color. Following the store's grand opening, the surrounding neighborhood would be showered in red confetti paper.

The second occasion where firecrackers made a presence was at a Chinese funeral, which years later I recognized as having amazing similarity to a New Orleans funeral. Firecrackers were once again torched to frighten away bad spirits.

The Chinese burial tradition called for forming a funeral procession with a band playing what could loosely be termed music. The band would usually be dressed in white and walk behind the hearse while playing unrecognizable dirge-inspired music. The burning of paper money was also part of the burial tradition. The play currency resembled Monopoly money and was burned so the deceased would have cash to spend in the afterlife.

Sometimes a large paper car would be burned so the deceased would have good transportation in the next world. To cap off this strange event, the hearse carried a big photograph of the deceased on the roof for all to see. Family and friends would follow behind the band, and professional mourners were often hired to put on a show of intense sorrow. The whole thing seemed rather macabre to me.

There were many Chinese holidays we enjoyed. A favorite was the Chinese lunar holiday. This festival was celebrated at night with all carrying colored paper lanterns with a candle inside for illumination. Lanterns resembled animals, fish, cars, airplanes - you name it and there was an appropriate lantern to carry. The brightly lit colorful shapes were a pretty sight, and particularly enjoyed by young children.

I enjoyed the mooncakes that were traditionally served on this holiday. Mooncakes were molded as a rich pastry surrounding a sweet interior of red bean paste, with a salty boiled egg often hidden in the center. I know it sounds unusual for Western taste buds to savor, but mooncakes really were quite delicious.

The team sports I loved playing with my English friends included soccer and cricket, but the sport I most enjoyed was kite flying. This was a favorite activity of children in the Chinese community. The kites I flew with my Chinese friends were not the pretty, long-tailed, decorated dragon kites often seen on the beaches in California. Our kites were built to fight and "kill" any high flying opponent. Kite flying was not a pastime; it was a competitive sport and had a huge following among the Chinese.

Many hot summer evenings I would catch the double-decker #9 bus traveling down Argyle Street to Yaumati. Like thousands of other young boys and men, I headed to a random roof atop a tall apartment building to indulge in my favorite Chinese sport. With me I carried three kites and a spool of kite string purchased from one of the best-known *tse-fus* in the kiting community. Standing on the rooftop, I was careful to get my bearings and keep my balance. I tried hard not to become one of the stories reported in the *South China Morning Post* telling of a young boy falling to his death because he was too heavily engrossed in kite flying to watch where he stepped. Usually a safety ledge surrounded the perimeter of the roof, but occasionally I would find myself on a flat surface with no barrier to prevent me from stepping over the edge. Of course I *never* told my parents about this chilling aspect of the sport.

So many kites littered the heavens! All sizes and colors rainbowed the azure blue South China sky on this evening. It was hot and humid, but a mild breeze helped offset the oppressive South China heat. It was ideal kite-flying weather.

I looked forward to fighting the kite fliers who were strangers to me, all boastfully weaving their kites from nearby rooftops. The breeze was blowing briskly, and it would be another two hours before the sun went down, a perfect South China evening for kite fighting.

I held the string in my right hand and with a quick tug, my kite leapt into the sky, twirling round and round as I fed it string. I was flying one of my prized kites, a *dai ma lai,* one of the biggest and best fighting kites made in China, and it cost me quite a bit of pocket money – thirty cents. The kite was constructed of thick tissue paper attached to a bamboo frame. The paper was painted with brightly colored symbols and images. This type of kite was extremely agile and could be maneuvered in any direction simply by pointing the head and rolling the string onto a big thread spool with bamboo rods projecting from both ends. Unlike decorative kites, fighting kites never had tails because that would limit maneuverability in the sky. A heavy tail would prevent fighting kites from spinning three hundred and sixty degrees and if that couldn't happen, the kite pilot could not point the kite in the direction intended.

I saw a kite several hundred yards to my left and another fifty yards in front of me. I let the wind pull my kite as the spool spun wildly in my hands, the string racing to be free. Round and round it twirled until I thought the distance looked right, and then I made my move. I waited until the kite's head pointed to the left and then started to roll in the string by putting the spool between my knees and rolling the bamboo rods over the tops of my legs. The string tightened as I wound it in. The kite immediately darted to the left in slow motion flight, much like a bird of prey stalking its dinner. When I thought I was directly above my "intended victim," I let the wind pull the string once more and the kite started to spin like a top. Once it was pointed down in the direction of my opponent flying beneath me, I again rolled in the string and my kite dove down like a swooping hawk so my string was positioned directly on top of my opponent's. When our strings touched, I once again let the wind pull my string from my spool, as did my opponent. Round and round the kites twirled with two razor edged strings running out at high speed, trying to cut the other's lifeline.

The true weaponry in kite flying was the string. Fighting string came in two varieties, cotton and nylon. Nylon string was far superior, but also ten times more expensive. Kite string was made fight-ready by covering it with a fine layer of glue and powdered glass. When the string moved quickly across a surface, it had the cutting power of a honed razor blade.

I suffered many vicious cuts on my fingers from an occasional careless lapse in concentration.

Sometimes my friends and I would make our own fighting string in a makeshift laboratory on an apartment rooftop, although the quality was lacking compared to the true masters' talents.

The process involved poking two holes in the bottom of a cheap plastic cup. The cup was then filled with a mixture of glue and glass powder made from pounding glass scraps. Reinforced cotton thread was drawn through the holes in the cup. One boy would hold the cup and a clean spool of thread and another boy would sit about thirty feet away, slowly winding the newly made fighting string onto a thread spool. This would typically be done on a hot day so the string would dry quickly after leaving the thick liquid in the plastic cup and before reaching the distant thread spool.

This particular evening I was fighting an anonymous foe for dominance in the Kowloon sky. My string flew out of the spool at a fast rate, landing on top of my opponent's string. I was trying to find a weak spot or knot so I could slice away his hold on the darkening sky. One thing to watch - as the string grows longer and longer, the weight causes the kite to dip, presenting the danger of getting snagged on a far-off rooftop.

I was on alert. Suddenly my enemy's kite was no longer twirling; it drifted away as lifeless as an autumn leaf and dipped below the jagged rooftops. Free from the threat of my opponent's string, my kite triumphantly soared high in the air and soon was only a speck of color because I had released so much string. This time around I was victorious, and as I reeled in the string, my eyes searched the skies for my next victim. When I pulled my kite to rooftop level, I had to watch that a scene had not been set for a "faked kill" strategy.

This carefully crafted maneuver occurs when an opponent pretends his kite is dead, but as his unwary opponent starts a victorious climb back into the sky, the supposedly "dead" opponent lets his string run free, cutting through the unsuspecting victor. Many battles were going on simultaneously, fought by kite owners usually unknown to each other, all flying their sails miles away on different rooftops.

That night my second fight did not go well for me; my string was cut and my kite drifted away. As I rolled in the string, it suddenly hit a mysterious snag on a rooftop about three hundred yards away. I strained my eyes and saw the snag was actually another boy who had grabbed my string and was holding it tightly. One of the hazards of serious kite fighting is the pirate who will try to steal your string so he can use it as his own. Eventually I had no choice but to pull my string until it snapped, hoping it broke closer to the thief than to me so my loss was minimized.

Some evenings I killed a dozen kites competing for dominance in the sky, while other kite pilots ran away and reeled in their kites when they saw my *dai ma lai* swooping and cutting through the air. This night I had seven kills and two losses, not a bad evening of sport.

Every flier knew when you unleashed your paper bird to fly in the sky, you had to be prepared for attack, possibly fighting to the death resulting in the loss of your pretty flyer. Only once did I come across a boy who did not know that flying a kite in the South China sky was an open invitation for a paper version of a dog fight.

Once I was standing across the street from my home, my kite soaring through the sky when I noticed a few *gwai los* launching a huge, clumsy kite from a nearby rooftop. The kite had a long ragged tale of colorful bows so did not possess the dexterity of Chinese fighting kites. It was the type of kite you would see at an American beach or a grassy park. A pretty kite, but definitely lacking the ability to maneuver around opponents. It certainly did not have a glass string to deal a death blow.

The *gwai los* probably brought the kite with them all the way from the United States and had no idea what they were up against. After several tries, they managed to catch the wind to launch their ungainly contraption. My friends and I watched the pitiful kite hang and bob in the sky.

Suddenly I couldn't help myself - I had to capture the foreign flier! The newcomers never knew what hit them, for moments later their kite was aimlessly floating over roof tops while they held a tangled mass of slack string. Sky warrior had struck! It was one of my few kills when the memory of victory stuck in my mind. Immediately after my assault, I felt pangs of guilt. The boys never had a chance to defend their kite and probably never even knew what had happened to it. I had given in to my mean and nasty side, and wasn't proud of what I had done. I won the kite battle easily that day, but when I checked my personal barometer, it told me I had lost something in the process.

The Chinese took kite flying very seriously and kite champions were widely recognized and honored for their skill and the quality of string they sold. Their kites were decorated with elaborate designs and markings and these champions would have followers similar to those who followed martial art *tse-fus*, or teachers.

Kite *tse-fus* designed special insignias and shapes for their kites so they were readily recognized. These markings could not be copied. The respected teachers were also known for their high tech nylon kite string and each would boast their string could easily cut through that of any rival. When a renowned kite *tse-fu* took to the skies, it was amazing how quickly word spread across the rooftops. Every kite pilot wanted to watch a *tse-fu's* masterful techniques

I can't think of an equivalent sport to kite fighting that is played in the West, and I often reflect on the good times I had with this sport. In my travels I've never seen anything like the high fliers of Hong Kong, although I have read that the sport exists in other Asian cultures.

The following day I once again headed out to Yaumati to fly my kites and little did I know what was to lie ahead. Climbing to a particularly high rooftop on a day I was feeling adventurous, I was annoyed to see another young boy standing on top of the elevator equipment hut with his kite already flying high in the sky.

An unwritten rule stated two kites could not be flown from the same roof because it would be too easy to get the strings tangled. This meant I would have to wait my turn, or go all the way downstairs and make my way to another building. It was still early so I decided to watch the action for a while and take measure of my competition.

The young boy flew a smaller, cheaper kite and was dressed in ragged shorts, a dirty t-shirt, and wore no shoes. He had climbed to the top of a small, square brick building that housed equipment for the apartment's elevators. These small buildings offered the highest point on the rooftop with the best view, but they were dangerous because there was little square footage to stand on and never offered a protective ledge. The top of the hut was smooth cement except for large handles attached to trap doors which led down to the elevator. An iron ladder marched up one of the access walls.

The young boy appeared reckless, giving his full attention to the kite fight he was battling in the sky. I noticed he was a skillful kite pilot and made several kills, even with his inferior kite and thin string.

The boy was madly jerking the string, becoming wildly animated as he danced with his kite. I was about to give a warning when suddenly he tripped on a trap door handle and went sprawling. I shuddered as I watched him slide across the slanted rooftop to the edge of the building. He managed to grab a handle with both hands as his legs hung over the side of the building. He was dangling over the side of a ten-story building with a panicky look screaming over his face.

My immediate reaction was to search for an adult to help, but a quick scan revealed I was the only one on the roof. I had to find a way to help him! Quickly I ran up the metal ladder on the side of the elevator hut and with one hand holding the opposing trapdoor handle, I used my right hand to grasp the boy's forearm. I started to sweat nervously; it was a grossly unpleasant feeling to have a life precariously held by a handgrip. Fortunately the boy was skinny and did not weigh much, but still I had a vision flash through my head of being dragged over the side and falling to the street hundreds of feet below. We were fighting the force of gravity but slowly with his help, inch-by-inch I managed to pull the boy back to the safety of the rooftop. When he was safely positioned on the cement slab, we both laid back to catch our breath and reflect on how close this adventure had been to becoming a tragic accident. I had his forearm clutched in my right hand, still afraid to let go. As I rolled over I spotted the familiar "sun scar" I had not seen in a couple years. I knew there was something familiar about this Chinese kid.

"Chow Chai?" I asked in Cantonese. "Is it really you?"

"Tong-nay! What good fortune it is for me to see you again at a time when I truly needed a friend."

We laughed at this unexpected reunion and climbed down from the small elevator shaft hut to a safer location on the main roof. It was then I realized my knees were shaking, a delayed reaction to the exceptional excitement I had just experienced. It had been several years since Chow Chai and I had seen each other and it was great fun to catch up on how our lives had been going.

Chow Chai told me he no longer lived in the squatter community because his family's shack had burned down. He had been adopted by what he referred to as "older brothers," and was now doing odd jobs for them in the Homantin market. I wondered just what he meant by "older brothers," and suddenly a warning flag popped up in the back of my mind. I had heard this term used before in reference to local gangs. Chow Chai had grown in height and was almost as tall as I was. I could tell his once bony body had developed musculature, probably from hard labor working for his "older brothers." Good thing, because it had taken a good degree of strength for Chow Chai to hang onto the trap door with the weight of his body hanging over the edge. After half an hour of chatting and catching up, Chow Chai told me he had to leave for a job that was waiting for him in Homantin.

As we said goodbye I handed him one of my nicer fighting kites and told him to make sure he did not try to follow this kite off the edge of the rooftop. A big smile creased his face.

"Daw-tse, Tong-Nay, ho pan yau." *Thank you, Tony, my friend.* "Choi keen," *Goodbye*, he called over his shoulder as he ran down the stairway of the apartment building.

The roof was now mine to launch my kite. Heavy competition once again filled the sky on that evening. Just before I flew my *dai ma lai,* I reflected on the danger that Chow Chai had confronted on top of the elevator hut. I was fearful that he might have chosen an even more dangerous path as poverty steered him into fulfilling "jobs" for his older brothers.

My early childhood in Hong Kong honed my competitive nature. Yo-yo championships, kite fighting, and all the other sports I loved instilled in me a strong desire to excel and win at whatever I attempted to learn and master.

I truly would gauge my early life in terms of winning or losing, and still tend to do so today. There was great diversity in the culture I called mine, and I was lucky to be exposed to people of all races and social classes - English, American, European, Chinese, and East Indian.

Isn't it interesting that growing up amid all this cultural richness, at the age of thirteen all I wanted to be was a WASP hailing from England, complete with blond hair and blue eyes? Interesting how societies sometimes influence the desire to be of pure Caucasian heritage. Monkey men, exotic street foods, kite fights, carrot patches, burial pots, firecrackers, and lunar lanterns were but a few of the fantastic experiences I had growing up in this British Colony called Hong Kong.

I often thought I heard a voice somewhere in the back of my head whispering that I was chosen to lead a very special life. I look back now to all these wonderful things that so enriched my childhood and feel incredibly lucky to have experienced them. With the modernization of Chinese society and the return of the British Crown Colony to China, I doubt a young Eurasian boy growing up in Hong Kong today would ever have the chance to enjoy all the wonders I embraced.

CHAPTER FOUR
"Here, There and Everywhere"
JOHN LENNON AND PAUL MCCARTNEY

Later in my life when I went to college, I was surprised at the number of people I met who had never traveled any distance from the town in which they were born, much less visited another country. Their life experiences seemed so limited and shallow compared to my own. Once again this was a reminder of how lucky I believed myself to be. Living in the premier cosmopolitan trading center of the Orient, I was constantly exposed to people from other countries and cultures, and frequently had the opportunity to travel to those countries.

The first adventure I took was a cruise from Hong Kong to Japan; it must have been in the late 1950s when I was around ten years old. My first cruise was a lot of fun, but the transport was vastly different from today's mega ships which offer multiple onboard activities to entertain and amuse travelers. All I can remember about that cruise is exploring the decks and playing countless games of shuffleboard with my brother. This was a great opportunity for my younger self to visit a country as different as Japan was and experience the excitement offered by a big city like Tokyo. Over the years I've met so many people who confuse Hong Kong and Japan, many believing Hong Kong is located in Japan.

49

I was too young to remember much about that first trip except that we visited scenic spots in the mountain resort of Nikko and were awed by the beauty of Lake Hakone. Typical of a young boy, I also vividly remember this trip gave me my first opportunity to go ten-pin bowling. I really took to the game. I was hooked the first time I saw the big black ball roll down the shiny wooden lane and crash into the pins with explosive thunder. I begged my parents to take me back to the lanes every single day. Most of the time they obliged their young son.

In Tokyo I visited my very first large amusement park – Korakuen. I had a great time on the rides until I took the one that spins round and round so fast that centrifugal force presses hapless riders flat against the wall. As the massive drum rolled faster and faster, the floor slowly dropped to show wide-eyed spectators peering down that riders were indeed pinned to the wall. When the ride finally stopped, I was sick as a dog and felt like puking for hours.

While in Japan I met my maternal Japanese grandmother who spoke only limited broken English. Everyone called her Mama and she lived with my Aunt Lois and Uncle Joe. We stayed with them during our visit.

Aunt Lois was my mother's older sister and her husband Joe was from Spain. Mama was very nice to me and I liked her, but we were essentially strangers and never had the opportunity to become close like many kids do with their grandmothers. My heritage was a quarter Japanese and yet I had absolutely no connection to my Japanese roots. Their house was typically Japanese featuring *tatami*, mats used as flooring in traditional Japanese-style homes, and sliding paper doors dividing the rooms. Following Japanese tradition, shoes had to be left at the front door.

I don't have much recollection of eating Japanese food other than my favorite dishes served were Kobe beef and tempura. Kobe beef was the tenderest steak I had ever eaten. The tempura was memorable because of the theater involved in the presentation of the meal. We sat at a circular table with the meal's ingredients piled behind a counter inside the circle. I wondered how the chef climbed over the wide counter to cook the meal. I didn't have to wait long for an explanation. As we sat around the table, a small circular section of the floor suddenly dropped and our chef appeared like magic, rising from the basement level. You can imagine the squeals of delight and laughter as he rose like an apparition.

Naturally my brother and I had to examine this amazing elevator firsthand so we quietly left our seats to explore. It didn't take us long to find our way downstairs and onto the small elevator platform. We thought we were hot stuff as the table rose and we confronted adults who were at first surprised to see two kids in the chef's place of honor, but then erupted into peals of laughter.

When our visit to Japan was over we flew back in a TWA Constellation. Now that's a piece of aviation history! This was my first experience in an airplane and I suffered a bout of travel sickness. Luckily it was a relatively short trip because I thought I was surely dying. But, after that first flight, surprisingly I never got sick again.

My next big opportunity to travel was marked by another aviation first – the jet airplane. This trip happened several years later when my parents took the family on a European holiday. The first travel leg was in a BOAC (British Overseas Air Corporation, later to become British Airways) jet known as the Comet. It was exciting to travel in such grand style, especially being one of the first to fly in this phenomenon known as a jet. The cabin was small and the seats very close together.

After a few hours of flight, seating became uncomfortably cramped, and there were many transit stops to come. Our plane made a total of five stops traveling between Hong Kong and London. We stopped in Bangkok, Bombay, Karachi, Istanbul, and Geneva before finally reaching our destination. The flight seemed to go on forever; it took well over 20 hours when transit stops were included.

The De Havilland Comet was memorable in more ways than one. It was the first commercial jet aircraft, but was widely regarded as an aviation failure and was grounded from the skies after a series of crashes, several of which were attributable to the aircraft design. The technology of jet aviation had not been fully developed before the prototype look to the skies. During the two-year period of time Comet crashes were under investigation, Boeing and Douglas leapfrogged ahead of the English company and American jet manufacturers soon ruled the aviation field. The Comet had disappeared from the skies, along with passenger confidence.

On that trip to Europe we visited England, Holland, France, Italy, and Switzerland and fortunately never dropped from the sky. My mother dragged my brother and me to every museum and church she could find. We were exposed to many works by the grand masters, such as Da Vinci's *Mona Lisa* and Michelangelo's *David* and *Pieta*, as well as a collection of cathedrals, castles and much, much more. Steve and I grumbled at being forced out of bed every morning to see all this "boring stuff." Years later, I was thankful my mother had insisted we visit the famous artworks and cathedrals as these early experiences vastly added to my education. Friends were amazed I had experienced things they had only read about or discussed in the confines of a classroom.

Of all the attractions we visited, my favorite place was the Tower of London with the Crown Jewels on display. We studied the history of England in school and I was quite familiar with famous British institutions. Seeing them made history come alive for me, despite all my grumbling.

Not all my European experience was memorable for cultural diversity; there was an incident in Venice, Italy that I will never forget. We had been traveling for several weeks and I was missing the company of the fairer sex so I insisted on going out by myself to meet local girls. After all, I was at the age when boys really notice pretty girls and was starting to think of myself as "cool."

After the stereotypical arguing and warnings to be careful around strangers, I was finally allowed to wander away from our hotel, but had to report back in exactly one hour. Off I went to St. Mark's Square where I was sure there would be many sweet touristas to meet. I was walking around the large square, smiling broadly as I searched for pretty faces, wondering what on earth I would say if I was lucky enough to find a girl who smiled back. As I wandered I saw a man in a raincoat standing thirty feet in front of me. He was grinning as he walked toward me. As he approached, he was still smiling, but I thought he was looking at someone behind me so I didn't pay much attention to him. I freaked out when the man turned one hundred and eighty degrees and started to walk right next to me. I looked at him curiously and he still had a smile covering his face, except now it clicked - he was smiling at *me!*

Before I could react and run, another raincoat-wearing smiling man appeared from nowhere and walked on my other side, essentially boxing me in. *My God, is Venice swarming with these guys?* I decided the best course of action would be to run like hell. I darted into the crowd and lost them in a quick minute. I noticed they didn't try to follow me. I ran back to the hotel at full speed and told my harrowing tale to my parents who were at first very concerned, but then realized I was okay and nothing really had happened. For days they teased me about my girl-searching adverse adventure and the episode became a family joke for years thereafter.

The next morning we had breakfast at the hotel and I swore "Raincoat Man" was sitting at the next table. I wanted my dad to go over and punch him a good one, but since I couldn't be certain of his identity, Dad wisely decided not to do anything. It was better than causing an international incident. Dad was a smart man.

Since I was raised in a British Colony, it was exciting to have the chance to visit England, our mother country. Steve and I were quite taken by the sights - Big Ben, Trafalgar Square, Buckingham Palace, and other famous landmarks. One of my biggest thrills was going to the Lord's Cricket Ground to watch my heroes play at one of the game's meccas.

Most of the time we stayed in the center of London, but we did travel to a few other places like Coventry where we saw the remains of the famous cathedral after the WWII bombing. The story goes that Churchill had a very difficult decision to make during WWII. The Brits had obtained a cipher machine and had broken the German code base. British intelligence was aware the Germans had planned a bombing raid to destroy Coventry, but the Prime Minister made the decision to let Coventry be bombed rather than reveal that the Allies had broken the code. This dangerous strategy would enable the Allies to continue to obtain secret information that otherwise would have been cut off. It took incredible courage to make that decision.

We also traveled to Liverpool to visit distant relatives and I met my Aunt Jack on my mother's side of the family. She eventually lived to be one hundred and eight and upon reaching her centenary, Aunt Jack received a personal letter from Her Majesty the Queen, as is the tradition in England. A nice custom that is so very British.

After hours filled with boring family chatter, a couple kids decided to sneak away to find something more exciting to do. My distant cousins asked if my brother and I would like to go to a music spot called the "Cavern" where a local group was starting to gain popularity. The group suffered a fair share of criticism by the establishment for their mop-headed haircuts and mod style of dress. Unfortunately we passed on that offer. It would have been quite a coup and memory to say we saw the Beatles in the early years before they became famous. Instead we decided to visit a gypsy fair. A big surprise waited when we walked out the door. Our transportation to the fair was going to be by motorcycle!

When my parents gave permission for Steve and me to go to the fair, I don't think they had any idea how we would get there. This was my first ride on a motorcycle and I found it exhilarating to race through the Mersey tunnel at high speed. I did not realize motorbikes would later become a big thing in my life; this experience planted the seed for adventures to come.

Most of the time we were in London, my family stayed at the Onslow Court Hotel, a nondescript, two-star hotel that housed mostly elderly people. The hotel was notorious for a series of murders that happened ten years before and, of course, this horrific event intrigued my brother and me. We had hardly unpacked before we started to explore the back hallways for signs of anything suspicious. Our search was rewarded by the discovery of an elevator that worked entirely on a rope pulley system. We imagined bodies being secretly carried out of the hotel using this creaky device. Up and down we went! It was wonderful fun and if anyone dared to disturb our imaginary world, we were positive it would be the murderer returning to the scene of his crime.

After an hour of elevator exploration, we heard *real* footsteps shuffling like the dead reportedly do. My pulse raced as I anticipated the appearance of hacked-to-pieces ghosts, or at the worst, an ugly, scraggly-haired, bearded murderer, perhaps a descendant of Jack the Ripper. The steps sounded closer and closer as Steve and I froze in position. Suddenly a silver-haired, octogenarian appeared leaning on a walking stick. He weighed no more than ninety pounds and couldn't hurt a fly. We later discovered he was one of the many elderly folks living in the hotel. But, in our imaginations, he *was* the murderer taking on a new form and disguise.

I believe travel is a wonderful form of education. I was blessed to have traveled as much as I did at an early age. I was happy I could tell my English friends about my visit to the Motherland and the sights many of them had never seen. Travel helped me feel a little bit better about who or what I was as my Eurasian struggle for identity continued.

CHAPTER FIVE
"Yesterday"
JOHN LENNON AND PAUL MCCARTNEY

Like Manhattan, land is a very scarce resource in Hong Kong and is extremely expensive. Almost everyone I knew lived in an apartment except for exceptionally rich locals and a few American expatriates who had accommodations covered by contract. Apartments were primarily high rises and provided little in the way of amenities, such as game rooms or swimming pools. If you wanted to swim, it had to be at a private club or huge government pool catering to countless thousands of locals.

An inexpensive swim option was to join the Hong Kong YMCA, which boasted a large indoor pool. The YMCA inhabited an old gray building built on prime land situated between the Peninsula Hotel and the Star Ferry dock. The YMCA was one of my favorite places to hit the water and my swim was always followed by a delicious hot snack of English-style fish and chips loaded with malt vinegar.

Even though our apartment was considered luxurious by most standards, we didn't have a swimming pool. On one November day in 1963 I was sitting on a double-decker bus headed down Nathan Road toward the Star Ferry terminal, looking forward to a swim in the Y pool. Before the advent of the Walkman, I carried a small transistor radio with a single earplug linking me to the pop sounds I loved. The sound quality was terrible with constant static buzzing in my ear, but radios were hot with Hong Kong teenagers.

As I was hopping off the bus, the music was suddenly interrupted and my ear was filled with a terse, serious English voice reporting shocking news had come out of Dallas in the United States. President John F. Kennedy had been assassinated, shot by a gunman with a rifle while he was riding in a motorcade. I was taken aback by this news, but since I looked to England and the Queen as my country and monarch, I was not completely shaken by it.

When I arrived at the YMCA, several American friends were already there and girls were unabashedly crying over the Kennedy assassination. The American guys were visibly teary-eyed as they tried to comfort the girls. I was impressed by the impact this leader's death had on my young friends; they truly looked up to him. If the Prime Minister of England had been shot, I guarantee none of my local or English friends would be affected nearly as much. It's been said most everyone remembers where they were the day Kennedy was shot, and in my case that is certainly true.

After the American kids gathered themselves, we decided to go for a swim and headed into the respective locker rooms. The narrow rooms had a security cage at the entrance where names were registered and valuables could be checked. The floor was covered in white tile and many times I was grossed out by the dirt tracked from the street onto the floor that was constantly wet from swimmers dripping water as they toweled off. I hated it even more when my bare feet were assaulted by the slippery brown grit.

The smell of chlorine was overpowering because it was dispersed in extra high levels to keep the water clean in the humid Hong Kong summer. The pool water was freezing cold and kids often perched on the narrow poolside deck with blue-tinted hands cupped under their shivering chins. My friends and I decided we had to get over the bad news of the day so we started horsing around doing crazy dives off the diving board.

One of the Chinese lifeguards tried to quiet us down, but in response the two guys on the board in front of me jumped in his direction, curling and tucking to make their bodies into a human water bomb.

I noticed the lifeguard wasn't too happy because he was wearing a dry t-shirt and had no intention of being blasted by the cold water. Nevertheless I followed in my friends' footsteps and figured my bomb was ultimately successful judging from the deep impact I made. My legs hit the bottom of the pool and as I started to surface, I wondered how impressive my splash had been. Just before I broke the surface, a body landed on top of me and I felt two hands grabbing my shoulders and pushing me back down. I struggled to get away and was desperate for a breath as I had emptied my lungs on the way up. The hands were strong and I found legs had wrapped around my body. I was helpless.

I started to feel my strength ebbing away and just as I started to take in water, I was set free. I spluttered to the surface in a state of near panic, coughing madly while frantically trying to restore oxygen to my screaming body. As I grasped the side of the pool, I saw my aggressor leap out of the water. It was the lifeguard! Apparently the man decided he had been on the bad end of harassment from young punks long enough and decided to teach me a lesson, and that he did.

My buddies told the lifeguard they were going to report him and he was wrong to try to drown me, but the big man just ignored them. As I clung to the cement ledge I thought - *This is one person I am never going to piss off again!*

I never reported him, probably because he scared the living daylights out of me and if he could do something that frightening and threatening in a public YMCA pool, what could the guy do to me on a dark street? No way was I crossing his path ever again!

Fast-forward a few years. I was standing on a balcony at my high school wearing my brown school blazer and blue school tie. I was yelling at a kid to do a better job cutting the lawn with a pair of manicure scissors. For half an hour the kid was intermittently laughing and complaining as he trimmed blades of grass with the small scissors. After finishing a section, the kid mouthed off at me, so what else to do but assign him five hundred lines to write, "I will not be a smart mouth."

This whole episode started because I saw the kid going into the morning school assembly wearing a pair of socks that didn't fit the school uniform code. To worsen his case, I caught him talking during the Bible reading. You might ask, just what was going on there?

In my last two years at King George V School (known as KGV) I was named a Prefect, thus given the authority to discipline anyone not abiding by the school rules, of which there were a bunch! KGV was a very English school. Students were educated by teachers from the British Isles and the school was directed by strong British tradition. About ten percent of the upper class was appointed Prefects by the headmaster of the school. I suppose the criterion was not dissimilar from how we choose managers and leaders today in the business world. Characteristics sought were leadership, presence, intelligence, and good judgment.

Despite these characteristics, I'm sure the under classes regarded us as the Gestapo of the school, especially since some kids were made Prefects although they never should have been given such responsibility and power.

Ian Buckingham was a good friend, a great guy, and lots of fun, but in my opinion one of the worst choices to be named Prefect. Ian was a drinker and a smoker (that was as bad as it got in those days) and often I had to ask him to put out his cigarette while on duty. But heaven help any poor, unsuspecting youth who Ian caught smoking in the bathroom or in school uniform off campus. There would be essays, lines, or detentions handed out for such behavior unbecoming a KGV student.

I was probably picked to be a Prefect because, in addition to the qualities identified, I had first-hand knowledge of all the things a student was not supposed to do. A couple of incidents in particular come to mind when I was a young innocent of age fourteen.

I was sitting in a history class bored out of my mind. I've always thought history was dull and found it particularly difficult to listen to Mr. Hollies lecture on the Magna Carta being signed in twelve hundred and fifteen and the consequences thereof. Next to me sat Anders Nelsson, looking equally as bored.

Anders was Swedish and a rock musician. He went on to form the Kontinentals, one of the premier rock and roll bands in Southeast Asia.

It was one of those inane moments when eyes locked and there was instant recognition that we were both wishing we could be anywhere but in this class. Wicked smiles flickered across our faces. Mr. Hollies was known for throwing the blackboard duster at students not paying attention but he had terrible aim, hitting innocent bystanders more often than whacking the deserving culprits. This time was no different; Mr. Hollies flung the duster at us to get our attention, but missed and hit a studious female sitting behind me. No apologies forthcoming, he carried on as if nothing untoward had happened to the now traumatized young lady.

A few minutes after the misplaced throw, Mr. Hollies did something out of the ordinary, something that left a lasting impression on me. Our history teacher walked nonchalantly down the row to stand before Anders. He did not say a word but looked him square in the eye and in a flash slapped him across the side of his face, full force. *Whap! Whap!*

Holy shit! I may not have been a genius, but I knew what was coming my way. Mr. Hollies turned away from Anders, looked directly at me and walked to my desk. I was prepared for what was to come but had quick reflexes, so as the big hand came swinging down I managed to deflect the blow with my arm while ducking my head. *Whack!* It still hurt like hell and I had great respect for Anders who took two blows by surprise versus my one blow with hand raised to absorb the sting.

Mr. Hollies glared and growled, "Now you two had better pay attention in class or else you will *really* get me angry!"

He then resumed his discussion of the Magna Carta as if nothing had happened. For Anders and me it was quite memorable and our heads were stinging and ringing for some time after. In traditional British schools, teachers were permitted to administer corporal punishment. Prefects were only allowed to give written assignments, but we would occasionally sneak in physical humiliation, like manicuring the grass. Back then Mr. Hollies would not be reprimanded for corporal punishment whereas today in the States, the man would be looking at the possibility of a stinging lawsuit.

The cane was another form of corporal punishment that only the headmaster or school principal could administer. As the name suggests, the cane was a long thin piece of flexible bamboo administered to the buttocks while hands were planted on the administrator's desk. For guys, a caning was not something to aspire to, but it was viewed by some of my peers as a required ritual for coming into manhood. I never thought I would be caned because the headmaster and I got on famously. We played cricket together and I knew he liked me, so how did I manage to get six strokes of the best?

Well, there was a kid named Anthony who was disliked by a few guys on the soccer team. One afternoon we were in the changing room after practice and Anthony was making a nuisance of himself by mouthing off to everybody in the room. To shut him up, we grabbed him, stripped off his clothes, and threw him naked onto the middle of the soccer pitch. He went home and cried to his mother. The next day she stormed into the headmaster's office to complain that Anthony's shirt had been shredded and demanded the culprits responsible be punished for the offense.

My name was not given because I was a good friend of Anthony's brother, Roger. However everybody known to be in the locker room was quizzed about the mischievous deed. During my one-on-one meeting with Headmaster Findlay, he gave me every opportunity to say I was not involved. I knew my friends wouldn't think much of me if I didn't stick with them. Besides that, I always had great difficulty telling a lie, so I 'fessed up.

I think it was one of those "this is going to hurt me more than it hurts you" situations. Six strokes on the butt will leave red welts and hurts like hell. Some on the soccer team were old hands at this punishment and stuffed padding into their underwear to lessen the sting. I didn't do that, primarily because I didn't know the trick.

Mr. Findlay and I remained on good terms after the incident and continued to play cricket together on the school team. I held him in great respect and I was saddened by his untimely death a few years later in an automobile accident in England. He was a very nice man and fair to his students. That was the first and only time I was caned.

At times I was incredibly naive and took honesty to such an extreme that it bordered on being stupid. At one of our morning school assemblies, the assistant headmaster announced he was annoyed students had been writing and carving on the wooden desks. He told the entire school population that he wanted anyone who had *ever* done such a thing to remain behind after assembly. Conservatively, this would include close to seventy-five percent of the student population, but guess how many stayed behind? Five of us!

I was one of the dummies, and so was my friend Anders. After the assistant headmaster reamed us out for vandalism, he recognized we were the only ones either stupid enough, or gutsy enough, to tell the truth so he took pity and let us go with a minor assignment. Our punishment was the worthless exercise of spending several lunch breaks mapping out the manholes on the school property.

If you were to ask how I was remembered in high school, no doubt it would be for my athletic ability. I've been blessed with natural abilities, including excellent hand-eye coordination that allows me to pick up any sport very quickly, much to the frustration of my competition. I would consistently rank in the top tier of any sport I chose to play. If Hong Kong had a feeding system that took high school athletes into the pro ranks, I'm convinced I had the potential to become a professional athlete. Most likely I would be a professional soccer player, with baseball and cricket being other possibilities. I was an intelligent kid and could always pass exams with minimum effort so my grades were never spectacular. I wasn't a prime student, but got by nicely. Sports were really my thing.

At KGV each grade level was further divided into A, B, C and D streams. I always landed in the A stream, except for one semester when I slipped on my finals and was put down to the B level the following year. I was so upset over this demotion that I really applied myself to my studies and the following year attained first position in the B class stream. But I wanted to be back up in the A stream!

My mother was the driving "encourager" in our family and would push me to do my best academically. I was quite proud of finishing first in my B stream class, but Mum clearly pointed out I had done so with a relatively low grade point average compared to the entire class. My mother taught me to compare myself to the very best in the class, not to the most convenient placement. At first I was disappointed I was not receiving the praise I thought I deserved for my B stream effort, but over time I learned the importance of my mother's valuable life lesson.

I proved to myself I had academic capability, it was only the matter of application I was missing most of the time. The problem was I seldom applied myself to studies as most of my free time was spent in sports-related activities since that was how I measured success.

In the main entrance hallway to my school, mounted high on the walls, were wooden plaques for all to see. They listed the names of the school's top athletes over the years in various sport disciplines. Not one name was displayed recognizing academic achievement, so clearly accomplishment in sports was held in higher esteem. Doesn't that sound right? It was a great feeling to see my name among others I had admired as I traveled through my high school years. I would love to go back to Hong Kong today, walk through the front entrance of KGV and see if my name still hangs high on the display plaques.

The sports I played best were soccer, tennis, and cricket. I took great pride that on my school blazer I wore "colors" that had been awarded for excellence in six sports - soccer, cricket, track and field, field hockey, cross-country running, and tennis. Colors were the equivalent to the felt "letters" awarded in American high schools, but instead were small metal shields worn on school blazer lapels. Each shield depicted one sport in which the color had been awarded. Most student athletes might wear one or two colors, so the six colors I wore on my blazer stood out quite distinctively. From my earliest recollection I always played to win, an attitude highly reinforced by my early achievement with a yo-yo. I was competitive as hell in sports and even though all were played at the amateur level, I managed to supplement my pocket money by excelling in cricket and winning bottles of scotch which I would sell to our *amahs* at a big discount.

Unlike cricket, I played soccer because I loved the game. I had a knack of always finding a way to weave the ball into the opponents' net. Scoring goals was such a great rush for me! KGV never had a championship soccer team, but we enjoyed great camaraderie and had a lot of fun.

As a kid I saw Pele and the Brazilians absolutely demolish a Hong Kong team. I also saw one of the greatest English right wings, Sir Stanley Matthews, play. My favorite team was Manchester United from the English F.A. league. This was around the time when that team lost almost all players in a devastating plane crash. My second favorite team was Tottenham Hotspur which fielded a great inside-left forward by the name of Jimmy Greaves.

Our KGV soccer team may not have been the most talented, but what a great collection of guys, including some of the toughest sons of guns you would ever want to meet. They had names like Sid Fattedad, Nick Barovsky, Pete Gonsalves, Norman Hope, Pete Turner, and Jose Barros. Maybe we didn't win every game we played, but with these guys on the team we sure could beat up our opponents. All of the guys were tough, but there was little doubt the toughest in the bunch was Nick.

I saw Nick in action many times and even though he was one of my good friends and frequently stayed at my house, it scared the hell out me when I saw him fight. One pugilistic event happened at a local church dance on the Hong Kong side of St. John's Cathedral. I'd heard Nick was mad at a Chinese dude, but didn't know the reason why. The buzz was a fight between the two was about to start outside the church doors. The fight was so quick and so ferocious that it was really quite incredible to watch.

One minute both boys were standing, and the next minute Nick kicked the guy in the crotch and after he doubled over, Nick kicked him in the side of his face. The guy was begging for mercy, which seemed to annoy Nick even more and he kicked him again in the face. The thing that struck me the most was the noise made by Nick's foot smashing into the guy's face. It didn't sound like what you'd hear in a movie soundtrack. Instead of the knocking, cracking sound artificially created for effect, the real thing was a muffled *Thwwup*. The fight was over in maybe seven seconds. Nick had quite a reputation around town and nobody messed with him. It was good to have friends like Nick - life would have been hell if he was an enemy.

It would be a big thrill for me to play soccer again with these rough and tough guys at a class reunion, provided we could still run in our old age. In our heyday, our soccer team never won tournaments or league awards, but I do have special memories of a particular championship game. I was selected to be on an All-Star, schoolboy representative team scheduled to play in front of tens of thousands screaming fans at the Hong Kong Soccer Stadium against a team of young Chinese professionals. Pete Turner and I were the only two from KGV invited to try out for the team and both of us made the cut. Interestingly, we were both left-footers.

The game was close but it was frustrating for Pete and me because our Chinese teammates did not want to pass to the guys from the English school. I guess discrimination can take many different forms. By the end of the first half I was really upset. As a forward I had to rely on the halfbacks and other forwards to pass me the ball. I had hardly touched the ball the first 45 minutes of play so Pete and I agreed we would have to work together if we were to make anything happen.

The score was 0-0 and I was playing in the center-forward position when a long breakthrough pass from Pete at center-half sailed over the midfield. There was a race for the ball, playing three opponents against me, but I was fast and managed to get to the ball first about thirty yards ahead of the penalty box. I tapped the ball forward and could sense the rush of bodies bearing down. Just before my legs were taken out from under me, I nailed the shot and as I tumbled to the ground, I saw the ball crash into the right side of the net beyond the goalkeeper's outstretched hands.

What a thrill - tens of thousands Chinese fans in the stadium went wild! It was a great goal. We eventually won the match 1-0 and I made the local newspapers the next day. Pete and I were ecstatic. My private "achievement meter" definitely registered WINNER on that day.

I stopped playing cricket the day I left the Colony but continued to play soccer in college and on a semi-pro level for years to follow. Soccer, actually called "football" every place on the planet except the United States, never really caught on in the U.S. at the professional level even though enthusiasm at the high school and college level is very high. I suspect the reason soccer hasn't broken into the big-time TV slots is that baseball, football, and basketball have the 12 months covered, and there is no room to include another sport. Another reason might be there are not enough points or goals scored to feed the average American viewer's appetite. Another fringe sport is ice hockey, which is televised but does not have the following of the big three.

In school we also played traditional American sports but they weren't a big part of our organized sport activities. We did compete against other schools in softball and the boys from LaSalle School were particularly adept at this sport. Basketball or American football weren't on our rosters. My school did compete in field hockey, which is a popular sport outside the USA. Other sports included tennis, badminton, table tennis, and track and field.

For those who think field hockey is a sissy sport for women only, you're wrong! When the game is played well, it is lightning fast and swinging sticks and a hard leather ball traveling at a high rate of speed can do plenty of damage. I once had the chance to see the Indian national team play Pakistan. It was real war on the field and it was awesome to watch the skill exhibited. Of course when those two countries competed, national rivalry came into play and very little love was lost. Forget about the hockey ball staying on the ground. At this level of play, it was common to have the ball whistling past at eye-level, especially on the short corners.

It might sound like I was a low IQ jock, doing nothing but spending my waking hours playing sports. That's not completely true - I enjoyed chemistry immensely. Of course that might have had something to do with my friend Sammy Fattedad and I pinching and patting the rump of a very proper English lass named Liz during Mr. Smart's chemistry lab demonstrations. Today I can hear the comments that would be thrown at us – male chauvinists, inappropriate sexual harassment, and so on. Heck, we were just horny teenagers, Liz included. She would protest and blush bright red, but we knew she really liked the attention. She never told us to stop and would beam the biggest smile our way as she mildly protested. Liz was great, one of the smartest and easiest-going kids in the school. Sammy and I were merciless, but I don't think we ever went over the line, at least according to the standards of the day.

While it's true I was a sports fanatic, I had parents who constantly reminded of the need for an education and wanted to give me the opportunity to go to university. I was a bright kid, but I simply was not terribly motivated by my teachers. In most English schools there is no "high school diploma" per se, instead at the age of fifteen or sixteen, students take the London General Certificate of Education exams (GCE) at the "O" or Ordinary level.

So after five years of secondary school, the future boils down to how a student performs in these final exams, generally taken in subjects like English composition, English Lit, math, chemistry, biology, physics, French, Latin, geography, and history. The average student would sit for eight subjects and pass five. I sat for seven and passed four, repeated two more, and passed them the second time.

At KGV a student had to pass a minimum of three exams to go to "Form Six" (somewhat equivalent to grades twelve/thirteen) to study two or three subjects at advanced levels for two years and then take the GCE "A" levels. "A" levels are recognized for full course credit by U.S. colleges. I studied and achieved passes in biology and geography.

I looked forward to having fun at our school dance that was held one Friday each month; we called it Friday Club. Looking back I realize it was really a non-event by today's standards, but back then it was an awfully good reason to have a party under relatively minor supervision by adults. Friday Club was nothing more than a tinny-sounding portable stereo system playing in the assembly hall with kids dancing to the music put out by scratched 45 rpm records. Some of the guys and girls really knew how to jive and I envied them dancing on the wooden floor to the sounds of Duane Eddy, Jerry Lee Lewis, Bill Haley, and other rock and roll musicians of the day. I didn't know how to jive dance and watched Sid and Sammy Fattedad, Alex Wernberg, Geoff Lyons, Peter Logan and others from the sidelines.

I remember when Chubby Checker came out with the Twist. It was considered to be an immoral dance and teachers would only allow us to play the record twice during the Friday dance. I guess a quota of two sins per night was acceptable. The Twist and the Mashed Potato were relatively easy dances so everybody would crowd the dance floor.

I always looked forward to the "group grope," otherwise known as slow dancing. It was the ultimate opportunity to see which guy had a crush on which girl. Friday Club was fun and a chance to let raging hormones smolder in the assembly hall until we were sure somebody would catch on fire. There was a long list of girls I had a schoolboy crush on at one time or another and in most cases it was unrequited. Rosie Bunton, Jackie Maché, Tina Gasten and Susie Baker were but a few I thought were absolute knockouts.

When the Beatles hit the scene their music instantly caught on, but they were not well accepted by teachers because their mop-head look was considered unruly and thus they were regarded as rebellious and disrespectful of authority. You can imagine the reception when the Stones became popular; God forbid if Kiss or Marilyn Manson existed at the time! I'm sure these musicians would have been considered demonic pagans and the straitlaced teachers at KGV never would have allowed us to dance to their beat.

One Friday Club night was not typical because we'd heard two of the toughest guys in the school were planning to rumble, but also because I had just bought a pair of very fashionable, but highly unusual, shoes. I knew I was going to be the object of good-natured teasing and harassment that night.

The Beatles were remembered for their collarless suits and hairstyles. What they were less remembered for was the introduction of "Beatle Boots." These were black leather, ankle-high shoes that were more toe-pointed than the usual shoe. With winnings from gambling, cricket, and scotch selling, I splurged on a pair of Beatle Boots and wore them proudly to the Friday Club. What happened when I walked through the door was not exactly what I had in mind.

The boots looked very mod, but there was something a bit peculiar about them. They were much longer than typical shoes. I tried them on at the store and even though I felt funny about the way they looked on my feet, I decided to buy them and wear them like a stud to the next Friday Club. When my friends gathered around me, I was subjected to more humiliation than I could ever have imagined. They remarked my boots looked about three sizes too long for my feet and assured me I could pass for Koko the clown.

"Look at Tony's clown shoes!" was the cry of the night. I could have died. What I had hoped would propel me into the "cool strata" turned out to be a staggering embarrassment. There was nothing I could do but endure the torment. What saved me from an entire evening of humiliation was word that the featured fight was going to start behind the buildings on a far grass field where teachers didn't patrol. Who knows what the reason for the fight was, probably some guy had been disrespectful to another guy and most likely a girl was somehow involved.

The two fighting adversaries were unevenly matched. Alex reared about six-foot and weighed over one hundred and ninety pounds. He was a tough athlete, competing in discus and shot put. Sonny was a tough, tough guy but at five foot ten inches tall and one hundred and fifty pounds soaking wet, he would have to do something special to win the fight.

Pushing and swearing got things started and things soon escalated when Sonny grabbed an empty Coke bottle and smashed it on a wooden crate, waving the weapon in Alex's face. This should have been a classic fight scene accented by taunts and jeers as jagged glass danced in the moonlight. One small difference, the bottle remained intact! Sonny smashed it again on the crate. The bottle still didn't break and before he could go for the third try, Alex jumped on him and wrestled the lightweight to the ground.

The pair rolled around and a few punches were thrown, but fortunately neither wanted to maim the other so after a few minutes the fight ended with Alex holding a hammer lock on Sonny's neck.

As the hammer lock grabbed, big commotion at the front entrance of the school commanded everybody's attention and kids quickly left the fight scene to find out what else was going on.

Our principal was an odd, bald guy by the name of Gore. He heard rumors that a boy and girl were making out (maybe more than kissing) on the soccer field and he wasn't about to let *that* happen under his watch. Principal Gore jumped into his car, his tires screeching as he pointed his English Morris Minor onto the darkened soccer field to see if he could catch the culprits in the act. There was nothing to see on the grass, but it was quite a sight to watch veins bulging on the principal's bald head as he searched fruitlessly for the "morally corrupt couple."

After all that excitement, it was time to leave the Friday Club and go into town to find something else to do.

It was only eleven o'clock, still quite early so six of us jumped on a bus and headed into downtown Kowloon to spend time at a hamburger joint called Queen's Kitchen. Buses in Kowloon came in two styles, single and double-decker, and were always painted red, just like the buses in England.

This particular evening we were riding a double-decker with KGV school kids taking over the entire upper deck. My pals on the bus included Norman Hope, Les Harvey, Alex Wernberg, Gopal Lalchandani, Frank Drake, and Peter Rull. We could be pretty loud and rowdy so I'm sure the noise discouraged people from joining us upstairs.

Queen's Kitchen was in a section of Tsim Sha Tsui just off Canarvon Road, an area populated by an excessive number of bars. Parading outside each bar were mini-skirted bar girls calling to the GIs who were visiting Hong Kong on R&R to come in and "have a good time." As we walked by the bars we flirted with the girls and they answered with salty retorts and giggles.

The hamburger joint was smack in the middle of Bar Row and was well-known for exceptionally greasy cheeseburgers and a jukebox chockfull of good tunes. A couple favorite tunes were "Mother-in-Law" and "Hello, Baby" by the Big Bopper. After eating, clowning around for a couple of hours, and strolling the bars, our next stop was usually Princess Billiards where we played serious snooker.

Snooker is the English version of pocket billiards. It is more difficult to master than pool and was a favorite late evening pastime for my crowd. We would often play for money, but not big stakes, just a couple dollars a game. On weekend nights we might play until three in the morning and then take a break for a late night snack of *pai kwut mein,* or pork chop noodles. We'd then play a couple hands of poker.

This was how my friends and I spent Friday and Saturday nights in our final years of high school. Obviously we weren't choirboys, but none of us ever got drunk and seldom had any serious liquor issues. Only a minority smoked cigarettes and none of us took drugs. Our vices were limited to staying out late, gambling, and chasing girls. We had a hell of a good time!

We grew up fast in Hong Kong. There was no drinking age. Nightclubs and discos were open to whoever had the money to pay the bill. Strange to hear, but marijuana, speed, and psychedelics were not easily obtainable whereas narcotics could easily be bought. I believe the reason for heroin and opium being more readily available goes back in history to the Opium Wars. A trained eye could easily spot skinny looking guys in the shopping arcades of Tsim Sha Tsui in downtown Kowloon. They would be leaning against pillars, eyes canvassing the crowd trying to spot customers. They would offer heroin in folded white paper packets for a few dollars each. Alternatively, little rolled balls of opium were easily passed. It really wasn't expensive…to start!

Growing up I remember seeing street people "shooting the dragon" on isolated street corners in the poorer parts of town. This was the term the Chinese gave to heating drug powder with a match until it vaporized, and then inhaling the smoke. Sometimes on back streets I would see addicts smoking opium through bamboo water pipes similar to bongs used by hippies to smoke hashish.

None of the guys I grew up with developed any kind of drug problem and I have often wondered why. I reached two conclusions. First, there were so many vices visible and available from a very early age that any "mystique factor" was eliminated. The second conclusion involved a social class phenomenon. The kids I hung around with thought drugs were for the poor and destitute and none of us wanted to be like that. Sadly for many of the American expatriate teenagers coming to Hong Kong with their parents, it was a different story. They sought drugs. This was probably related to the hippie movement and the growing popularity of marijuana and psychedelics sold on the black market in the States.

In the '60s some of my American friends smuggled grass into Hong Kong when they came back from home leave. One of my buddies left for the States and came back from spring break with a stash. We lived in the same apartment complex so I ran upstairs and knocked on his door to welcome him back. Bobby was a character, a guy who was naturally wound like an eight-day clock. You'd swear he was on amphetamines. I liked Bobby. He had a fun personality, always seemed to be in a good mood, and had a generous nature. On this particular evening, we were listening to music in his room, just hanging out. Bobby pulled out his travelling bag, dug around, and came up with a jar of Noxzema.

"Bobby, you really don't need to apply face cream to make yourself more beautiful," I teased. "Nothing can help *that* face."

"No, I'm not interested in the goddamn Noxzema, this is what I just remembered I had stashed away."

As he spoke, Bobby pulled out a small baggie of grass from the bottom of the jar and shrieked like a leprechaun who had just found his pot of gold.

"This is real good stuff, guaranteed to be from Maui, at least according to my supplier in San Diego. Let's do some."

I had never smoked grass before and Bobby's place was a pretty safe environment so I thought to myself, *Why not?* Bobby produced a pack of Zig Zag papers, another introduction to the hippie antiestablishment movement. He showed me how to hand roll the paper, lick the edge, and twist the joint to produce the classic shape.

I tried to roll one but wasn't very successful and eventually settled for the joint rolled by Bobby, the professional. Bobby lit the joint and we both took a few hits. He instructed me to hold the inhaled smoke as long as I could. First time I tried I hacked up a storm since I didn't smoke and was completely unprepared for the harsh taste of the marijuana. Amazingly, it only took a couple more hits before I adjusted to my new vice.

That first night I thought pot had little impact on me. Bobby was laughing and gobbling cookies he had loaded on a plate in the kitchen, but I really didn't notice much effect other than feeling good and laughing over dumb things. This was the only time I ever smoked dope in Hong Kong and I never tried anything stronger.

Not all my American expatriate friends were into experimentation with various forms of mind-bending drugs. Two friends bring a smile to my face - Mark Kogan and Scott Moyer. Both were capable baseball players, but their efforts to play cricket, well, that was another story. Much to his chagrin, Mark could never adjust to hitting a ball that bounced in front of him. Scott was a bit better with a bat, but neither could master the ability to bowl a cricket ball straight-armed.

Mark went back to the States with an amazing capability to speak Cantonese after only two years in Hong Kong, and Scott went on to become a first-class drummer in a band playing California surf music. Music has remained his passion to this day.

Having expatriate friends had a downside. They would always be gone in two or three years, and such was the case for these two. One day I heard Scott was back in Hong Kong for brain surgery and was staying at the Mandarin Hotel. I grabbed Sammy Fattedad, a mutual friend, and went to cheer him up. We had a good time reminiscing about the old days and laughed uproariously. Sammy even tried to teach Scott how to play the guitar. Sammy was an accomplished musician and a member of the famous Kontinentals.

The fun evening was drawing to a close when something strange happened. Scott was clowning around with a Zippo lighter, flicking it on and off. I was talking to Sammy when a searing pain assaulted my wrist. Scott had heated the Zippo cover and as a joke pressed the metal cap against my wrist, never expecting the skin to sizzle and blister.

The pain was incredible and it was all I could do to keep control. I kept reminding myself that my friend was scheduled for brain surgery the next day and I should not upset a patient prior to something so serious, so I played the incident down.

Sammy and I left in short time and found a 24-hour pharmacy where I purchased antibiotic ointment to prevent infection. It was late and the Star Ferry had quit running so we had to grab a small *wallah-wallah* boat to cross the harbor. I was in severe pain as we chugged across the choppy water. Looking at my blistering flesh, I noticed something eerie. The burn's outline bore a striking resemblance to the scar I had noticed on the back of Chow Chai's hand so many years before.

CHAPTER SIX
"Rock and Roll Music"
CHUCK BERRY

I was wakened from a deep sleep by the pounding of deafeningly loud music and insistent drum thumping. It was Monday morning, the first day of my two-week Easter break. Like most sixteen-year-olds, I was looking forward to sleeping until noon.

This was not to be because at the ungodly hour of 9:00 a.m. my brother Steve started practicing his drums in our living room, just 30 feet from where I slept. Steve set up his drum kit surrounded by stereo speakers which were blasting the Rolling Stones begging, "Can't Get No Satisfaction." My brain was not fully functional, but recognized I was probably hearing Hong Kong's latest rock drumming idol.

My younger brother was spoiling my attempt to catch up on much needed sleep after a night of cavorting. I tried putting a pillow over my head to shut out the sound. Fat chance that would happen. The *boom, boom, boom* emitting from the base drum shook the walls as my bed vibrated to the beat.

I dragged myself out of bed and opened the door to the living room. With the door open, the decibels ascended three-fold. Perched on a drum stool behind a set of blue Premier drums capped with Zildjian cymbals sat a slender, pale boy with long, curly Afro-styled hair. The idol was pounding his tom-toms, thumping the bass drum and crashing cymbals in sync with Charlie Watts.

Funny how Steve was born with curly hair and mine was dead straight. As a young kid, he hated his hair because it was difficult to manage, but when the Afro look became classic '60s rock 'n roll a la Jimi Hendrix, Steve landed at the top of the heap.

"Steve," I implored, "give me a break, it's too early to start that pounding. I need to sleep for a few more hours!"

Without resistance, but displaying evidence of annoyance, Steve put down his drumsticks and turned off the stereo without saying a word. My brother had a tendency to play the silent type, especially when he wasn't happy with what was going on. He shuffled off to another room and left me to catch a few more zzzzs.

I can't remember how many dozen times this scene was repeated in our household during Steve's upward spiral into Hong Kong's drumming notoriety. This was the era of the Mersey beat, and teens in Hong Kong were tuned into both the English and American music scene, although British bands were usually at the top of the hit parade.

Several British bands visited the Colony and I had a chance to see some of the classic acts of the '60s, including the Beatles. A lot had happened in three years; my interest in yo-yos had given way to a passion for rock and roll music and of course …girls.

When I saw the Beatles at the City Hall in Hong Kong, they still wore collarless suits and looked fairly well-groomed, except for their outrageous mop-head hairstyles. Unfortunately Ringo was not with them. He was recuperating from the removal of his tonsils so the Fab Four was temporarily the Fab Three.

Other groups performing in Hong Kong included Manfred Mann, The Searchers, and The Kinks to name just a few. They found their Hong Kong fans to be as boisterous as any others. We were as crazy about the new sound as every other teenager on the planet.

Steve started drumming at age twelve and drove me crazy with his practice sessions in the living room of our apartment. At thirteen he was already the equal of many famous English drummers and I thought he easily rated among the best in the world, unbiased as I was. Steve had certainly developed a reputation as being the best young drummer in Hong Kong, and as his fame grew, things began to change in our relationship, as well as with the outside world. Steve was no longer known as "Tony's kid brother." Instead, I became "Steve's older brother." A subtle, but very noticeable difference. I was so proud of him! It was great to be on the dance floor and hear the crowd cheering when my little brother went into one of his drum solos or provided a well-recognized backbeat to a famous song.

But on this early morning I was not one of his adoring fans. I couldn't get back to sleep after my morning wake-up call, so I decided to get up and venture on a gambling trip to Macau.

I called my friend Les Harvey to set up our day. Les was a year older and we'd been friends for many years, competing in track and field events together. Les's forte was discus and shot put and mine was javelin. Les and I also shared a passion for gambling. This day we planned to catch the noon hydrofoil to Macau for a day at the casinos and planned to return later that evening. I checked my wallet for the two hundred dollars I'd saved, ran downstairs, and grabbed a taxi (we were all too young to drive) to collect Les, he lived nearby on Kadoorie Avenue.

"Hi Les, are you ready to bust the bank in Macau?" I asked as my friend slid across the seat. We couldn't wait to get started on what would surely be a winning streak.

"You bet," he assured me. "I'm going to win big at the blackjack table, and I've got a new system I want to try out on the dice game."

"Well," I replied, "I don't know about your new system, but what I do know is that I have a feeling in my bones that this is going to be our lucky trip and I'm going to make big bucks this day!"

We laughed as the cab made its way downtown. The hydrofoil pier was on the Hong Kong side of the harbor so we had to take the taxi to the Star Ferry, and then take the ten-minute ride across the harbor. Our last leg was a short walk along the waterfront to the docks which moored the sleek Italian hydrofoils.

We bought our tickets and made our way to the seating area that resembled a short, wide airplane cabin. Within minutes we were skimming the waves at high speed on our way to the Portuguese colony where gambling was legal. We flew over waves for an hour and a half to cover the forty miles to Macau, a small town with little to offer except the annual Macau Grand Prix and casino gambling.

The hydrofoil ride was enjoyable, especially standing outside on the deck. The boat started at a relatively slow speed, but once away from harbor traffic, the captain gunned the engines and the bow elevated on hydrofoil wings allowing the boat to fly across the water at high speeds. We passed Stonecutter's Island, Chung Chau, and Lantau in a whiz. Those days there was little habitation on islands other than Hong Kong and the Kowloon peninsula so the only way to get onto the outer islands was by ferryboat. These islands were remote and not frequented regularly.

Occasionally a gang of us camped on Lantau Island at a site we found in a hilly section of the island. Our hideaway featured a stream and small pool, perfect for cooling off on hot summer days. I was an amateur camper and barely had the necessities to fill a backpack. However, I did have a canteen and sleeping bag. Others like Peter Rull and Norman Hope had equipment up the kazoo and fancied they were amateur soldiers carrying full army gear.

On one of our camping trips Norman was gloating over a box of donuts he brought with him. He bought them at Cherikoff's, a popular Russian bakery in Kowloon. Norman was letting everyone know how much he was going to enjoy having the sweets for breakfast. Next morning, much to his chagrin, a local ant colony had captured Norman's donuts and the box was occupied by thousands of little red guys marching over hills of sugar. We had a good laugh at his expense.

"Serves you right, Norman, for all the gloating. Now you'll eat baked beans like the rest of us," we teased.

Looking back, we really didn't do much on these trips. We played card games like hearts and gin rummy, hiked, explored, and roasted and toasted food as we thoroughly enjoyed friendship around the campfire. Such simple pastimes left me with so many fond memories.

Apparently not all camping trips were so uneventful, at least according to stories told by Eddie Xavier. Once the gang was encamped on a level piece of ground above a beach and noticed a Cub Scout troop had come for the day. Nobody paid much attention to the young boys, but when scanning the beach with a pair of binoculars, Eddie noticed something very disturbing was happening. The troop leader and a couple boys were undressed and the adult supervisor was copping an occasional fondle. *Gross!*

Eddie also told of the time a guy they nicknamed "Bluebeard" was on the beach romping with his lady friend in the buff. The gang watched the couple for some time. With no TV at camp, we had to find other forms of entertainment.

As our hydrofoil got closer to Macau, the water changed from blue-green to muddy brown. Shallower waters coupled with the flowing of a major river, the Pearl, into the sea destroyed the perfect blue. Macau was a Portuguese colony, but entry was simple. All a visitor needed to do was show a passport and you were in. Five minutes at the max.

The Portuguese settled Macau between 1554 and 1557 and the territory served as a vital base for merchants as well as Christian missionaries ministering to China and Japan. The settlement of Macau pre-dated that of Hong Kong (1841) but with the settlement of the British Colony, the importance of Macau declined.

At sixteen I was legally too young to gamble, but nobody ever tried to stop me. I guess they were willing to take money from gamblers at any age. This was Asia where money didn't just talk, it shouted.

Les and I sauntered into the Estoril Casino and surveyed the big gaming room. On one wall slot machines lined in formation but they never interested me because I regarded their payouts the result of pure luck requiring no skill. I considered myself a skillful gambler so the games that held my interest were blackjack and a Chinese dice game called *dai-sai*, which translated means "high-low."

Three dice are used for *dai-sai* and the object is to bet on the many possible combinations paying out differing odds. In many ways *dai-sai* betting is similar to roulette. The dice-shaker sits in the center behind the table and shakes the dice inside a big bowl covered with a glass dome.

When the game is ready to start, the shaker cries *Hoi* (open) one time and betting begins. *Hoi* is shouted a second time and betting continues. After the third and final declaration of *Hoi,* the dice, which were all this time hidden, are shown.

The dice-shaker's ceremony added drama to the betting and gamblers would bet either high or low which paid even odds, hence the name *dai-sai*. Next to the dice-shaker mahjong-like blocks were displayed which showed players the high-low sequence for the past twenty throws (as if that made any difference to the outcome of the next throw).

I parked my butt at the *dai-sai* table and proceeded to make several ten dollar bets, alternating between high and low using my intuition. Occasionally I bet certain combinations, such as pairs or certain numbers between three and eighteen, each bearing different odds depending on the difficulty. I felt luck was with me and was having a good day. Within an hour or so I pocketed a healthy pile of money so I decided to break away and play a few games of blackjack.

Once again lady luck was with me and I hit several blackjacks. I decided to take a break and wander around to check out other Chinese games, but most never really interested me. *Fan-tan* is a game I found incredibly silly. The croupier dips a bowl into a pot of ordinary white buttons and then turns it over so the buttons are hidden beneath the bowl. Gamblers bet on combinations displayed across the gaming table. After bets are put down, the croupier removes the bowl, takes a bamboo cane and counts away the buttons in groups of three until one, two, or three buttons remain. The object of the game is to bet on how many buttons will remain after the division by threes. This game didn't hold my interest for long and I didn't make any bets.

After a short walk around the casino I found Les and we decided to get something to eat. Since we were both doing quite well we thought we would treat ourselves to a special meal at a well-known Macau restaurant called Posada's which offered a specialty a dish known as African Chicken. African Chicken is a baked chicken covered with an array of spices and was quite a treat in those days. During lunch Les asked how I was doing at the tables.

I had a winner's smile on my face and answered, "I'm doing really well. In fact I'm up almost a thousand dollars! How are you doing?"

Les confided, "Wow, that's great, we're both hot! I'm also doing well. In fact I'm almost winning as much as you are." This was a first as most of the time one of us would be up a couple hundred at the most, but more often down a few bucks. We wolfed down our delicious chicken and were anxious to get back to the tables. Like most gamblers, we could never get our fill of the game.

Back at the Estoril we continued to have good and bad spells and played a little longer than planned. We decided to catch the six o'clock hydrofoil back to Hong Kong as big, big winners. We seldom gambled at the same table; it was a superstition among friends so we went different ways.

Once more I headed to the *dai-sai* table and laid down my bets using the same pattern I had used before. After playing for twenty minutes I was getting frustrated – I'd lost almost half my winnings, five hundred dollars! Les must have decided he had enough too because he came over to catch the action at my table and make a few small bets. He said. "Let's go, you may as well quit while ahead."

By now I was really angry at having lost back half my stash.

"No way! I want to walk out of here with my thousand bucks. I'm going to make one big bet, five hundred on low!" I retorted.

"Don't be a moron," admonished Les. "I won't let you lose all your winnings.You'd be really miserable company on the hydrofoil ride back." With that final comment, Les reached across the table and pulled back half my bet.

I looked at him and debated whether to demand he put back the money, but decided to let the reduced bet stand. We listened as the dice-shaker cried *Hoi* once, *Hoi* twice, and finally *Hoi* for the third time. A one, two, and three, it was a low combination and I won two hundred and fifty dollars! It was good to win, but annoying that Les had pulled back half my bet. I still wanted to win a thousand; it was a goal I had to achieve, and the sum had a nice ring to it. I continued to play with my two hundred and fifty win, but after a half dozen games had once again lost it all back. By now my frustration level was over the top. I told Les

I was going to bet the full five hundred dollars, only this time on high. I was a lost cause, sick with gambling fever.

"You are really impossible," Les sighed. "I can't watch you lose your money." With that my friend walked away. I took the big five hundred-dollar bill from my wallet with a flourish. I put it down on the high bet and immediately started to squirm. A five hundred dollar Hong Kong bill is about fifty percent larger than a one hundred dollar bill; its presence on the table was really quite impressive, and was a huge amount of money to me. My bet was the only five hundred dollar bill on the table. I had never had that much money in my life and here I was putting it all down on a single bet because of gambler's greed.

Hoi once. *Hoi* twice. *Hoi* for the third and final time and the dice were shown. It seemed the dice-shaker was uncovering the bowl in slow motion. My eyes strained to see the numbers as my heart pounded. I felt dizzy and my mouth was dry. The numbers were presented for all to see and count. Four, five and six. My God, I thought, that adds up to fifteen high! I won! I shouted wildly for Les to see my stash.

"Alright, that's enough!" I grabbed my money and Les and I walked out without looking back. I was glad we were gambling with cash and I didn't have to stop to cash chips. I would have been tempted to bet along the way to the cashiers' cage.

Once out of the casino, Les and I laughed at our good fortune. Both of us walked away as big winners. We stopped at stores on the way back to the pier and bought gifts for our families. I decided to buy Steve a Spanish guitar, which was something he had wanted for some time. Maybe he would forgive me for interrupting his drumming practices.

I found a bottle of Mateus Portuguese wine I thought my parents would enjoy. No problem with sixteen year olds buying booze in Asia.

The hydrofoil ride back to Hong Kong was exhilarating because we were returning as winners and that was a great feeling. We savored the high while we could because trips home were not always so pleasant. We were winners this time, but I can't imagine how bad I would have felt if I'd lost my five hundred dollar win, and then lost my own bankroll trying to get it back. I would have had trouble sleeping for days, maybe weeks, afterward.

Gamblers inevitably have a string of bad luck. A few months later we took another gambling trip to Macau that was far less pleasant. The downfall of every gambler is believing a big score will certainly lead to another win. Things were very different on that second trip. It was an experience Les and I would rather forget. Once again, we were planted in the Estoril Casino placing bets, only this time lady luck wasn't smiling. After several hours my well ran dry and I decided to ask Les for a loan.

"Sorry, but I'm busted. In fact, I was going to ask you for money," Les answered.

"Ask me? I'm down to my last dollar, how are we going to get home?"

We were angry and embarrassed by the stupidity of our situation. Never before had we been in such a position and we now had to do something desperate. After deliberating, it was obvious there was only one solution. The two big gamblers had to go to a pawnshop to hock watches and then head back to Hong Kong to borrow money to redeem them. Instead of the more expensive hydrofoil ticket, we took the ferry back. It was a long boat ride home, almost three times as long as it took the hydrofoil to cross the harbor. To make matters worse, the sea was choppy. As we ferried back to Hong Kong we tried to think through what we were going to do next. We left relatively nice watches with a pawnbroker and needed to go back and claim them ASAP, but where to get the money? Finally we settled on a plan.

When we arrived at the Hong Kong dock we went to borrow money from my mother, hoping she would feel sorry for us. It was a slow, miserable walk from the pier to Prince's Building located in the Central District of Hong Kong. We went to my mother's office on the 17th floor and I felt sick at what I had to do. Losing my savings and the bout of seasickness from the ferry trip added to my misery, but knowing I had to ask for a loan was the worst.

After the obligatory parental lecture on the perils of gambling with Les standing sheepishly behind me, we got the loan and headed back to Macau for the second time that day. The return trip was miserable in more ways than one. We were physically and emotionally sick. The spring was absent in our step as we walked from the ferry dock to the pawnshop. Once there we forked over the money for our watches along with what seemed like an exorbitant broker's commission and dragged our heels out the door.

"What do you want to do now, Les? We have almost an hour and a half to kill before the next ride home." Les shrugged indifference.

"We haven't eaten all day and even though I'm not really hungry, I don't want to take the trip back on an empty stomach. I feel close to puking as it is," I admitted.

"I've got an idea!" I finally shouted. "We don't have enough to do another African Chicken at Posada's but a hot *won ton mein* at a food stall down by the dock could hit the spot." My idea seemed to invigorate Les and he nodded in agreement.

We found a typical outdoor food stall for our meal. The owner/cook stood inside a covered, square-shaped structure that was slightly elevated. Hanging from roof beams on all four sides of the stall were a collection of meats, including duck, chicken, fish, and sausage. Mystery meats were also hung high. A big black wok sat on a gas stove in which virtually everything was cooked. It didn't take him long to whip up our hot soup.

"Starting to get a little nippy, and soup is a good idea," I commented as I zipped up my light nylon jacket and slurped my broth. It turned out we were hungrier than we thought and within minutes our bowls were clean. Visitors from Europe would probably recoil in horror at the unsanitary conditions at food stalls, but Les and I were locals and had no problem with the bizarre food service.

"You ready for the trek home?" asked Les.

As I stood to leave, somebody bumped into me enough to make me stagger. It was a young Chinese man and I saw incredible fear filling his eyes. I thought he was worried he had hurt me and I started to assure him I was fine. Then I realized the guy wasn't looking at me - he was looking *behind* me and within a split-second was off again. Les and I turned and saw three men twenty yards away running at full speed in our direction. The men were dressed in traditional Chinese clothing and wearing the black Chinese slippers often associated with kung fu. Yikes, they were waving meat cleavers! Les and I moved aside, we were not going to get in their way, not while they were waving choppers. The trio dashed by us, hot on the heels of the young man who had bumped me.

"Shit! What the hell was that all about?" I screamed in a hoarse whisper. I sat back on the bench as color drained from my face.

"Triad thugs," answered Les casually. "Chopper attacks are the traditional way Triads use to teach their enemies a lesson. It may be old-fashioned, but bloodiness sure gets the point across. You don't want to cross their path when they're on a mission. They're probably *sze kaus.*"

"What? How did you get to know so much about Triads?" I demanded. Les just smiled.

"I know you don't think of me as a wealth of knowledge, but this is an area I took an interest in and I wrote a paper for one of my Asian history classes about it." With that admission Les proceeded to give me a quick lesson in Triad lore.

"There's a good deal of myth when it comes to the origin of the Triads. Some say they began as a resistance movement to Manchu emperors. In the 20th century they were reported to collaborate with Sun Yat Sen, the founder of Republican China. Later Triads were said to work with Chiang Kai Shek to fight the communists under Mao Tse Tung, and were even reported to work with the Japanese during the occupation of Hong Kong in World War II. When Mao's communists were victorious in 1949, Triad members were dispersed to Hong Kong, Macau, and other places."

"Shit, Les, and here all the while I thought you were just a pretty face. I never thought of you as a historian."

Les flipped me a bird, grinned, and continued his dissertation.

"Triads have an interesting way of appointing their hierarchy. Major positions are given a name and a number, the latter being derived from Chinese numerology. The head of the Triad is called the *Shan Chu,* sometimes referred to as *Tai-Lo,* or elder brother. Under the *Shan Chu* lists a sub-boss and these men have the power to order the execution of any foe.

Additionally there is the incense master who is called *Heung Chu.* He is responsible for watching over Triad rituals, oaths, and the initiation of new recruits. The individual responsible for military activity is the Red Pole or *Hung Kwan* and the chief financial officer is the White Paper Fan. All these individuals are given a three numeral identification; for example the *Shan Chu* is a 489, the *Heung Chu* is a 438, and the *Hung Kwan* is a 426. And there you have it, a quick background on Triads."

"Well, I'm impressed, Les. I've lived all my life in Hong Kong and learned more about Triads in the last ten minutes than I picked up over the last 16 years." Little did I know at the time I would become even more intimate with Triad activities over the coming months.

We found our way to the dock and boarded the proverbial "slow boat to China." The trip seemed even longer than usual. Losing our stake and witnessing the attack by the Triad gang was not our idea of a good time. To this day my mother reminds me how sheepish and sick we looked that afternoon in her office pleading for a loan. She uses that occasion as a lesson to remind me of the evils of gambling. Pity her words weren't much heeded.

While our first love was casinos, Les and I were also avid poker players and were always searching for action. Quite often several guys from school got together at somebody's house and shuffled the cards until the wee hours of the morning. Les was always there along with Gopal Lalchandani, Phillip Morias, and Derek Turner. Most of the time I was lucky with poker hands, but there was one terrible time I took a beating which required six months recovery time.

Did you think Les and I learned our lesson from the Macau fiasco? No, we did not. We thought we were ready for a higher stake poker game with working adults. Oh boy, two high school teenagers wanting to get into a big stakes game with working adults. Not too bright. We got wind of a game on the Hong Kong Peak and through a mutual friend managed to get ourselves invited to play.

The stakes were high, but not exorbitant. At the beginning of the night, we held our own playing various hands of draw and stud poker. Nothing dramatic. I was up a few dollars and Les was about even. At midnight a new game was introduced and that's when we bit the hook and they reeled us in. The game was "Whirlpool" because it had the seductive capability to suck you into playing for a pot of money when you had no business being there.

The object of the game was quite simple. One card would be dealt to each player and then each betting round the players would be asked if they wanted another card. Play would stop when no more cards were requested. Each player totaled the face value of their cards with aces counting one or eleven, and picture cards valued at a half. Players closest to five and a half (low) or twenty-one (high) would split the pot. It was the type of game when experience and location to the dealer gave a big edge, but I was too young and cocky to recognize the clues. I instantly loved the game, and even though I was losing, elected to play again and again.

The hours went by quickly and it seemed I was always being sucked into the pot but seldom won. It was indeed a whirlpool! When my bank account ran low, I turned to Les for a loan. I was obsessed with the game.

To make a long story short, I lost about five hundred dollars, of which two hundred was borrowed from Les. Les didn't do as badly as I did, but managed to fall into the hole for two hundred. We left at seven the next morning feeling as miserable as we possibly could. We walked down the mountain to the Star Ferry and took a cab home. It was almost as bad as the infamous Macau trip. It was not the first time we were taught a lesson that separated the men from the boys. I remember the sick feeling I had after losing so much money, and every time I paid a few bucks on my loan from Les, the feeling came back full force. What's funny is in the years since I've recuperated my losses with interest by teaching the game to "Whirlpool virgins." First-time players rarely leave the whirlpool table as big winners, but the fever springs eternal.

Another form of gambling my friends and I readily embraced involved snooker. As mentioned, snooker is a form of pool originated by the English. It is played on a larger table with smaller pockets and balls and is a much more difficult game than pool to master.

The snooker ball must be hit directly into the pocket for it to drop, whereas pool tables offer a much larger margin of error. On a pool table the ball can bump the cushions at the mouth of the pocket and still fall in. We'd play snooker for small sums of money and I had an aptitude allowing me to make a few dollars. I even had my own cue; it was a "Joe Davis 500 Century Break." Joe Davis was an English snooker legend and the line of cues recognized his five hundred runs of over one hundred points. The best run I ever achieved was forty points, which doesn't sound that impressive, but was really quite respectable. Among my circle of friends, the player with the most talent was Steven Wong and he had the most beautiful and most expensive cue that I had ever seen.

The basic rules of snooker involve sinking a red ball enabling you to then sink a colored ball. The latter vary in points from two to seven. The black ball is worth seven points and the key is to position yourself to maximize your turn at the table and score as many points as possible. When betting is involved, the player who leaves the opportunity for a score to occur is the one responsible for payment of the points accumulated. We generally played for fifty cents a point with ten dollars at stake per game. Four or five players were in the game.

You often hear stories about the "bad element" hanging around pool joints and I'm sure those stories are true in many cases. My friends and I were among the "baddest dudes" at the Princess billiard tables because most other players were everyday Chinese guys just enjoying the pastime with an occasional wager. Admittedly, the smoke-filled, low ceilinged dark rooms did not do much for the image of the game and some of my snooker-playing friends weren't exactly angels.

At the Princess I would occasionally play with a band of young Thai boxers who were the nicest guys, unless you faced them in a fight. These guys loved to rumble and it was almost a form of recreation for them. I'm not talking about fighting in a gym; I'm talking about street fighting. The young men were lethal with their legs and possessed the incredible ability to kick an unfortunate opponent in the face two to three times before he knew what hit him.

A guy named Raymond was the leader of the group and we became good friends after meeting at a local nightclub. For Raymond fighting was a fun way to pass the time and he once invited me to join his band of "Merry Thais" for a rumble. He enthusiastically told me the rumble was going to be eight Thais against a gang of ten Chinese kung fu fighters. I thanked him for the opportunity, but explained I was a lover more than a fighter and politely declined the invitation.

The day after the big rumble, I saw Raymond and asked him how things had gone. He had a few bruises above his left eye, but said it was a short fight and the Thais once again kicked butt and sent the other gang running after a few short minutes.

A mutual friend witnessed the action and said he had never seen anything like it. The small number of Thais kicked their opponents with a ferocity he never imagined such nice guys could possess. They were merciless and extremely effective. Despite being outnumbered, the Thais easily beat the Chinese boys.

After hearing about this fighting power, I was enthused and decided I should learn how to Thai box. Raymond introduced me to their teacher and I took lessons from their *tse-fu* for a couple weeks. In one of my early lessons, my teacher instructed me to hit him and he would evade my punches. For awhile I thought I might enjoy learning to fight especially since the punching was only going in one direction. This soon ended when I walked into a block for a punch I had thrown. My teacher never punched me, he only blocked my effort, but I still ended up with a shiner. This confirmed I was definitely a lover and not a fighter.

One evening my friends and I played snooker for several hours before most of the guys decided to go home, leaving only Les, a few regulars, and me in the room. Before long we were hungry so we ordered *pai kwut mien* from a noodle house around the corner. The steaming pork chop with noodles in a soup broth arrived twenty minutes later and for just a couple dollars we enjoyed a delicious early morning snack.

After the meal the cards came out and five of us played stud poker with house employees until the early hours of the morning. At three a.m. we were ready to call it a day and head for home. As Les and I walked we heard loud yelling in the streets. As safe as I felt in Hong Kong at night, it was uncomfortable to hear ugly sounds at this hour so we cautiously walked down the steps into the alleyway leading to the main thoroughfare, Nathan Road. We hugged the wall on the dark side of the alley and peeked around the corner. We could see the noise was coming from a jewelry shop about fifty yards away. The road was deserted but fairly well lit by bluish-white street lamps. We saw three young men dressed in traditional Chinese black clothing. They were grabbing merchandise from a broken shop window and throwing it into a travel bag. One of the boys was clutching his arm and it appeared he had accidentally cut himself on the shattered plate glass and that's what brought about the yelling.

Another held a chopper in one hand, ready for any possible trouble. Guns were almost unheard of among the criminal element, only the cops and British army had firearms. Somehow this band of thieves had disconnected the alarm and stationed their getaway car next to the building so it was ready to whisk them away when the job was done.

Les and I stayed behind the wall out of sight, but I was curious and wanted to get a better look at what was happening. The heist was over and the thieves were getting into their car when I stepped out of the alleyway shadows. The last one into the car stopped and looked directly at me, our eyes locking. He shouted something to the others and they drove away, fishtailing as they fled. I had been foolish to take the risk of being seen and I cursed myself. We were damn lucky that the three guys decided to drive away and not take issue with a curious onlooker. Les and I flagged a taxi and within a few minutes and we were safely on our way home. Ten minutes later, the cab dropped Les at his place on Kadoorie Avenue and gave the taxi driver directions to my home in Cantonese.

As I stepped out of the taxi I thought about what I had seen when my eyes locked with those of the thief… it had been many years, but I could swear those eyes belonged to Chow Chai!

The familiar pounding on the drums once again awakened me the following Saturday morning. I looked with one eye at the alarm clock and it showed nine on the dot. It wasn't too bad because that Saturday I had to be at the Kowloon Cricket Club for a tennis match at ten-thirty.

I jumped out of bed, put on my tennis gear, and threw my cricket kit into a bag. KGV was playing their annual cricket match against a rival school at the same club later in the afternoon. I had loads of energy so playing two sport events in one day was no sweat.

The KCC was one of many social clubs in Hong Kong and my parents were members. Apart from cricket, the club provided tennis courts, lawn bowling, and a swimming pool. I felt very fortunate to be a junior member. When I was younger, my mother was an excellent tennis player and I enjoyed being her ball boy whenever she played. Mum played on the ladies' "A" team for the club and won several trophies, including one for being on the Ladies' Championship team in the Hong Kong league. She told me the day I could beat her at tennis, she would no longer have any interest in playing the game. She announced on that day she would become a spectator and my official cheerleader. That day arrived when I was thirteen. As promised, Mum watched me play, but never stepped on the courts again. I'm fairly certain her reasoning had nothing to do with my win.

Tennis is a great game and my natural ability allowed me to play with the top adult players and hold my own. My bread and butter shot was a deadly strong topspin, western forehand and I could hit the ball with substantial pace. In the days before metal and fiberglass rackets, my pride and joy was a TAD wooden racket strung with genuine animal gut.

The racket was a gift from my Aunt Lois who would occasionally leave her home in Manila to spend a couple weeks playing mahjong with her Hong Kong friends. I persuaded my Aunt Lois to buy me this present after months of nagging and occasionally locking her in the clothes closet, refusing to release her until I extracted a promise of a new tennis racket. Or maybe it was because she threatened to end my youth in a violent fashion if I didn't open the closet door. In any case, she bought me the racket of my dreams.

I loved to play singles and men's doubles, and occasionally enjoyed a game of mixed doubles on the KCC red clay courts. The main reason I enjoyed mixed doubles was because I would often play with Sue Hewson, a teacher from KGV. Sue was petite, buxom, and quite cute. She always wore a mini-tennis frock and her underwear flashed continuously. It was hard for a horny teenager to concentrate with this peep show going on, but I would usually play well enough to win so she would keep me as her partner. When I was playing with Sue, I seemed to hit the balls into the net fairly frequently when she was in the forecourt. This meant Sue would have to bend over to pick up the balls, thus presenting me with an excellent view of her frilly panties. Chinese ball boys also picked up tennis balls, and they were quick learners so it didn't take long before they got lazy about picking up balls within Sue's range at the net. Sue wasn't the greatest tennis player, but I was always a willing partner. Another wonderful mixed doubles partner was Muzzie Fincher, a great all-round, fun person who treated me like a little brother.

Tennis at the KCC wasn't just "puffball" mixed doubles. I played well enough to get into matches with several of the male "A" players. Not too many youngsters have the opportunity to develop their game on red clay, and before long I was playing for the club in league matches throughout Hong Kong. Most tennis courts in the Colony were of red clay, but there were also a significant number of grass courts. Hard courts, the norm today, were few and far between.

My memories of high school tennis always call to mind Yogi Berra's expression, "It ain't over 'til it's over."

I was playing Dave "Fudd" DeVelder in the finals of the school tennis championship and I was leading in the final set, five to zip. Everything was going great, my serve was on, my shots were hitting the lines, and I was killing Fudd. Then for some inexplicable reason I began to choke. Instead of bringing my focus on winning the game, I started to think about how I would feel if I lost. My arms felt like rubber and my stomach was queasy. I lost one game after another and could feel things slipping away. It was horrible. I couldn't stop my downward slide and eventually lost the final set and the championship, seven to five. From that day on I realized whenever I competed, I had to fight to the very last point, goal, run, or whatever, and to go for the jugular showing no mercy. I never wanted to experience a competitor coming back and beating me like Fudd did that day. It was one of those painful life lessons.

After a morning of KCC tennis, my young legs were very willing to continue with another sport in the afternoon. A quick sandwich and shower was all I needed. I changed into my white slacks, white shirt, and white cricket boots for an afternoon of cricket. This day we would play for the "Youngsaye Shield" against Diocesan Boys School, otherwise known by foes as DBS or "Dirty Buggers School." There was no love lost between the rival schools. Mr. Youngsaye was a principal at DBS and a big cricket fan, but he had absolutely no athletic ability. The only way he could make a name for himself in the sport was to present a trophy for the annual match.

Our team won the coin toss and elected to bat first and let DBS chase the score we would undoubtedly post. I felt playing tennis in the morning helped me prepare my eyes to watch the ball better when playing afternoon cricket. Today I was seeing the red cricket ball like a watermelon and smashing it to every corner of the cricket ground. My teammates were also playing well and we were building a good score. I personally scored seventy-five runs including a couple of towering "sixes" hit out of the field into a neighboring park. Watching the ball sail over the fence bordering the cricket ground I worried the rock-hard leather ball might bean an innocent kid, but fortunately there were no casualties.

When it came time for DBS to take their turn at bat, I was to have as much success bowling the ball as I had experienced with the bat. Along with my teammates we were successful at taking all the DBS wickets and I managed to "bowl out" six DBS batsmen. The KGV team played a great game and we won the coveted shield by a handy margin. Of course it was great to rub it in DBS faces because there had been times when they had taken us to task.

The next day I opened the sports page of the *South China Morning Post* newspaper and there was a big headline shouting, **Tebbutt Towers in School Match**. I had achieved the occasional press clipping for school athletics and soccer, but not since the yo-yo championship had my name appeared in such bold headlines. It felt good to have the recognition, and once again I was motivated to seek excellence in all I tried. My personal scorecard was again registering in the WIN column.

Cricket is an alien pastime to people in the U.S. They can't understand the game and find it very boring. What amuses me is most Brits think the same about baseball. Having played both sports I can tell you that cricket is indeed more boring, but does have its high points. Every time I try to discuss cricket with an American they confess to complete ignorance of the rules and ask for an explanation. Occasionally an American kid living in Hong Kong who had been good at baseball would try out for the cricket team and one or two actually made the cut. The greatest difficulty these kids had involved batting because they were not used to hitting a ball that bounced a few feet in front of them and changed direction because of the spin gripping the earth. Most found this tougher than hitting a baseball pitch that crossed the plate without a bounce.

Good hand-eye coordination enabled newcomers to hit the ball hard when they made contact, but often had trouble learning the defensive aspects of the game. Another hurdle many could never master was the straight arm required when bowling the ball, a very unnatural action for someone not familiar with the game from an early age. If a batter bowled out on the very first ball he faced, he suffered the humiliation of what was known as the "golden duck." A "regular duck" was getting out without scoring any runs, but not on the very first ball.

Trying to explain the rules of cricket to anyone not familiar with the sport is a monumental challenge that I've botched every time I've attempted it. Let me try to make a fool of myself again, this time in writing and I really hope I can do a reasonable job of not confusing those of you who give a damn.

There are two teams of eleven persons. For baseball players, think of it as only one inning of play instead of nine and there is a time limit on the game, generally five hours for one afternoon of amateur league play. A common misunderstanding is that a match lasts several days; this is only true for international "Test Matches" played between countries. The first team bats and scores runs until the entire team is out, or they can "retire" because they think they've scored enough runs and then give the other team a chance to beat their scored number of runs. If the second team manages to score more runs, they win the match. If they are all out before scoring enough runs, they lose. If at the end of five hours they are still batting but have not scored enough runs, the game is declared a draw.

Batting takes place in the middle of a large, oval, well-cut grass field with a finely cut center tract that is rolled so it is flat and firm, this is called the "wicket." A "sticky wicket" would be an expression for a playing surface that is not well prepared or develops an irregular surface making it not "true."

Two sets of three sticks (called stumps) are set twenty-two yards apart and it is the role of the batter to protect these stumps from being hit by the bowler (pitcher). A run is scored when a batter strikes a bowled ball and runs the twenty-two yards to the other side without getting tagged out.

An automatic four runs are scored if the ball is struck and crosses the perimeter of the field on the ground surface, and six runs are counted if it crosses the perimeter in the air without a bounce. Bowling is alternated with six deliveries from one set of stumps, followed by six at the other and so on throughout the allotted time.

A batter continues to bat until he is out by hitting the ball in the air and the ball is caught. He is out if the bowler manages to get the ball past the batter and it hits the stumps causing the bales to fall, or the umpire rules the ball would have hit the stumps if the batter had not put his legs in front of them, and is hit by the bowled ball. This is given the very logical name of LBW, or Leg Before Wicket.

A big difference between bowling and baseball pitching is that in the former a run-up is allowed before delivering the ball. A fast bowler is referred to as a "pace bowler" and will often take a run-up of about twenty yards or so before hurling the ball down the cricket pitch. A "spin bowler" would normally only take four to six steps before delivering the ball. The ball must be delivered with a straight arm, which Americans find extremely difficult to do because they are so used to bending the arm at the elbow when making a baseball pitch. The aim is to curve the ball in the air and bounce or spin it off the grass onto the stumps.

Batsmen wear protective gear in the form of leg pads, protective cups, padded gloves, and today a helmet and face mask, although we did not have those when I played the game.

So there you have a description of cricket, not that difficult to understand, right? Then again, I wonder how many people in North America have ever given a second thought to this sport.

I had mixed feelings about cricket because it was mandatory for the most talented students to play on the school team and matches were almost always on Saturday afternoons. The school team also included one or two teachers who wanted to make certain their team was fielding the top players. I actually enjoyed the game, but didn't like being compelled to play and having no freedom of choice in the matter. Giving up Saturday afternoons during the season when friends were at the beach or partying was sometimes a pain in the ass.

The school cricket team played in the Hong Kong men's second division. I may have been the team captain, but I had a little help from the teachers on the team telling me what I should do. Two of my favorite teachers who played on the school team were Mr. Findlay and Mr. Reeves, both great gentlemen.

League sponsors gave prizes every week to players who had good results bowling or batting and since I was good at both, I would frequently win a bottle of scotch. It would be "Vat 69" for scoring at least sixty-nine runs or a bottle of "Long John" for taking at least five wickets, i.e. bowling out five or more batters.

Since I did not like drinking scotch, I would sell my bottles to make extra spending money. This was one of the best perks of an otherwise boring game. It allowed me to supplement my pocket money and gave me additional incentive to play well.

After high school I played First Division Cricket and represented Hong Kong against a British Commonwealth touring team that boasted some of the best professional cricketers in the world on its roster. I must admit, even though I had ambivalent feelings about cricket, it was a thrill to play at the top level of competition. I almost wet my pants when I had to face one of the fastest bowlers in the world, Harold Rhodes. Imagine watching a gangly six-foot three inch Englishman, with the reputation of being one of the world's fastest, taking a twenty yard run and hurling the ball at the ground in front of you at 90 mph! The batsman's nightmare in cricket is to get "out" on the very first ball faced. I was so thankful that against Rhodes I was able to survive more than one ball. In fact I was able to score a few runs before I was caught out by a beautiful diving catch made by one of the fielders. I did not distinguish myself, but neither did I embarrass myself.

Since the ball was bowled with the intent of bouncing in front of the batsman, it was quite common for the ball to bounce awkwardly off the pitch and hit the batsman on a part of his body. I'll never forget playing in the intramural championship game of Crozier vs. Nightingale. Teams were named after former Headmasters of KGV.

Upsdell and Rowell were the other "House" teams and at times the intramural competitive spirit would run very high. On that particular day, I was facing the fastest bowler in the school, if not all Hong Kong, a fellow by the name of Gerald Laishley. (Gerald was another member of the Kontinentals). The other team had already batted and our team was rapidly approaching their score and was on the verge of winning. We needed six runs to win and I was facing Laishley as he ran up to bowl the ball. I had good reflexes, but wasn't prepared for what happened. Instead of the ball coming at an angle to bounce in front of me, Laishley let go of the ball at top speed right at my head. I tried to duck but could not move out of the way and it hit me square on the left side of my face, just below my ear.

I don't think the act was deliberate; Gerald just lost control of the ball. The pain was incredible and the hit caused a ringing in my head that sounded like an alarm clock. I staggered about in a stunned daze, almost to the point of being knocked out. I was in a pretty bad way and the game had to be suspended so I could be taken to the hospital for x-rays.

It turned out the ball had cracked my mastoid bone. For several days after I had to sit in class, with my head tilted to the side. It felt like water was flowing out of my ear, but it was actually blood draining in my middle ear.

Three weeks later both teams were back on the cricket pitch ready to play and finally decide the winning team. I was nervous and didn't know how I would fare against Laishley. I was worried I would be intimidated at the thought of getting hit again.

I settled in to my stance and watched Laishley take his run up and hurl the ball down the twenty-two yards at the stumps behind me. Instinct and ability took over and I smacked the ball to the outfield for a couple of runs. What a relief! I hadn't folded; I met the challenge and gave it my all.

From then on no fear filled my heart. I was determined to help my team win the championship. My batting partner and I managed to put together the effort needed to score enough runs to beat our opponents and win the trophy.

It was one of the greatest triumphs of my cricket career.

CHAPTER SEVEN
"I Wanna Be Your Man"
JOHN LENNON AND PAUL MCCARTNEY

It had been another great day of tennis and cricket and now I was ready to party through the night. Several friends and I decided to go to the Bayside nightclub where the Kontinentals were playing rock.

The Bayside was a popular hangout located in Chung King Mansions on Nathan Road, across the road from the Hyatt. The Kontinentals had developed a fantastic following since most of the band members were from KGV. Their music was great.

As I walked down the steps to the club, I saw school friends sitting around drinking rum and Cokes or making moves on the dance floor. Rob was one of my American friends and was looking a little high when he called me to his table. This was the same kid I had punished by making him manicure the grass during my Prefect days at KGV. Rob was visiting Hong Kong on break from high school in the States. He was now a solidly built teenager and had grown several inches, much taller than I was.

"What's happening, Rob?" I asked, happy to see my old friend.

"Hey, Tony. I have to run an errand and need somebody to go with me. It will only take about half an hour. We'll be back in no time at all. Will you keep me company while I get the job done?"

"Sure," I answered without asking what was going on. "Just let me buy a drink and have a couple dances and then I'll come with you."

I walked over to a table where my friends were hanging and sat down to talk with them while enjoying my first drink of the night. The music was loud and kids were having a great time making moves on the floor. Almost half the clubbers were high school students since there was no age restriction for nightclubs. The only restriction was the money needed to purchase at least one drink, but often that drink was nursed for several hours. The majority of clubbers were adults from all walks of life, but we hardly noticed them.

I was dancing with a Korean girl in my class named Theresa. She was teaching me how to jive when Rob tapped me on the shoulder and ordered, "Let's go."

I groaned because I was having fun, but a promise is a promise.

"Okay, as soon as this dance is over I'll find you."

After the song finished, I thanked Theresa and headed over to Rob. He saw me coming and gestured to wait a minute, he had to make a phone call. Thirty seconds later, we walked out of the club, turned left, and walked down Nathan Road toward the Star Ferry. As we made our way through the crowd and were assaulted by blinking neon signs and smells mingling from restaurants, I wondered what Rob was up to. We walked to the end of Nathan Road and into a multi-level car park, or parking garage, across the road from the Peninsula. Rob started to climb the stairs and I followed.

"Where the hell are you going?" I asked, trying to hide my discomfort over this strange situation. Neither of us had a car so I had no idea what we were doing in a parking garage.

"I'm meeting someone and I need you to watch my back. This will only take a minute."

I was starting to get curious about *exactly* what was going on. Earlier I thought Rob was high, now I was sure he was trying to score drugs.

Rob turned quickly and told me to stay near the door to the stairwell as he walked to a railing overlooking the main road. Like a ghost, a thin Chinese man wearing dark glasses with a cigarette hanging from his lips appeared out of thin air. The man had a few words with Rob and I saw

Rob hand him money in exchange for several small paper packets. I was right, it *was* a drug score and, damn it, I was involved! Like it or not, if the cops showed up I was an accomplice. My eyes surveyed the garage for any movement and then I saw them, several Chinese men leaning on a black Ford, the obligatory cigarettes draped from their lips. They didn't look like they were satisfied with the money Rob handed over.

"Rob! Let's get the hell out of here!" I shouted. He ran to the stairwell and in a few seconds we were rushing down the stairs to the busy road.

"You asshole, you should have told me what you were up to!" I roared.

"Hey, everything's cool. I just had to have somebody watch my back while I made a buy. Hold on a minute."

Rob ducked into a doorway, pulled out Zig Zag papers and began to roll a marijuana joint. He liberally sprinkled white powder from the packet onto the grass. The white powder was heroin.

"I'll share some with you, here take a hit."

I was really getting pissed off. First Rob tricked me into being party to a drug buy and now he was carelessly flashing narcotics and smoking a joint in a busy part of downtown Kowloon. I declined the hit and headed back to the Bayside. Rob caught up to me and I blurted, "You had me watching out for you while you were making a drug buy and didn't bother to tell me what you were up to? What the hell where you thinking?"

I was wasting my breath talking to him. Rob tuned me out, he was happy with his score and everything now was lookin' good for him. I made a mental note that this was the last time, the very last time, I would ever do a favor for Rob. While he was a nice guy, he was weak and I could see he was caught in a drug infused spiral that would pull him further and further down into its ugly depths. I was no angel, but I had no use for drugs. If there was one thing the police handled firmly in Hong Kong, it was being caught with narcotics. I fumed, knowing I could have been set up as an accomplice to a narcotic buy which would guarantee a stint in Stanley prison. That would have done wonders for my future. The agony that such an ordeal would cause my parents would have been devastating.

Rob and I headed back into the Bayside in silence. I was still furious. Rob had tricked me and was now high without a care in the world. We walked down the circular stairway to the nightclub and sat down at a table. Without a word, Rob left.

What a shitty night this had turned out to be, one bad thing after another. As I sipped my rum and Coke I noticed the Kontinentals were taking a break and a Beatles song was piped over the loudspeakers. Anders, the leader of the Kontinentals, saw me sitting alone and motioned me to his table by the stage.

Anders and I had a friendship dating back many years when we shared that memorable moment in Mr. Hollie's history class when the Magna Carta led to blows. That incident was far behind and now Anders had become quite a musical celebrity. While we were not bosom buddies, we'd remained good friends over the years. Many guys in school were jealous of the pop singer; Anders was a Swedish, tall, blond, good-looking guy, along with being a rock star.

A bigger reason for jealousy, Anders was one of the few guys in high school who was "getting it" on a regular basis. Many of us just fantasized about sex, few had actually experienced going "all the way." Anders was one of them.

Groupies in those days were known as "ballroom girls" and Anders was dating one of the most popular of the flock. Ballroom girls were generally in their late teens to mid-twenties and worked as dance hall hostesses in ballrooms scattered across the Colony. They were frequented almost solely by Chinese businessmen and were a popular Hong Kong phenomenon in the 1960s.

Ballrooms were usually visited after an evening of Chinese business dining and were generally considered respectable establishments, akin to the Japanese geisha concept, but on a far less grand and ceremonious scale. Chinese ballroom girls didn't have the status bestowed a true Japanese geisha. Men went to the ballroom to have a few drinks while the pretty girls kept them company with conversation or dancing. For the Japanese, geishas were a highly respected and talented cultural phenomenon.

Every fifteen minutes lights in the ballroom would change color as the signal for the girls to move on to the next group of guests at another table. Sometimes the girls were paid extra to stay at a particular table. To boost club revenues, the girls ordered expensive champagne (which actually was a lemon-lime soft drink) and an additional cover charge was added to the evening's bill. These girls were not prostitutes. They were just pretty young women, uneducated, and looking for a night of fun and easy money.

Of course "private arrangements" could be made on the side for favors, but that was personal business. The girls did not have pimps either through the establishment or on the outside; this distinguished them from call girls.

The Hong Kong pecking order for loose girls from "naughty to bad" would ladder out as: ballroom girl, bar girl, call girl, and the lowest rung would be the brothel prostitute.

Anders introduced me to his girlfriend Jackie and she surprised me by saying one of her friends had a crush on yours truly. Jackie wanted to know if I was interested in meeting this girlfriend. Is the Pope Catholic? Does a bear shit in the woods?

I could scarcely restrain my enthusiasm. I could sense the possibility of taking a huge step in my life – the loss of my virginity. Here at the Bayside was an opportunity to meet a woman of the world at a most tender age. A minute before I had been swearing about my circumstances, but now life never sounded sweeter.

Jackie told me her friend had been watching me at the club for weeks and would be stopping by around eleven o'clock. The friend worked in a ballroom too but she had the night off. I told Jackie I would be sitting right at this table - it would have taken Bruce Lee and a team of his martial arts students to persuade me to leave!

My watch showed it was now ten; I had an hour to kill. A stream of thoughts crossed my mind. What would she look like? Would she be nice, or a brazen tart? Would she like me once she met me?

Rum and Cokes flowed as I pondered my near future. I was feeling a light buzz as I thought about my early sexual encounters and wondered if this meeting was going to lead to the "big event." Like most guys, I flirted and dated in my early years of high school but never had a serious teen romance.

The first time I fondled a girl's breasts was quite a comical sequence of events, and the story goes something like this . . .

Girls from St. George's, the English Army School, were reportedly faster and easier than those at KGV, a rumor that was probably unfounded. Naturally I set out to meet a few of these easy women at dances held at St John's Cathedral Hall on Hong Kong Island. I met a cute blonde named Theresa. After the usual awkward preliminaries, we discovered we liked each other so we went on a few movie dates.

One evening I took her home and while heavy necking in the shadows, I thought to myself - *This is the moment, now or never! I must find out what it feels like to fondle a girl's breasts.*

Theresa was showing, or feigning, enthusiasm, but every time I tried to unbutton her blouse, she wouldn't let me touch her. It was really confusing and frustrating. I figured the rumors about St. George's girls were bullshit generalizations, or else I just wasn't her type. It never occurred to me that maybe she just wasn't the tart type.

It turned out Theresa was a really nice girl; I enjoyed her company and she was very attractive arm candy. We continued to date and my original Neanderthal, crass motivation for dating her soon disappeared.

Weeks later after a particularly passionate kissing session, I found my hands wandering over her blouse buttons once again, but this time my fumbling was not met with opposition. I soon discovered how difficult it was to unbutton someone else's shirt as I struggled for what seemed an embarrassing eternity before achieving my goal. I fondled my first female breast and felt like I had taken a giant step in my ascent to manhood! No longer would I just read about such glory or hear about it from my more experienced brethren. I was now one of the experienced ones!

From what I could tell Theresa was equally pleased, which was a relief because I didn't want her to feel she was under my manly carnal spell. Later I asked her why she had been so reluctant the first time I tried this stunt, yet so cooperative later. In no uncertain terms she said I was too forward initially and she wasn't an easy girl. That sounded reasonable.

She added another reason that really surprised me. Theresa had a pet cat and while playing together on the floor, the cat had given her a swat across her breasts and scratched them all to hell. The scratches had not yet healed on that evening of my first fumble so she wasn't about to let me touch them. How weird is that?

I owe this girl big time because my future sex life might have been ruined if, when fondling my first female breasts, I encountered a mass of crusty scabs! Worldly Tony had dog-eared the pages in Philip Roth's book, *Portnoy's Complaint*, and who knows, a scabby breast experience might have led me to be as neurotic about sex as the lead character in that book was.

While waiting at my table I daydreamed about Theresa, breasts, scabs, and cats, and where it all could lead. Suddenly Rob pulled up a chair next to mine and seemed to be coming down from his high. He was beginning to feel edgy and remorseful.

"Look, Rob, it was a dumb thing to do, but I know you didn't mean to piss me off. I'm okay so let's not talk about it anymore," I said, hoping he would leave after a drink.

Rob was surprised how well I was taking all this. When he left earlier I had fire in my eyes, but now I was relaxed and in a pretty good mood. Hell, Rob wasn't going to argue with his good fortune, so he ordered another drink and the two of us kicked back, relaxed, and listened to the Kontinentals belt "Mashed Potato."

I kept checking my watch. Rob finally got the message and headed off into the night.

Eleven o'clock came and went and I started to get anxious. Was I going to be stood up and miss a great opportunity? A few minutes later three gorgeous Chinese girls in *cheong saam* dresses walked slowly down the stairs in high stiletto heels and slid gracefully to Jackie's table.

The combination of that particular dress style and high, high heels looked exceptionally sexy. Nonchalantly I watched the band with one eye unobtrusively glancing at Jackie's table. The girls were giggling and chatting. My supercharged brain started to question whether my admirer had changed her mind and if she and her friends were now laughing at my expense.

Which one was she anyway? The taller woman in the middle had a sultry way about her and a beautiful smile. The other two were sure pretty, but I made up my mind, she had to be the girl in the middle. Finally Jackie waved me over and I tried to act cool by taking my time sauntering to the table. Internally I was ready to sprint across the night-club stage if need be.

Jackie made introductions. "Tony, this is Cerena." In front of me stood the tall one, a beautiful woman with features suggesting Vietnamese-Chinese descent. Jet-black long hair, doe eyes, and uncharacteristic, but exceptionally attractive, full lips formed a gorgeous mouth. Cerena's skin was the color of milk chocolate and her figure was sensational.

I nervously muttered, "Hello," and sat down and struck up a conversation with the girls about music and dancing. I thought it was best to include everybody so I would appear friendly and not on the prowl.

Cerena was unbelievable. She was beautiful, sweet, and I instantly felt comfortable around her. I knew I was in lust, honest-to-goodness lust. Cerena had a husky voice and spoke better English than I spoke Chinese; we must have talked non-stop for half an hour, although it seemed like five minutes. She wanted to dance so we joined the pulsating mob on the floor, right in front of the band. Anders gave me a wink. No surprise - this woman who worked in a ballroom was a terrific dancer. With her great looks and body, the men in the club were probably wondering what the hell she was doing with a young Eurasian teenager. It felt fantastic to be with her. We drew stares from both men and women as we danced first fast and then slow. We looked good!

Cerena and I hit it off that night and after several slow and close dances I felt I had met the woman of my dreams. I was used to dating younger girls; it felt incredibly different to be with an adult woman, especially such a striking one.

After the club closed Anders, Jackie, Cerena and I went to a Chinese noodle restaurant for a late-night meal. One of the great things about the

Tsim Sha Tsui district of downtown Kowloon, was that restaurants were open all night to serve delicious food at great prices. Cerena and I were having a wonderful time and I hated to leave her, but it was three in the morning and time to call it a night.

She gave me her phone number and I promised I would call. I put her in a cab, gave her a light goodnight kiss, and felt miserable as she drove away. She looked out the back window and waved. I jumped into another cab and headed home, stumbling into the house in a delirious stupor. My dreams were delicious that night.

I called Cerena the next day and we dated steadily like any couple in high school. There was bit of an age difference - she was nineteen and I was sixteen. We went to movies, dance halls, and partied at clubs all over Hong Kong. Cerena confided she loved the beach so we went to Clearwater Bay and took a small boat to Hebe Haven and spent the day on the beautiful white sand. We had a great time lying in the sun and splashing in the warm waters. Needless to say, Cerena looked great in a bikini. My feelings for her were genuine and growing stronger and stronger. I wondered where lust left and love began.

At first I was thinking only about sex and how far I could get with a dance hostess, but now my feelings were deepening. I was falling for her.

We brought a raft with us to the beach and enjoyed floating away from the crowd. As we paddled around our legs touched and she playfully teased me by wrapping her legs around mine under the water, then squeezing them around my waist. I was definitely aroused and falling hard for her. What a great day - I can almost sense the smell of the beach and the fragrance of her skin even today.

I brought Cerena home a couple times to meet my parents, although they never knew what she did and never asked, probably thinking she was a girl from school. I never went to the ballroom where she worked, but knew how they operated. Generally they were ridiculous rip-offs. I couldn't afford to go regularly anyway on my allowance, but I was with the main attraction during Cerena's off-hours. I didn't need to pay for her company. We were growing more attached every time we were together and I knew our relationship would soon take the next step. I had dreamed of the ultimate sexual encounter since I browsed my first *Playboy* magazine.

You never forget your first lovemaking experience, and mine was no exception. It's much more vivid than my recollection of where I was when President Kennedy was shot. I was sixteen years old and horny as they come. My imagination was driving me crazy, all I could relate to were erotic dreams that ended with an embarrassing wake-up. How does one dream about an event never experienced anyway? Usually erotic dreams end at a pivotal moment because the mind has no subconscious memory to draw upon to continue.

Cerena and I had been dating for several weeks and for our big evening, full of hope and anticipation on my part, I planned dinner at one of her favorite Chinese restaurants. Cerena loved Hakka food and ordered for us, as I was not that familiar with this style of Chinese cuisine. After dinner she wanted to go to a club so we went to the Firecracker Bar at the Ocean Terminal and danced up a storm for a few hours. As the evening wound on, softer music was played and we held each other close. After we closed the place down, we decided to walk though the main streets of Kowloon. We talked and held hands as we wandered down Nathan Road past the closed shops and tailors scattered throughout downtown. She looked up at me and a mischievous smile crossed her face. I knew she wanted to say something. I asked her what was on her mind. Cerena answered softly, "Tony, will you stay with me tonight?"

I flushed, thought I was going to have a heart attack and almost gasped out the words "Yes, of course, you know how much I want to stay with you!"

When I first spoke to Jackie about meeting this girl, sex was on my mind. Over the few weeks I developed deep feelings for Cerena, it was no longer just about sex, but having her ask me to stay with her made my blood surge. I held her and we kissed for a long time. She never looked prettier.

We soon checked into a small Chinese hotel, a typical rental for amorous adventures. As the saying goes, "I entered as a boy and left a man."

It was a very special night, very sexy, and very beautiful, everything a first sexual experience should be. I was attracted to Cerena and she was attracted to me. Perhaps we were even in love a little. We slowly and amorously helped each other undress and then she peeled herself from me and slid on the bed. I wasn't totally nervous, but she was a beautiful woman and the first woman I had ever seen lying completely naked on a bed.

I felt a shiver run down my spine and hoped I wouldn't disappoint her. I got into bed beside her, held her tightly, and shivered with anticipation. Cerena gently kissed me and guided my hands around her body. This was everything I thought lovemaking was supposed to be, and more. She taught me how to give her pleasure, which in turn gave me great pleasure. She was such a wonderful teacher. I can't remember how many times we made love that night, but I do remember each time seemed better than the last. Practice does make perfect! That night was a great sensual experience and I felt incredibly close to this beautiful woman; I believed I was experiencing my first true love.

After a sound but short night's sleep, the wonder of finding myself lying next to this beautiful woman amazed me. Cerena looked even more beautiful in the morning light than she appeared the night before. I watched her sleep before she finally woke up and smiled at me through half-closed eyes.

Though my night had been dizzy with pleasure, I was aware there was something important I had to do. I was respectful of my parents and did not want them to worry. I pulled on my clothes and went to find a telephone to call home to tell my dad I was fine and had spent the night with a friend. I didn't bother to tell him my friend was my beautiful Vietnamese-Chinese girlfriend. Perhaps he knew, but it was a family rule that we had to let our parents know if we were staying out all night, but fortunately the rule did not include the requirement to divulge details.

I went back to our room to find Cerena wide-awake and holding her arms out to me. I didn't need to be told what she wanted. We had another passionate morning session before setting off in different directions. I was on Cloud Nine, but craved sleep. Our tiny room had no shower and I could still smell Cerena's body on mine as I rode home in the cab. I went straight to bed and her sweet female fragrance stayed with me as I drifted off.

I didn't wake until late afternoon, then showered, dressed and headed back downtown. It was a Saturday afternoon and Cerena and I arranged to meet at the Bayside for an afternoon tea dance. I walked down the stairs to the club and there she was with her ballroom girl friends sitting at Jackie's usual table. My woman looked fabulous.

I was feeling pretty good about myself when suddenly one of the girls yelled across the room.

"So, Tony, you lose your cherry! How was it?"

I was mortified and sure everybody in the entire club had heard her. I turned crimson and the girls started to laugh. I was the butt of their jokes for the rest of the afternoon. It was one jab after another and every one made Cerena blush and look even more beautiful. She loved it! I was secretly pleased to be teased as Cerena's lover, there were many at the Bayside who would have given their right arms to be in my place, including the guys in the band. I had indeed lost my cherry and for a young man in his teens, this was a very special moment, it was my coming of age.

What a great life I had – I was a student, had no job worries, enjoyed all the sports I wanted to play, and experienced fantastic sex with a beautiful woman. Life was definitely good!

Entering into a sexual relationship was certainly a lot safer back then in the early sixties. The horror of AIDs had not been encountered and the worst sexually transmitted disease could be treated with a shot of penicillin. How different the case is today for young adults who face risks associated with a sexual encounter. It's almost like Russian roulette, you never know until too late if the chamber is loaded with a deadly bullet.

What followed for me were months of happiness, good times, and lots of lovemaking. Cerena and I had fun together and I had deep feelings for her, but the time inevitably came when I realized ours was not a relationship made in heaven. The obvious differences in our backgrounds would be a problem. I was a sixteen year-old high school student and she was a nineteen year-old "working woman."

In all the time we dated, I never went to her house and had no idea where she lived or who she lived with. She could have lived with her parents or with other girls, I just didn't know. I never bothered to ask, it didn't seem important. I didn't think my parents would be delighted if they knew Cerena's background, liberal though they were. I knew I had to finish my studies and there was University somewhere in my future. But here I was jumping way ahead, thinking about marriage to a woman I had known for just three months. It was so typical of me to analyze and plan ahead in great detail, the ultimate Virgo.

The dreaded day had to come. The ending of our relationship was nothing like I expected. My own petty jealousies and immaturity brought closure to the affair. It had nothing to do with Cerena.

Late one night I was walking with my buddy Norman down the driveway of the Hyatt Hotel on Nathan Road where we had stopped for a late night coffee. Cerena and two Chinese men, probably customers from the ballroom, entered the coffee shop. Of course I knew she went out with other men, it was part of her job and I trusted she didn't sleep with anyone but me.

I had always been in denial about Cerena's extracurricular activities until I saw them paraded in front of my face. She smiled at me as she and the men walked into the coffee shop, pretending we didn't know each other. I knew it wouldn't be good business on her part to drop her companions and leave with me. After all, she did have a job she had to keep. Still, I raged when I saw her in the company of other men. A fire-bomb went off inside my head and I went absolutely out of my mind. I was irrational. I was furious at seeing her all dressed up and in the company of these guys. I, I, I . . . I went home and sulked.

I was jealous, angry, and behaved much as would be expected from a high school teenager. I decided that night we were finished as a couple, so the next day I phoned her to let her know it was over. I caught Cerena completely by surprise, it never occurred to her she had done anything wrong, and in truth she hadn't. She listened to me quietly. After awhile she started to cry and pleaded with me to understand that nothing happened between her and the two men. The three just had a snack and she went straight home. My crazy reaction wasn't making any sense to her.

I was heartless. I simply didn't want to see her anymore because I didn't like her being with other men. She reminded me it was part of her job to accompany men and that nothing sexual ever occurred with them. She insisted I was the only one she loved and the only man sharing her bed. Nothing she said made any difference, I decided the affair was over and nothing would sway me from my decision.

After I hung up, I didn't expect to hear from Cerena again and for the next couple weeks, my usual routine took over. My friends and I visited clubs but I would be alone, no pretty girl beside me. I spent more time than ever before at the snooker parlor. It was a sad period for me as second thoughts crowded my mind. I really cared about my beautiful first love. I went to school, told my buddies we had broken up, and really didn't think much more about it. I missed Cerena, but did not regret my decision to call it off. There was no future to our relationship.

I had no clue I was about to receive one of the most frightening telephone calls a sixteen-year-old high school student could ever get.

I was spending a quiet evening at home watching TV with my dad. We were big fans of *Star Trek* and would religiously watch the show together. My favorite character was the Vulcan Mr. Spock played by Leonard Nimoy. The Vulcan philosophy that logic ruled the world struck a chord with me and I thought Mr. Spock would be a great role model. The episode we were watching that night was about a planet on which all the adults had died and the children had taken over. The children referred to adults as "Grups" and this became an affectionate term my friend Norman and I would call each other over all the years. The telephone rang; I thought it was Grup calling as I picked up the receiver. It was Cerena. She said, "Hello, how are you, Tony?"

I was surprised to hear her voice and in a very cool Mr. Spock-like voice I answered I was just fine. Several minutes of awkward small talk about absolutely nothing followed. I was anxious to hang up. She then said four words that drained the color from my face.

"Tony, I am pregnant." This was followed by an outburst of quiet sobbing on the phone. I thought I was going to be the first sixteen year-old to have a massive coronary, brain hemorrhage, and puke session all at the same time. I didn't know what to say or do; all I could remember was my dad's advice that if I was going to date girls and had thoughts about sex, I had better take precautions. Yikes! I was literally in a panic state as I struggled with the shocking news. It took all I could muster to form the words that eventually come out of my mouth.

"Are you sure? What makes you think so?" She stopped crying for a while and became annoyed. Cerena reminded me that she wasn't a little girl and knew about these things. Besides, her period was three weeks late. I contemplated asking her if she was sure the baby was mine, but wisely decided against it. I can hardly remember the rest of the conversation; my mind was in a dull fog. I told her I needed to think about the situation and assured her I would call her back so we could figure out what to do next. I felt sick.

The next day I decided to seek advice from the more "experienced" guys at school, including my friends Anders and Nick. Most said the same thing. They believed Cerena was likely using the possibility of a baby as a ruse to get us back together and that she wasn't really pregnant. On the other hand, she could be telling the truth. I knew very little about abortions and none of my friends could be considered experts on that subject matter.

Anders had spoken to Jackie and she told him she thought Cerena really was pregnant. Cerena and Jackie were good friends so I couldn't be sure whether she really believed Cerena or was her confidential cohort. Jackie indicated Cerena was going to see a doctor about terminating the pregnancy and that made my ears perk up.

The following evening I was with my friend Alan Sloan at the Hong Kong Electric Club swimming pool. There was nobody else swimming that evening and I shared my terrible predicament with a friend who was a good listener. Alan convinced me of two things that evening. The first was that it would not be a good idea to drown myself in the club's pool. The second was that I needed to restore a relationship with Cerena

After listening to the wise high school advice, I decided the best thing to do was remain on friendly terms with Cerena and convince her to seek medical help to end the pregnancy. The option of having the baby was the worst case scenario and marriage was certainly not in the cards.

A couple schoolmates had fathered children and they went through very difficult times and suffered incessant gossiping behind their backs.

I telephoned Cerena that evening hoping to work things out. After an awkward conversation she told me that she had seen a doctor and he had given her an injection to end the pregnancy. I had no reason to disbelieve her, even though I was not aware such injections existed. Following that stilted conversation we spent time with each other over the next several days, but it really wasn't the same. The special feeling we once shared was long gone.

Ten days later Cerena told me she finally had her period and my sigh of relief could be heard across Hong Kong and Kowloon, possibility even into the New Territories. This announcement ended two weeks of pure hell. To this day I will never know if Cerena really was pregnant or if it was a ruse. If she was pregnant, I am unaware of any abortive shot existing at that time. The experience impacted me greatly and when I became involved in future relationships, I became paranoid over the possibility of pregnancy and became almost obsessive/compulsive over taking precautions. Call me a cold cad, but once I heard there was no baby, I knew it was definitely all over between us.

I think I was lucky my first sexual encounter was a tender and passionate experience and not a "cash transaction." Hong Kong in the '60s was the proverbial place where you could find whatever you wanted - all you needed was money. Selling sex was big business and it seemed Chinese males were more promiscuous than most. Brothels were everywhere, the most famous one was in the Wanchai district where U.S. and English Navy personnel came ashore for R&R. Wanchai was made famous by the movie *The World of Suzie Wong* starring William Holden and Nancy Kwan. The story was of a love affair featuring a Wanchai bar girl and a British artist.

Stories of seamy sex for sale were rampant, but one that always fascinated me was sex for sale on sampans, little Chinese boats, floating in the Causeway Bay region of the harbor. The rumor was many of the prostitutes were blind and had developed incredible skills at satisfying their clients. Sad enough that young women were being drawn to prostitution, but I thought the marketing of sex with blind women to be repulsive, yet several Chinese friends used their services regularly.

Other forms of sex for sale were plentiful on Hong Kong streets and sometimes my school friends and I found our entertainment in unusual ways. We often wandered through the all-Chinese section of Mongkok looking for the sex peddlers. These guys carried rattan baskets and inside there would be an assortment of items including small pornographic books that looked like hymn books, fancy colorful condoms, outrageous dildos, and stimulating sex potions. We would look through peddlers' wares but I don't remember anyone buying anything except for an occasional dirty book.

On one of our excursions, my friends and I found ourselves bored silly and searched for something, anything, to do. Somebody came up with the bright idea to tour brothels, just to look, not touch. This sounded like a brilliant idea so off we went to the sleazy part of Kowloon. We walked around for a while and didn't have to wait long before a pimp approached us and offered "pretty girls." We said we were interested, but the girls had to be *really* beautiful before we would pay.

"Yes, yes, yes. I will show you pretty girls," he cried. That pimp was working hard for his money. We visited at least five brothels and in every one played the charade and had the women paraded in front of us as we shook our heads with disappointment.

Each brothel looked the same, a small apartment with partitions forming small rooms, each holding little more than a bed. The partitions did not extend all the way to the ceiling so a customer could easily hear what was going on next door.

The Chinese women working in these places were generally in their late twenties or early thirties and not the most attractive. These were not expensive brothels, costing around thirty Hong Kong dollars (US$5) for a short time of pleasure. If the girls had been younger and prettier, they would be working the ballrooms or bars.

After an hour of sleazy amusement, we gave our pimp guide five bucks and went to a bar for drinks and laugh about our perverted experience. Not the usual Saturday night entertainment for teenagers and perhaps slightly depraved, but not at all outrageous for local guys growing up in a place like Hong Kong.

Although I did not frequent brothels, I did contribute to the delinquency of a high-school classmate who was intrigued when he heard my tale of touring houses of ill-repute. My friend Peter was a kid I had known since the age of five. Peter pestered me to take him on a tour of brothels until I finally agreed. To my surprise, Peter decided he was not going just to tour the sites, he planned to sample the "flower ladies."

I soon discovered I had unleashed a demon. Peter enjoyed himself so much that he became a frequent patron, along with an assortment of converts he roped in. Peter would be the guy telling the spicy stories from then on. Peter's mother always thought I was such a nice boy; I shudder at what she would think of me if she knew I led her son astray. My mother always thought of Peter as such a nice young gentleman, she certainly didn't know about his mischievous sensual streak. Go figure.

Back to the famous bars in Suzie Wong's Wanchai district. Hong Kong had hundreds of bars but they really took off in popularity during the early '60s when U.S. armed forces visited the Colony for R&R. These guys would arrive from the jungles of Vietnam looking for recreation and companionship in a place known to be safer and friendlier than the streets of Saigon.

GIs described Saigon as a corrupt, money-grubbing city where nothing except the almighty buck had any meaning. In Hong Kong, money talks, but the city was a far cry from war-torn Vietnam where sheer survival was a priority. Many times my friends and I would be in a nightclub listening to music and downing drinks when a young American serviceman would overhear us speaking English and approach our table. Typically the soldier was plain lonely and drawn to friendly company with people not trying to take his money. I talked with a few soldiers more than once during their two weeks in town and became close enough to correspond. I thought it would mean a lot to them to receive a friendly letter when they were back in the jungles of 'Nam.

The influx of servicemen created a boom in the demand for bar girls and many young women left textile factories in the satellite town of Kwun Tong to search for a better life offering more money, and hopefully more fun. Driving down the back streets in Tsim Sha Tsui, we often saw these young girls standing outside bars in incredibly provocative ultra-mini-skirts, calling guys in for a drink and the proverbial good time.

It was during this period I first saw Chinese girls dye their hair blonde or red - it looked *really* strange. Unlike ballroom girls, bar girls were known to be available for the night, provided you had the money and were not too obnoxious. These girls did not have pimps so they could refuse a customer and the barkeeps offered muscle if needed. Several friends had brief flings with bar girls, but no lasting relationships. The girls tended to be rough around the edges and a bit tough. Bar girls were definitely in a different category from ballroom girls like Cerena. They used a salty vocabulary and elegance and sophistication were not their strong suits.

During the Viet Nam years, it was interesting to watch the bars in the Colony segregate and become known as "black" or "white" hangouts. This race phenomenon was definitely imported by the GIs; I had never seen anything like it before. Over time certain nightclubs took a similar route and patrons made choices - Motown and jazz or the Beatles and other British/American pop groups. Locals like me had grown up in a multi-cultural melting pot of Chinese, English, Americans, East Indians, Portuguese, Europeans and a representation from the four corners of the globe. We had never seen what we now witnessed with the GI influx.

I once had a fling with a bar girl. It was soon after Cerena and I broke up. My buddies and I were once again bored and looking for excitement so we found our way into a bar in Tsimshatsui. The place was relatively empty with a juke box playing popular music. Since we were locals, the girls didn't hustle us, but did come to sit and talk. We offered to buy them drinks provided they were not the famous "champagne cocktails," otherwise known as 7-Up bubbles in a champagne glass.

I had my eye on one of the girls, a real cutie, and I think she took a liking to me because I looked mixed - European and Oriental. Her name was Julie and I asked her to dance to the blaring jukebox music. After several drinks, lots of laughing, dancing, including slow numbers, it was two in the morning, time to close. During our last dance, Julie whispered into my ear, "Do you want to come home with me, Tony?"

Julie seemed very nice, had a mischievous personality so I said, "Sure, as long as this is not a 'professional sleepover.'"

She laughed and said, "No, I ask you because I like being with you."

She did have one question before I could spend the night with her. "Do you have a girlfriend?" she asked.

"No I don't, not for many months," I responded with a laugh.

"Okay, then! Since you don't have a girlfriend, I will be your girlfriend tonight and we will have a good time."

"Sounds great to me!" I enthusiastically agreed. We grabbed a cab and rumbled off to her apartment. What struck me about Julie was the loneliness I saw in the eyes and life of this young, pretty woman who spent her time in the company of many men. She rented a room in an apartment owned by an older man, and she did not say anything about their relationship. I reflected that he could have been a relative, a friend, a lover, a protector or even a serial killer! Metal security gates blockaded the front door, which worried me because not only did it keep people from getting in, it also kept people from getting out.

There might have been other renters in the apartment, but since we walked in so early in the morning, it was difficult to be sure. Julie's room looked like any teenager's room, although I had pegged her to be in her early twenties. Relatively small, the walls were painted Pepto Bismol pink and pictures of musicians were plastered over them like stamps. A large makeup mirror jig-sawed with pictures of American movie stars drew my attention and pieces of costume jewelry hung down from the bevels. I was surprised to see stuffed animals, teddy bears, and fuzzy frogs spread on the bed.

We walked in and sat on the bed and talked for a little while. Julie walked to her dresser, lit a candle and turned off the lights, putting on soft music to set the mood. She slowly undressed and smiled at me coyly, knowing she was having the desired effect. When she was down to her panties she stood before me. She motioned for me to stand up and she quickly unbuckled my belt. As she tugged at my pants I pulled off my shirt and before I knew what was happening Julie was kneeling in front of me introducing me to a new form of sex that I found extremely enjoyable. When she thought she had me fully aroused, she got into bed, pulled me on top of her and started to moan. Now I had something new to work with! Sound effects!

Julie wrapped her legs tightly around my waist, so tightly it bordered on being uncomfortable. We had a great night together, made love several times in many different ways as we enjoyed each other's bodies.

One memorable trick Julie knew involved crossing her legs behind my back and cracking her hips. It was so strange that I found it erotic.

When most men think of women of the night, their image is often of a hard woman who wants to get the act over with so she can pocket the money. Julie did not fit the stereotype; she was bubbly, had a sense of humor, and outwardly enjoyed having sex.

We slept like babes and the next morning she gave me a wallet-sized picture with her phone number on the back so I could remember her. First things first. I called home to let Dad know I was fine, and then I said goodbye to Julie and went downstairs to catch a cab.

I kept Julie's photo for several years, but I never did see her again. It was another no future situation and it made no sense to prolong the inevitable. I did feel guilty about my "wam, bam, thank you, ma'am" performance that night and probably reinforced the idea that all men are the same and are only really interested in one thing. But, then again, I could have been her "wam, bam" for that particular night.

CHAPTER EIGHT
"Money"
BRADFORD AND GORDY

My parents were middle-class folks working hard to make a good living for the family. My father worked his way up the ladder from a clerk position to purchasing manager for the British American Tobacco Company, manufacturers of such well-known cigarette brands as Lucky Strike and Pall Mall. In reality, my dad had probably peaked in his career, but in my mind he was a VIP in the company and I was extremely proud of him.

My mother was a formidable executive assistant to one of Hong Kong's leading *Tai-Pans* whose family had originally emigrated from Iraq to Hong Kong, then Shanghai, and then back to Hong Kong after the communist takeover of China. The Cantonese translation for *Tai-Pan* is "big shot" and is customarily applied to senior business executives or entrepreneurs who have gained considerable status. Mum worked for the family for 28 years and became a trusted insider for both business and personal matters, so much so that our family was blessed to have the Kadoories consider our entire family as more than an employee/boss relationship. Lord Kadoorie and his brother Sir Horace were known to us as Uncle Lawrence and Uncle Horace, along with Aunt Muriel (Lord Kadoorie's wife), The Hon. Sir Michael Kadoorie (son), and Rita (daughter). The Kadoories were all very kind to the Tebbutt family.

Some of my fondest memories of growing up in Hong Kong were visits to Boulder Lodge in the New Territories. Several times a year Steve and I would pile into the family car with my parents and drive (on the left side of narrow, single-lane country roads) to the nineteen and a half milestone in the New Territories known as Castle Peak. On the waterfront stood Boulder Lodge, the country home of the Kadoorie family.

The family patriarch, Sir Elly Kadoorie, was a British merchant with roots in Iraq and became one of Shanghai's wealthiest men. The former Kadoorie estate in Shanghai was built in 1924 and represented the city's finest colonial architecture. The mansion was built primarily of marble, hence the name Marble Hall. Today the building is known as the Shanghai Municipal Children's Palace, a place where children enjoy extracurricular activities. After the communists took control of the area, most non-Chinese immigrated to Hong Kong to start new lives.

Sir Elly's sons, Lawrence and Horace, were philanthropic businessmen who had investments in hotels (including the world famous Peninsula), the local power utility (China Light and Power), and numerous other enterprises. Lawrence's primary focus was building the businesses while Horace dedicated most of his time to philanthropy. Their generosity and concern for peasant farmers included the purchase of a barren hill at Paak Ngau Shek in the New Territories. They turned this desolate space into an experimental farm where research was carried out to improve livestock, vegetables, and fruit trees.

Horace Kadoorie led the experimental program, and adhered to the philosophy of "helping people to help themselves." The program was particularly beneficial to widows living in the New Territories. Widows were thought to add little value to their rural communities and were looked upon as a burden. Horace gave widows well-bred cattle and swine, hence raising their status in the village. Horace was also a benefactor to the many *Gurkhas* who served with the British Army.

Gurkhas were known as fierce, loyal warriors from Nepal who fought side-by-side with British and Commonwealth troops during WWII. Over time the British army restructured and reduced their numbers so many *Gurkhas* found themselves remaining in Hong Kong when their garrison was disbanded. These men only knew soldiering, but were taught skills at the Kadoorie Agricultural and Experimental Farm to help them survive when they returned to their native mountainous land.

The mountain on which the farm was established was planted with varieties of beautiful flowers and provided scenic picnic spots. The actual farm was on private property not open to the general public without special permission. Our family was privileged to have open access to this showplace, which was visited by dignitaries from all over the world. Our friends and visitors from overseas had a chance to see a great humanitarian effort not available for all to visit. I felt like a big shot when my friends would ask if they could tag along when we visited the farm.

Horace had another hobby which brought joy to the younger visitors to Boulder Lodge. My brother and I were always thrilled to see Horace's Fairyland. Fairyland was a collection of minerals clustered in a darkroom that emitted beautiful colors when a black light was shone over them. It makes me laugh when I think years later black lights would come into vogue highlighting Hendrix posters accompanied by a few tokes on a joint. I can't imagine what Fairyland would look like while high on pot. In my mind's ear I can hear a toker muttering, "Wow, far out!"

Boulder Lodge was a beautiful, large, granite two-story house built on a rock cliff overlooking beachfront property. A small private beach was separated from the public access by a natural rock wall and a private boat dock served the spectacular speedboat that was used for water skiing and cruising local waters. Two levels of balconies provided opportunities to enjoy outdoor dining, drinks, or afternoon tea. A sea wall surrounded the mansion with several large black iron cannons facing the bay to protect the property from pirates of old. My little brother Steven and I would straddle the cannons and imagine they were pointed at pirate ships in the harbor. This was a place to let our imaginations run wild. Heavy black cannonballs scattered about added to the ambiance. At least there were cannonballs until Steve came up with the idea of rolling them down the hill into the sea. It became quite a topic of conversation during one afternoon tea when a guest known as "The Captain" queried in a strong English accent, "I wonder what ever happened to those cannonballs?"

A hilarious English tea conversation followed, reminiscent of a scene from a Monty Python sketch. Numerous theories were put forth as to how the cannonballs came to disappear.

"I say, Major, do you think a wild dog pushed them down the hill?" One theory.

"I daresay not, old chap. It was more likely one of the local chappies who thought he might confiscate the cannonballs and sell them for scrap," answered the Major.

"How reprehensible," was the reply.

"Indeed, tut! tut!" And so went the conversation.

The property at Boulder Lodge included a garden the size of a city park. Beautiful and exotic flowers and shrubs were plentiful, but the garden's centerpiece was an enormous porcelain dragon pagoda. The pagoda was about three stories high and approximately ten feet in diameter with a wickedly beautiful, winding ascension.

There were caverns in the basement section and two small observation rooms were placed on the climb to the top. Intertwined within the cave-like tunnels was the dragon's reptilian body. Our favorite point was the peak where we could sit atop the dragon's head and overlook the entire garden landscape.

The dragon had a white underbelly with red scales covering its back. Two bulging eyes and a thick red tongue stretched from the summit of the pagoda. Dragons are a symbol of good luck in Asia and so this monstrous dragon was built to protect the garden, but not from the Tebbutt brothers.

My earliest memories of Boulder Lodge dated back to the early 1950s when we were invited to Boxing Day celebrations. Boxing Day is held the day after Christmas and its name is derived from the many empty boxes left after opening presents.

Celebration days at Boulder Lodge were wonderful fun and very British affairs with a dozen or more families in attendance. Foot races were held in the gardens and side events like target shooting ping-pong balls from a pump-gun made for good times. I loved to watch the assortment of parents participate in egg-in-spoon and sack races. Grand prizes were awarded to all each evening when everybody gathered in a huge living room in front of a roaring fire with the spicy fragrance of Indian curries simmering in the kitchen.

Michael Kadoorie, Lawrence and Muriel's son, was seven years older than I was. He had a bubbly, gregarious nature and also had very nice and very expensive toys. When he was younger, Michael had one of the biggest Lionel train sets in the world. The layout was built on a platform featuring mountains, multiple tracks, houses, stations, water tanks, you name it and it was part of the display. Trains could blow their whistles and had smoke curling from their stacks. It was an awesome spectacle, a dream collection by today's standards.

In his early twenties, Michael took up competitive go-kart racing and whatever he did, he did in a big way. My brother and I were absolutely thrilled when a cement go-kart track was built to wind through the garden at Boulder Lodge with several go-karts available for all to enjoy. Steve and I raced go- karts against adults and often beat them. What a tremendous thrill to be in your early teens and racing your mum and dad on a racetrack around a magnificent garden. We were on top of the world!

Did I mention Michael had nice toys? After building up a sweat racing the karts, we would cool off by going to the boat dock and jumping into Michael's speedboat to go water-skiing behind his hot Cigarette boat. The Cigarette boat was made famous for reaching high speeds to escape customs officers off the coast of Florida as smugglers carried drugs to waiting buyers. The boats were long, sleek and powered by twin Cadillac V-8s so they were a joy to ski behind. We cut through the waters between the many islands in the South China seas. We took turns skimming over the waves on one or two skis depending on our level of skill. Michael was the best and slalomed competitively.

Michael tried ski kiting until one day an unexpected wind turned the kite upside down, crashing into the water along with a shaken-up Michael. There would be no more ski kiting after that incident.

I managed to become proficient on one ski and learned to love the sport. After all this effort, we were plagued by huge appetites but our arms were so weak and tired from hours of skiing that it was difficult to hold a knife and fork.

Michael had plenty of other toys and although I was too young to drive, I did appreciate his E-type Jaguar, the first classic sports car of many more that were to come. I have to say Sir Michael Kadoorie was, and still is, a great guy, obviously wealthy, but never did I detect a rich kid attitude. I greatly enjoyed his company and mischievous sense of humor. Michael has continued the family tradition of success in business blended with philanthropy.

Michael got his taste in cars from his dad Lord Kadoorie, who bought a new Aston Martin every time the model changed. The third Aston he owned was the DB4GT, and it was the silver model similar to the one made famous in the early James Bond movie starring Sean Connery (a DB5). I clearly remember the first time we saw it at the Lodge and the big impression the car made on all of us lucky enough to observe this classic up close and in person.

Lawrence Kadoorie was a great man, but one of the scariest drivers ever to sit behind the wheel of a car. I once sat next to him when he drove through town and it was one of the most harrowing experiences of my life. Lord Kadoorie possibly needed new glasses because he never saw stop signs along the way and by the time we arrived at our destination, I was a mumbling mess.

A favorite story about the Kadoorie family involved the "Ivory Garden." Norman Hope, my best friend whom I have known forever, asked if I could arrange for him to see the special Kadoorie secret ivory collection that he had heard so much about. There was not much hidden from the Hong Kong community, but I wondered how he had come to learn of the garden.

Personally, I had never heard of this collection and didn't know what he was talking about, but since Norman was my best buddy I asked my mother if she could show it to us. Mum said she would be happy to escort us on a tour and we arranged a time to meet her at the office. The Kadoorie offices were in St. George's Building, the tall skyscraper built to showcase a grand waterfront view of Hong Kong's famous harbor. A few years later the Jardines Company built their corporate skyscraper and partially obstructed the view. The Jardine Building came to be known by the Chinese as the "House of One Thousand Assholes" because of the hundreds of unusual circular windows that dotted the façade of the building.

The Kadoorie offices housed spectacular Chinese carvings in malachite, tiger's eye, and other semi-precious stones. I had become jaded (so to speak) because I had seen these beautiful carvings so many times I no longer fully appreciated the magnificence of the office. By any standard it was a priceless private mini-museum of Asian art.

After Norman and I spent time looking at the richness displayed throughout the main office, Mum took us to another floor and used her key to open an innocuous looking door without markings. Once that door was opened, another key was inserted into the wall and a metal door slid into the ceiling, just like a Hollywood spy movie. We passed through the metal door and as a button was pushed, the whole contraption came down and locked us in. It was pitch dark in the room and when the light was snapped on, a long, narrow, yellow-carpeted room with rosewood paneling was revealed. Glass shelves lined both sides reaching to the far end of the room. On every shelf pieces of ivory took residence, each labeled and identified with a short history. Jade bowls half-filled with water were dispersed throughout the display. I asked Mum why the jade bowls were there and she replied, "You have heard me say on occasion that I had to water the garden after work, remember?"

"Yes," I answered, "but I don't understand what you're getting at."

"Well, what I was doing was making sure each jade bowl had water in it to keep the humidity in the room at an appropriate level. We don't want this ancient ivory to dry and crack."

A nice metaphor, I thought to myself.

The ivory was breathtakingly beautiful, much of it dating hundreds of years before the birth of Christ. Every piece stood out in its own right as a unique piece of art, but there was one piece I will always remember.

It was an ivory chain about two feet long capped with ornate ends. It had been carved hundreds of years before Christ, and what was so amazing was it all came from a single elephant tusk. It took the artisan his entire lifetime to create this piece. I wondered about this artist, how he felt about his work, and how he had lived his life.

On either side of the room's entrance were Chinese fans about two-and-a-half feet wide by two feet tall carved from latticed ivory and studded with brightly colored semi-precious stones. These fans had mysteriously made their way from the Imperial Palace in Peking to this quiet room in St. George's Building. There were only a dozen or so such fans in the entire world. What Norman and I were looking at is difficult to describe, it was stunningly beautiful!

I never asked how these rare pieces of art found their way from the Imperial Palace to a private collection in Hong Kong. Interesting that I didn't even know about this ivory museum, although I'm sure my mother must have mentioned it at some point. It was only because my good friend Norman had heard the stories and asked to see the collection that I ever bothered to find out about it. Today I often wonder whatever happened to that collection, whether it's been turned over to the British Museum as rumored, or whether it sits quietly somewhere ready to bewitch the next visitor with its beauty.

Every year the Queen of England creates an Honors List and makes awards to people who have made significant contributions to the Empire. For his outstanding business leadership in Hong Kong, Lawrence was awarded a C.B.E. (Commander of the British Empire), followed by a Knighthood (Sir Lawrence), and finally a Peerage (Lord Kadoorie). Horace was awarded an O.B.E. (Order of the British Empire) prior to receiving his Knighthood (Sir Horace).

I think I was extremely lucky growing up knowing the Kadoories as Uncle Lawrence and Uncle Horace.

CHAPTER NINE
"Girl"
JOHN LENNON AND PAUL McCARTNEY

My years of teenage dating did not *only* include encounters with fast women of the night. There were several girls at school I dated and took to dances, movies, and parties, but never to bed. I didn't date any one girl for very long. I guess none really appealed to me, or vice versa. Perhaps my relationships with older, experienced women clouded my perceptions. I never found schoolgirls very interesting, until I found Jenny.

I first met Jenny when she was a pretty, young girl in my brother's class, and it was clear Steve had a big crush on her. I was sixteen and Jenny was fourteen, an age difference that would normally have kept me from even considering dating her in high school. What kind of ragging could I expect if I dated a girl two years my junior? Not gonna happen.

As is always the case, nobody, including me, expected anything to spark between us, it just did. Steve would walk Jenny home from school and I occasionally ended up walking with them for company. Next thing I knew I was the one waiting for Jenny to come out of class so I could walk her home, with or without Steve.

The awkward young girl was transforming into a very beautiful young woman. Initially my brother Steve was pissed with me for hitting on the girl he liked, but he got over it and it never developed into a problem between us.

Out of respect for Jenny, her age, and the situation, I was on my best behavior for the first year of our relationship. We got into heavy petting, but never actually "did it." By the time Jenny was fifteen, I was looking at a gorgeous young woman with a bloodline that was part American and part Spanish. The guys who teased me when I first started dating Jenny had pretty much shut-up. She was really a knockout, and she had me hooked.

Dating Jenny meant you were part of her family. Jenny's mother Sandy was of Spanish descent and was very dear to me. I often referred to her as my second mother.

Robin, Jenny's younger sister, was a great kid and more importantly a great friend. Robin's nickname was Bob and she told everybody I chose the wrong sister to date. If Jenny hadn't been around, I think Robin would have been fun to date, except she was even younger than Jenny and I was already stretching it. Sam, Jenny's father, was a nice gentleman but seemed a little spacey and our relationship wasn't as close as those I enjoyed with the women in the family.

Sandy always insisted we all go to the New Territories on Sunday, known as "family day" in that household. I acted as Sandy's translator as we walked through the markets in Shatin, moving from one outdoor stall to another. One of her favorite places to visit was the Buddhist temple in Shatin. The pathway leading up the hill to the temple was lined with street peddlers who sold every trinket and household article imaginable. In Hong Kong bargaining was how things were purchased so every time Sandy wanted to buy something, I bargained for her.

Sandy's favorite pastime was trying to embarrass me, and sometimes she managed to do it in spades. She especially enjoyed embarrassing me in public places, like the lobby of the Peninsula Hotel or a restaurant. Sandy would pretend I was her younger, kept boyfriend and would keep up the charade until I turned bright red. She would burst out in a deep, throaty laugh at my expense. Come to think of it, if Jenny hadn't been her daughter, being Sandy's kept toy-boy wouldn't have been all bad. After *The Graduate* featuring Mrs. Robinson hit theaters, I received relentless teasing about Sandy from several friends, especially Norman.

Jenny and I dated for four years and I thought for sure it was the real thing and we would eventually get married. Unlike Cerena or Julie, I thought this relationship had a future.

Jenny was petite with long dark hair, nice legs, and big beautiful brown eyes. One of the funny things I remember about this slender young woman was her voracious appetite. It was amazing how somebody built so small could eat so much. We loved to go out for Korean barbecue. If you've never tried Korean barbecue, you're missing one of life's great pleasures. Slices of thinly sliced marinated beef are cooked on a metal hat-shaped inverted cone.

During cooking the air reeks with wafts of garlic and spices. Each cone has a funnel above it to suck the fumes so diners don't suffocate of garlic asphyxiation. The cooked beef is eaten with white rice and a variety of side dishes ranging from pickled cabbage to tiny, dried salty fishes. The mini-fish gross out some people because they remain whole and have their little black eyes intact.

The variety of food offered in Hong Kong was tremendous and when not eating Asian dishes, Jenny and I went to the other extreme and gorged on escargot at French restaurants. One of our favorites was Au Trou Normand, a great bistro located behind the Peninsula. Whoever came up with the saying "The way to a man's heart is through his stomach" got his sexes confused. I think Jenny enjoyed eating as much as she enjoyed another sensual activity – sex.

Jenny and I did not become lovers until we dated for several years, but it was not for my lack of interest or trying. She told me she just wasn't ready for sex. I respected and loved her too much to force the issue. I was convinced it would eventually happen; it was simply a matter of the right time. I just hoped Jenny didn't want to wait until we were married.

Marriage! Boy, was I a teenager in love, or what! I was also deeply respectful (and fearful) of Sandy so I behaved. Painful but happy memories are appropriate ways to describe some of our early dates. Those of the male persuasion can recall teenage years when prolonged sexual foreplay without relief could lead to a bizarre state known as "blue balls." This condition was so terrible that death seemed like an acceptable alternative. Remembering a party at a friend's house on Repulse Bay carries particularly vivid memories that make me want to bend over in pain just thinking about that night.

It was a great party, lots of dancing, groping, and kissing on the couches. Jenny and I walked outside to watch waves crash on the shore. It was a beautiful starry night and Jenny looked particularly beautiful. We stayed outside for quite a while, kissing and fondling each other. Finally we walked back to the house and then it hit me - a dull, gnawing ache in my groin that made it miserable to walk or stand. At first I thought I was suffering from some form of weird constipation and went to the bathroom hoping for relief. Unfortunately relief did not come. I was almost doubled up with pain, yet completely unaware of its source. I remember Jenny and my friends were really concerned about me and were wondering whether I should go to the emergency room.

Perhaps I had appendicitis? What a joke! If they knew the reason for my discomfort they would have all died laughing. Later when I thought about, I wondered how somebody with my vast and fast experience could not have heard about blue balls. Once Jenny and I knew the reason for this pain, we also knew how to relieve it. It was amazing how often I felt the pain coming on after that!

Unfortunately, life is never without a few bad memories and our intimacy did not begin until after a painful incident that almost split us apart.

During the summer Jenny and her family vacationed in Hawaii. Although Jenny was gone only three weeks, I wrote to her often and was slightly bent out of shape when a week went by without receiving a letter in return. When the family returned I soon tired of hearing about the beaches, parties, and other activities. The jealous young soul in me resented Jenny had such a good time without me, and I almost asked why she bothered to come back. Mine was definitely a juvenile reaction, but quite typical of any male my age.

A week later I noticed Robin was acting strangely; she seemed to be upset about something. The two of us were close and I considered her as my little sister. In conversation she spilled the beans that Jenny was with another boy while in Hawaii and that was the reason I had not received many letters. Robin never went into detail, but her body language told a distressing story. The more we talked, the more I feared the worst. Soon after, Jenny, Robin, Steve, and I were walking home from school. I pulled Jenny to the side of the road and demanded, "I want to know if it's true you made out with some guy when you were on vacation? Is it true?"

When her eyes searched the ground, I had my answer.

"Jenny, did you just make out, or was it more serious, you have to tell me."

She hesitated and guilt spread over her face like an eclipse. She paused, looked up at me and said, "I'm so, so sorry, Tony. I got in with a crowd of great kids when we first arrived and met a guy who was really nice to me. We were just friends, but one night we were at a party and things got carried away and next thing I knew we were in the bedroom."

Bedroom!

She started to cry, but her tears meant nothing to me. To say I was hurt and angry would be an understatement. I was enraged and my immediate reaction was to break it off with her. I didn't say one word the rest of the way home. I was like a volcano ready to erupt. How could a girl who loved you do something like this?

Jenny kept telling me how sorry she was and how I was the one she loved, but her words ran hollow. By now I was near tears myself, but anger held them back. We each went home and I wondered what she thought when alone. I know I went through great agony as I mentally listed the ways I could break up with her.

I sulked for a few days and breaking up was still on my mind, but deep down I knew I cared for Jenny too much and wanted to stay with her no matter how badly betrayed. The following week I met her outside her classroom after school and we walked the usual route home without saying a word.

As we came closer to my place Jenny put her hand in mine and squeezed. While trying to reconcile events in my mind, it had become essential that I become her lover. I could not go on knowing she had given herself to somebody she had known only a few days, but had not been my lover all the time we dated. I knew this was an unhealthy reason for demanding intimacy, but I simply could not help myself.

After the confrontation, I knew it would be difficult for her to deny my advances. By now we had reached my home and Jenny asked if she could come in and listen to music. Both of us knew music wasn't really on her mind. We went to my room and locked the door. It was mid-afternoon so my parents wouldn't be home for hours. And it happened. Once we became lovers, the feelings we had for each other grew deeper, and with time my wound healed.

For all the years we were together, I was always faithful to Jenny, but there was that one humorous evening I behaved badly and the whole high school heard about it. It was the last night of the annual school play and there was going to be a big cast party when the curtain went down. One of my friends, Ian Buckingham, persuaded me it would be fun to load up on drinks at the party, just the guys. I had never been much of a drinker but thought I would give it a try. We weren't going to be driving and I foolishly figured I would be in a relatively safe environment.

Wrong! I got so shit-faced on straight gin that I did a number of things I would seriously regret the next day.

I discovered I became amorous and quite fearless when drunk. At the party I found a mop in a closet and ran through the crowd hugging the stick accosting every good-looking girl I could find. My ultimatum was they could kiss my girlfriend Miss Mop, or they could kiss me. I managed to kiss a whole lot of girls that night; it seems I caused quite a stir. I was darn lucky some jealous boyfriend didn't beat the hell out of me. One girl named Jackie Fischel took advantage of my inebriated state and I kissed her more than once. I know darn well I kissed her many times. She had a crush on me so I was ripe for the taking.

Luckily nothing happened apart from kissing. Honestly, I was probably too drunk to perform anyway. The next day I got a well-deserved monster hangover and a brutally cool hello from Jenny. We both knew I had been a complete idiot to get so drunk, but fortunately I had not done anything permanently damaging, like ending up in somebody's bed, so Jenny forgave me.

Having mentioned Jackie Fischel, I must tell you about her brother Pete. He had the most amazing bar-trick talent I have ever seen. Pete and I were having a drink at the Scene, a disco in the basement of the Peninsula. Pete bet me he could blow smoke out of his eyes!

This sounded so ridiculous that I was immediately ready to put down hard cash to take the bet. Pete said he didn't want to take my money and I figured this was his way of backing out of the wager.

But with great ceremony, Pete lit a cigarette and inhaled deeply as a strained appearance swept over his face. Two thin spirals of smoke wafted from his tear ducts. *Unbelievable!* If I had not seen it, I would have thought it was a trick, but this was the real thing! Some weeks later, Pete showed me a variation of the trick at the beach. We ducked underwater and tiny air bubbles could be seen coming out of his eyes. This guy was talented!

CHAPTER TEN
"Things We Said Today"
JOHN LENNON AND PAUL MCCARTNEY

The English school system is very different from the American educational system. From ages eleven to fifteen, students study a variety of core subjects. At the end of each year exams are given in each subject and must be passed before a student could move to the next grade level. This was the way it was at KGV.

Depending how well you performed, a student would be assigned to an A, B, C or D class within the grade level. As expected, students in the D classes were not terribly motivated as they were classified at the bottom of the heap. After five years of study, all students took the London University General Certificate of Education exams at the "Ordinary" ("O") level in each subject.

This system, in which a set of exams is scored by a teacher who doesn't know the student and is sitting thousands of miles away in England, is a stressful way of measuring the culmination of five years of study. I much prefer the American system that enables students to study and pass exams in different subjects over the entire course of their high school career.

I had advanced to "Form Six" (equivalent to US grade 12) where I spent two years studying two subjects at the advanced level. The first year was relatively fun and pressure free and I managed to find enough time to pass two more exams at the "O" level. Results in "O" and "A" level exams were reviewed for entry to British universities, and "A" levels were recognized for credit at American universities.

I studied biology and geography and passed both subjects, which meant I was eligible to apply to a British university. I was surprised to discover in my A-level geography class of six kids, a class where I was the class clown and not exactly the teacher's favorite, I was the only one who passed the exam. This achievement made me wonder about my "un-actualized academic potential," but that pondering lasted only a couple days before I was back in my world of sports, Jenny, and music.

What was even more interesting was my geography teacher Miss Roberts told me she always thought I had the ability to do very well and was not at all surprised I had passed the tough exam! That was a surprise – I thought Miss Roberts didn't like me one bit. I passed two "A" levels, which meant I was now ready to move onto the next stage of my life – University. The big question was where to go?

When I was in high school it seemed my classes would never end and I'd forever be seeing the same old friends, teachers, and sitting for the dreaded exams hoping to pass so I could move on to the next stage in my life. I think most high school students long for the day it will all be over so life as a young adult can begin.

When my commencement day finally arrived, I found I wasn't quite so sure about what was ahead and what I was going to do for the rest of my life. The prospect of freedom from high school suddenly became scary and at the age of seventeen I sensed becoming "old."

My parents drummed into me that I was going to University after high school, no question about it. Neither Mum nor Dad had the opportunity, so by God, Tony *was* going to be the first in the family to receive a college degree.

I was easy going and this sounded fine to me and, yes indeed, I should definitely strive to achieve academic greatness, although I had no idea what it was I was aiming to achieve. In Hong Kong there were three options following high school: 1) Attend the University of Hong Kong; 2) Attend a university in the mother countries of England or America; or 3) Attend a university in Australia.

Standards at the local university in Hong Kong were high because of the large number of applicants, but this wasn't a good option for me. Let me ask you this. Would you be impressed by a degree from the University of Hong Kong, even if I told you the curriculum and standards were extremely high?

Option #2 was the most popular. But for me England was a long way away and the cold and wet held no appeal. I remembered the bad weather from family travels years before. British prejudice positioned American universities as not having the same high academic standards as those in the UK. American universities definitely represented a more expensive proposition too.

The third option, and one that held greatest appeal for me, was to study "down under." Australia sounded like a neat place, the last modern frontier. Having ties to England, this country would not be drastically different from Hong Kong and the weather certainly seemed far more hospitable.

I sent applications to the universities of Sydney, Melbourne, and Perth and was accepted by all three institutions. I am normally a very rational and analytical person, but at times my impulsive streak rules. When it came to choosing a university in Aussie, my impulsive nature reigned supreme. With little research into the different locales, I decided the City of Lights was the place I was headed. Did you know Perth became known as the City of Lights because astronaut John Glenn could see the city from space because the entire city population turned on their lights for him? Cool. *Sounds like a fun place.* Was I in for a surprise!

So it was decided, the first Tebbutt to gain a university education was headed to Australia. I graduated from KGV in June 1965 and had six months to loaf around before the school year began in Oz. Perth is in the Southern Hemisphere, so the scholastic calendar geared up in January instead of September; I was in for an extended holiday. I was to find those six months passed very quickly, in more ways than one.

From a very early age, I had the need for speed, and as the saying goes, the only difference between men and boys is the size of their toys. When I was a toddler, my parents nicknamed me "Flash Gordon" (FYI,

Gordon is my middle name). I zoomed everywhere and I could run like a rabbit.

The first toy I owned which increased my personal speed was a pair of roller skates. I was an absolute spitfire on wheels. Remember, early skates had steel wheels that lacked traction, suspension, and were exceptionally noisy. The next technological innovation was rubber wheels; this was like moving from a four-cylinder car to a V8 with enhanced suspension.

Soon after roller skates came bicycles. I worked my way up from the leisurely recreational bike with upswept handlebars to a racing ten-speed Raleigh built in England. Once again speed was my burning need and I tried my hand at road racing in the New Territories.

At each stage of my development I had an idol representing the epitome of whatever sport I followed. For cycling I admired the Frenchman Jacques Anqueteil, the five-time winner of the Tour de France. My love for bicycle racing didn't last long because I discovered racing bikes seriously was an incredible physical challenge requiring more physical fitness and training than I was prepared to give. One time I did really well in a bike road race, but was disqualified because I was drafting behind a speeding truck for part of the competition. I didn't know this was against the rules, but I did know it was dangerous.

Another time I did quite well to finish in the top ten of a race, but was so exhausted by the effort I didn't have the energy to ride my bike home. I had to telephone good old dad to drive ten miles into the New Territories to get me, and then rode home with my bike stuffed in the trunk and my body and mind half-comatose. Speed demons were still on my shoulder when I graduated from KGV and were growing stronger than ever (must have come with the raging hormones). I had six months before heading off to University so I started to lobby for what most boys at that age want – a motorcycle.

Big problem. I had no driver's license and there was a long waiting list to get one in Hong Kong. It was a full nine months before a driving test could be booked. This was a substantial barrier to getting a motorcycle and I could see no obvious solution.

Fate smiled! My parents asked Steve and me if we would like to go to the Philippines to visit our cousins for a couple weeks. Since we had little else to do, we both said sure, we would love to have the opportunity to travel, especially since several years had passed since we last visited the Philippines. That had been an occasion that Steve and I would never forget.

My cousin Sydney lived with her husband and family in Urdaneta village in the district of Makati, a suburb of Manila. Her three children lived with her, along with my Aunt Lois (mum's sister) and Uncle Joe, her husband.

Steve and I were particularly fond of Uncle Joe. He was a bit of a rebel with a touch of piracy in his blood. Uncle Joe had personal economic ups and downs and dabbled in all sorts of businesses, primarily in the import/export field. He was always generous to Steve and me when money was flowing. Unfortunately for Uncle Joe, he was currently experiencing a depression in his personal economy that forced him to move in with his son-in-law, Sydney's husband Martin.

Martin was a very successful American businessman and this really galled Uncle Joe; he hated living in his son-in-law's house. I thought Martin was remarkably tolerant of the whole situation, and gave him a lot of credit for putting up with a father- in-law who was not particularly grateful for the help. Martin was always good to Steve and me, but he was not a warm man, although generous with good intentions. That made gave him a big bold OK in my book.

The day after I arrived in Manila, I discovered a big surprise in the garage. Martin owned a Honda motorcycle! It was a black Honda 250cc and it was a beautiful machine. I immediately began to plot and figure out how to sweet talk my cousin's husband into letting me drive his motorcycle. It really wasn't that difficult.

As I said earlier, Martin was a decent guy and was willing to allow me to ride his bike as long as I knew what I was doing and was not in danger of maiming myself. Martin gave me a quick lesson on how to handle the bike, paying special attention to the gears and brakes. I was allowed to ride around the village of Makati, only because it was a walled and guarded compound. Martin insisted I had to be cautious, not speed, and not do anything dangerous because if I didn't follow his rules, I would be grounded. No problem! I would have agreed to anything just to ride that bike.

For the next five days my daily routine was simple: Get up, eat breakfast, and ride around the village, sometimes with Steve on the back. Most of the time I rode alone. Day after day, I followed the same routine, enjoying myself immensely. I'd ride from one end of the village, greet the guards, turn around and hightail it to the other end. It never got boring and I was able to get comfortable with the powerful cycle. On day five, my Uncle Joe, ever the instigator, asked, "Hey, aren't you tired of riding around and around in the village?"

To which I responded, "Sure, Uncle Joe, but since I don't have a license I'm not allowed to drive on the outside roads." I saw a smile slip over his face.

"Well, why don't we get you a license?" I really wasn't sure where he was going with this because my Hong Kong experience told me there was a long wait to get a driver's license. My uncle's mischievous side was kicking in. He had found a way to stick a barb into his son-in-law's side. Uncle Joe resented that Martin had given me the opportunity to ride his motorcycle while he had nothing of his own to give me.

"For twenty bucks we can get you a license, this is the Philippines!" Bribery! I knew Manila was corrupt, but was Uncle Joe serious? Could I really get a license?

"I'll get you one tomorrow." True to his word, the next day Joe walked into the house with huge grin on his face. I anxiously approached him with hopeful words, "Did you get it?"

"Has your Uncle Joe ever failed on a promise?" With that he handed me a red piece of paper that was indeed a driver's license bearing my name. Wow! What a great gift! It was the first time I had been exposed to such corruption, but since I was on the receiving end with nobody getting hurt, I was delighted with the gift. I could hardly wait until Martin came home so I could ask him to drive his motorcycle outside the village and on the streets of Manila.

When Martin came home and heard about Uncle Joe's administrative manipulations, he was really a good sport about the whole thing. He didn't have a problem with me being on public roads as long as it was okay with my parents and I continued to be very careful. Next mission, a phone call to my parents. After much pleading, they finally reluctantly agreed, but couched it with warnings that if I did anything the least bit reckless, I would have the privilege taken away pronto.

For the next several days I explored Manila roads close to our house and found my way to the American school where Steve and I parked the bike and struck manly poses to impress the young pretty things coming out of class.

We must have impressed somebody because out of the blue, I got a telephone call from a friend of the family who said a model was needed for a cola ad shoot and asked if I would be interested.

Never one to back away from a new experience, I quickly agreed. My decision was solidified when I found I would be paid for the gig. A few days later I was on the lawn of a mansion in another village suburb called Forbes Park. This development was where the real money was - unbelievable properties and beautifully landscaped gardens were everywhere. A "shoot crew" commandeered the property, ready to photograph the cola advertisement. All I had to do was hand a bottle of cola to a young American beauty sitting on a magnificent white horse. *Quite the dramatic setting for a soft drink ad,* I thought.

It didn't take long for my ego to plummet. I discovered the shot would be taken behind me so the blonde would have the frontal shot, leaning down from the horse and taking the cola from my outstretched hand. It sounded simple enough, and what the heck, even if I wasn't in the full shot, they were paying me a hundred bucks for easy work.

For what seemed like hours, but in reality was only about twenty minutes, the crew posed us and took photos from dozens of different angles. The whole deal was beginning to get boring and I was losing interest.

Then something happened that quickly got my attention. The thousand pound horse stood on my foot! Pain shot through my leg but I couldn't pull away - the damn thing was so heavy that I was trapped.

I didn't want to embarrass myself in front of the pretty blond, but tears were welling in my eyes. The horse was wearing thick metal horseshoes and I was wearing thin slip-on leather shoes! This was a real mismatch.

The blonde was reaching for the cola but I was waving my arms like a madman. The camera crew couldn't figure out was going on. After an eternity the stupid animal finally got off my foot and I let loose with a delayed yelp of pain. People rushed to me, but when I told them what had happened, I received no sympathy. All I got were gales of laughter. Blondie high on the horse apologized, but not without a giggle. My moment of fame had not turned out to be as glamorous as I hoped. My cousins later sent me copies of the ad in the local newspaper and sure enough, the back of my head only showed in the photo so I had the hardest time convincing people that I really was the male star.

One Saturday Martin said he had a surprise in store for us. We were all going to the go-kart race track. Steve and I would be allowed to drive the karts around the course. Martin had always wanted to race cars and several of his friends were Filipino Grand Prix race car drivers competing on the Asian circuit, which included the Macau Grand Prix. To hone their skills when not on the big track, these guys would race high-powered go-karts on weekends. The star racer was a nice, young Filipino man by the name of Dojie Laurel.

Dojie was the son of a politician and as such was from a wealthy family. All Filipino politicians were rich, the wealthiest being the famous, or infamous, Ferdinand and Imelda Marcos. Dojie had a brother wilder in spirit and while we were in Manila his brother was caught in a controversy involving a shooting at the original Bayside nightclub. Coming from a gun-controlled British Colony, it was strange to see people walking around wearing holsters and brandishing handguns. But today at the track nobody was armed with a gun, at least that I could see.

The go-karts were being tuned and the high-pitched whine of their engines was like music to my ears. The smell of the fumes was an aphrodisiac. Steve and I patiently waited our turns to take a spin on the quarter-mile track that included hairpin turns, S-curves, overpasses, and loads of thrills. These karts were much faster than those we raced around the Kadoorie's garden at Boulder Lodge, thereby increasing the danger factor and increasing the thrill.

Most racers brought two karts, their main machine and a backup. Martin's backup was substantially slower and older than his racing kart, but he told me I could race his #2 buggy in the main event. My excitement was building by the minute.

Steve was out on the track in the kart and it wouldn't be long until the main race was set to begin. Steve was coming round the final corner and my heart flipped. The kart he was driving was in obvious difficulty, spluttering and limping as it maneuvered into the pit. It only took a few minutes for the diagnosis, it was a terminal problem. There would be no more racing for this machine.

The look on my face must have been genuinely pitiful. I felt so bad because I was really looking forward to racing with the men; my hopes were dashed. Dojie must have seen my forlorn expression because he very kindly mentioned to Martin that I could drive his number two kart in the race. I was wild with anticipation! This was an incredibly generous offer by Dojie and I was only too willing to take him up on it. I slammed on the helmet and snuggled into the seat for a few practice laps and soon discovered this buggy was not only faster, but handled much better than Martin's kart did. Cool! Bring on the competition; I was ready to race!

My competitive kart race was less than spectacular. The big boys quickly demonstrated they not only had the horsepower to blow me away, but had the *cojones* to make sure nothing got in the way of the checkered flag, not even a teenager filled with determination to show his racing prowess. More than once they nudged me off the track as they set their sights on the finish line.

Kid, if you're going to be out here with the big boys, you better be prepared for real racing treatment.

I pushed the limit until I went over the edge and lost it in a hairpin corner. I eventually stopped by bumping into a tree that had suddenly jumped in front of me. With Herculean effort, I managed to lift the front end of the kart onto the track and finished the race only a couple laps behind the winner, who happened to be Martin.

As I drove to the pit, I noticed stiffness in the steering that had not been there before. *Whoops, this is not good*, I thought. I sheepishly told

Dojie that I had mangled his kart and messed-up the steering, not sure what his reaction would be. I was feeling awful about the accident. He had been kind enough to lend me his spare and I had botched it. But Dojie was terrific; he blew off the accident as part of the sport and insisted I not worry about it. What a great guy, what a great day! Even Martin was happy. He had managed to win a trophy - finally - against top racing talent and take another step in his goal to race in the Macau Grand Prix.

Our visit to Manila was drawing to a close and Steve and I were ready to go home to Hong Kong. Our cousin Pablo, (Sydney's brother), had taken a liking to Steve several years earlier when we first visited Manila (pre-Jenny), probably because they both had a wild streak. In his mid-twenties, Pablo was the black sheep of the family. He was a happy-go-lucky, two-hundred-twenty pound, black belt judo expert who never took life too seriously. I was never quite sure what Pablo did for a living. I think he was in the import/export business, but didn't seem to be terribly successful. That particular visit to Manila had a somewhat rascally ending for the Tebbutt brothers, more so for Steve who was only thirteen at the time. It was one of the last days of our visit and we were told a drive in the countryside was on the agenda. Pablo would be giving us the tour. I should have suspected something because Pablo was not the type to play tour guide. We took off after lunch and when we hit the suburbs of Manila, Pablo announced we were going to visit an old-style bordello where Steve could lose his cherry. Steve and I were somewhat at a loss for words upon learning of this new development.

Soon we found ourselves in front of an old, but well-kept house reminiscent of a plantation. I had apprehension about this adventure, but on the other hand, I wasn't complaining since there was an element of sexual excitement about the prospect of what lay ahead. Steve was eager, but also a bit nervous about expectations surrounding this "first time" event. The front door opened into a large foyer with several armchairs placed appropriately. We sat down and were served soft drink refreshments while Pablo talked to the mama-san about the arrangements. Soon after the mama-san left the room and quickly came back with six young, smiling women and we were told to take our pick. I noticed one young Filipina was quite attractive and quickly made my choice.

It went differently for Steve because an older woman (in her twenties) made the choice for him by taking him by the hand before he had much chance to consider. I think she relished the thought of having fun with the "virgin."

We marched up a grand flight of stairs to nice private rooms where we were to do the dirty deed. There was not much to say about my experience. The pretty young girl motioned for me to undress; she put a condom on me, and we went through the motions in a mechanical manner. Within twenty minutes I was back out the door and seated in the foyer. Another twenty minutes passed and no sign of Steve. Finally, almost an hour after he first walked up the stairway, down came Steve with a goofy grin plastered on his face. His partner told us Steve had "represented himself well," which made him quite proud of his performance. I never got to the bottom of who was the real instigator of this foray into the seedy side of the Philippines, but deep down I had suspicions it was good old Uncle Joe.

Our cousin had a mischievous streak and he was determined to expose my younger brother to more of the seamier side of life in Manila, without his parents knowing what he had in mind.

The night before we were to leave, Pablo and his judo buddy Robbie drove by the house and told Aunt Lois we were all going out for a final night of fun. Aunt Lois assumed we were going bowling or some such thing and told Pablo to get us home early.

Pablo and Robbie got into the front seats of the car and Steve and I sat in back. Pablo, sitting in the passenger seat, turned and said to Steve, "Tonight you are going to see your first *live show.*"

Steve and I looked at each other and laughed, we weren't sure exactly how to interpret this proclamation.

"What are you talking about?" asked Steve, chortling nervously.

"Tonight your cousin and I are taking you to a part of Manila where you can see a man and a woman doing the dirty deed. It'll be a good laugh and something by which you can remember the Philippines," Robbie answered with a chuckle.

Steve and I weren't too sure we wanted to do this and tried to tell the two big lunks maybe we could find something else to do. Problem was, we were much younger and you know how younger kids don't want to be uncool, so we half-heartedly went along for the ride.

And what a ride it was! We drove through a section of town where bars and the women on the streets looked pretty raunchy. In those days Manila was reminiscent of Chicago in the twenties, lots of corruption and guys wearing guns. I have to admit I was getting nervous and was happy we were with two really big guys who were judo experts.

We finally came to a seedy apartment building and Pablo jumped out of the car to talk to a woman leaning on the doorway to the staircase. Her hair was dyed red and she was a little porky. This woman had certainly not won any recent Miss Manila contests. I was praying she was not going to be a part of the show, whatever the hell it was. I looked at Steve and I could tell from his expression he was thinking the same thing. Pablo stuck his face into the window opening.

"Okay, Robbie, park the car, we'll head on upstairs to the apartment."

"Hey, guys, what say we go to a movie or go bowling?" Steve quickly nodded in agreement to my feeble suggestion.

"No way!" bellowed Pablo. "We're going to have some real fun!"

We parked the car, headed across the street to the stairway, and marched up to the second floor. The door was already open. It was a hotel apartment, nothing more than a bedroom and bathroom holding a couple chairs. Only a few feet separated the walls from the bed, but wide enough for four chairs. We sat in place for an eternity. By now Steve and I were really uncomfortable with the whole situation. Pablo was having a great time and kept kidding Steve. He insisted Steve and I would enjoy the show. Soon enough the red-haired, porky woman came in with a skinny, slimy looking dude with greasy black hair and a mustache.

I started to feel queasy. This wasn't going to be pretty, and it certainly wasn't my idea of sexy. But Pablo and Robbie were into it and were laughing and talking with the "performers" as they took off their clothes. Like I said, it really wasn't pretty; they looked much better with their clothes on.

Before they got started the couple practiced an unusual version of safe sex. Slimy pulled out a bottle of rubbing alcohol and a couple hand towels, soaked the towels with the alcohol, and rubbed the towels all over his gonads. I shuddered as I thought about how much this would sting the old pecker. Porky did the same thing to her anatomy and then proceeded to use everything in her arsenal to arouse a rather limp Slimy. After excessive sucking and spitting, Slimy became moderately erect, enough for the show to go on.

For the next ten minutes the two engaged in multi-positional fornication that was anything but erotic, and eventually terminated with the most pathetic simulation of an orgasm imaginable. I glanced at Steve and could tell he was just glad the whole thing was over. Unfortunately our ever-happy cousin Pablo had not had enough and wanted to prolong the fun and games.

"Hey, can you do any tricks for us?" he asked Porky. She had a stupid grin on her face and replied, "You wanna see me slice a banana?"

Pablo and Robbie were like cheerleaders, egging her on. What happened next was the most amazing feat of vaginal dexterity I have ever seen. She took a banana, fully inserted it into her vagina and pushed it back out cut into pieces, ejecting one piece at a time! When this gross show was over, Pablo still wasn't satisfied, he wanted more so he turned to Steve and demanded, "Have you ever felt a woman's pussy?" Steve was horrified and muttered something unintelligible, which Pablo took for the answer no. Pablo beckoned for the woman to slide over on the bed and told her to put both legs against the wall on either side of my brother, literally pinning him in with the straddle.

"Touch it" Pablo ordered.

"No way am I touching her," Steve insisted. Pablo responded by grabbing Steve's index finger and sticking it right into Porky's crotch! I thought I was going to puke right then and there. The look of horror on Steve's face was indescribable. Pablo was laughing hysterically as Steve sat mortified. Porky removed her legs from either side of Steve and asked if anybody wanted a turn with her.

Steve and I simultaneously and very emphatically shouted, "No, thanks!" We were raised to be polite after all.

To our great relief Pablo and Robbie weren't interested in her proposition so they paid the two performers their fee and we left the apartment. When we got downstairs, Steve was holding his right hand in front of him and looking at his finger like it was infected by the plague (God knows, maybe it was). Pablo and Robbie thought this was incredibly amusing and teased him unmercifully, warning him to be careful where he put his finger next. At his point Steve was beginning to lose patience; he had not enjoyed the experience and he certainly did not like having his finger dipped into the crotch of a gross prostitute. Steve turned to Pablo and said, "If you think this is so funny, why don't you take some of it?"

As he spoke, Steve wiped his finger on Pablo's hand. What seemed so funny a few seconds before now had a different effect on our cousin; he jumped back as if touched by a cattle prod. On the other hand, Robbie thought the whole sequence of events was hysterical and started to egg Pablo on about the "stuff" that now covered his hand. He taunted Pablo, "Maybe if you rub it on your lip you'll be able to grow something other than that sorry excuse you call a mustache."

The two started to banter angrily and Pablo made a motion to touch Robbie with his "infected" hand. Robbie immediately went into a judo stance ready for combat. Within seconds the mood had changed from one of jocularity to one of intensity. The two black belt judo experts were ready to do combat in the middle of the street in a not-so-nice section of Manila, all because a finger had been inserted into the vagina of a prostitute! I didn't find the situation to be at all amusing and was getting genuinely concerned so I yelled to the two of them, "Hey guys, stop behaving like stupid kids. This is no place for the two of you to fight."

Maybe it was the shock of me speaking out and the embarrassment of someone much younger chiding them for their bad behavior or maybe sanity prevailed, but whatever the reason, they stopped dead in their tracks. We drove home with a bare minimum of conversation and when my Aunt Lois asked where we had been, we simply answered like teenagers normally do, "Nowhere special, Aunt Lois."

Only the seediest and most disgusting place I have ever been in my life!

Steve and I hardly ever talked about that night. I think it was a time we weren't proud of and would just as soon forget the whole ordeal. However, the episode remained forged in our brains.

The next day we flew back to Hong Kong and I never told my parents what we had experienced. They probably would have made a big stink and got Pablo into a whole lot of trouble. If it turned out Uncle Joe was the instigator, the trouble caused would have been intense and neither Steve nor I wanted that to happen.

Now that I had my motorcycle license, begging and pleading my parents for my own motorcycle increased in intensity. To this day I'm not sure why my parents gave in because I know from the very first day I had my bike they worried about my safety. My parents would never sleep well until they knew I was back home and safe in bed, although this was often in the early hours of the morning.

I lobbied for what was popular with several of my friends at the time, a Honda 250cc. I was surprised and thrilled when my dad (who also loved toys) said I could get a BSA because the Japanese bikes were not as well built. Like in so many other areas, Japanese motorcycles have since moved on to become the leaders in the industry and English bikes have all but disappeared, although in recent years there has been a revival of the Triumph brand.

We went to the BSA dealership in Wanchai and there in the window sat the most beautiful machine I had ever seen. It was a 650cc Thunderbolt Rocket. The "Beeza" was a beautiful combination of royal blue and chrome. The gas tank was shiny blue with a chrome speed flash and emblazoned on both sides was the bold BSA insignia. The fenders were chrome and glistened brilliantly in the sunlight. This was a *big* motorcycle with slightly upswept handlebars and twin chrome exhausts. Leather tasseled grips flew on the end of each handlebar.

After seeing this bike, I had to have it. Dad negotiated the price as was typical in Hong Kong, eventually coming to an agreement. He paid for the bike and I was in heaven. The dealer gave me instructions how to operate the beast and I jumped in the saddle.

I noticed how heavy the bike was compared to the Honda I'd been riding and I almost laid it on its side just getting on it. This bike didn't have an electric starter, it had to be kick started after playing with the gears to find neutral. Kick starting the bike in gear guaranteed sooner or later you'd be snapped in the shins. Today's cycles have electric starters and kick starting might be considered a lost art.

I'd never mounted a motorcycle this big and wobbled as I drove down the road. I could tell Dad was having second thoughts as he watched me weave, but soon I got the hang of it. It's exhilarating to accelerate hard on a big bike; it's like no other sensation of speed and very few cars even come close. The sound from the dual exhausts is deep and throaty compared to the whine and chatter of the high-revving overhead cam Hondas. The Beeza was a beauty!

Kowloon is not very populous and connecting with other riders was easy. I hooked up with several guys who rode BSA Thunderbolt Lightnings, Triumph Bonnevilles, and Norton Commandos – all big English motorbikes. We wore the typical leather jackets and when we rode through the main streets our roar and style commanded attention. Helmets weren't mandatory so dark sunglasses blackened most faces. We were hot, really hot.

We were definite bike lovers, and not troublemakers as many may have pictured us. But when our squad of guys in black leather roared through the streets, we looked like bad asses. We simply loved our speed demon pieces of steel and chrome and the thrill of maneuvering at high speed on country roads. We had no interest in causing trouble and certainly had no gang tendencies.

I soon discovered it's safer to race on roads at night because oncoming headlights give good warning. In daylight if a car in the oncoming lane overtakes a corner, the bike rider has no warning until he's a mass of road kill.

I loved weaving around corners at high speed following the rear lights of the front rider - it was magical. Going through the S-curves, leaning first one way then another, was almost like dancing as rhythm took over. Many times we'd blast through a deserted piece of road in the wee hours of the morning and hit the magic "ton," which is slang for 100 mph.

Early morning drag races determined which bike was the fastest. The surprise winner was the Norton, with the Triumph Bonneville a close second. Although my Thunderbolt was plenty fast, it had a single carburetor engine thus not as fast as others with twin carbs. Racing at 100 mph isn't much of an accomplishment for today's equipment, but it was pretty fast in those days and we raced on relatively short spans of roadway. Today's "rice machines" are so fast it's downright scary to think sixteen-year-olds are on the roads. A modern Kawasaki Ninja would make English bikes look like they were standing still!

Our bikes didn't have aerodynamic fairings or dropped handlebars; most of us had upswept handlebars seen only on Harley-Davidson bikes today. Even so, we were nuts to go as fast as we did, particularly around corners when our big bikes would lean over so low that kickstands scraped the road, sending a shower of sparks.

Although helmets weren't mandatory, I was more cautious than the others and frequently wore mine, especially on long night rides. My heroes were world motorcycling champions Mike Hailwood and Giacomo Agostini, both rode MV Augustas, a great Italian marque.

Another racer I admired wasn't as famous, but known for his unique style rounding corners. John Cooper rode a Norton single banger 500cc classic, and when leaning into the corner would take his entire body out of the seat and hang onto the motorcycle like a sidecar. Cooper was also known for the pair of "mooneyes" on his helmet front. Today his style wouldn't be radical; most Grand Prix racers hang out of their seats in corners, but back then Cooper was a revolutionary. I enjoyed mimicking Cooper and would occasionally hang over the side of my Thunderbolt Rocket speeding through twisty corners. Did I ever fall and hurt myself? Of course I did, but fortunately never had a serious accident with lasting consequences.

Two falls are well-remembered, even after forty plus years. Fall #1 happened as I was driving off the vehicular ferry that crossed the harbor from Kowloon to Hong Kong. Vehicles entered and exited along the same route so oil and sludge collected on the wooden gangway bridging the ferry to the dock. As I exited, I hit a greasy spot and it sent my bike sliding sideways with me tumbling after. Damage was minimal to self and bike, my pride took the bigger fall. I unceremoniously performed this little trick at low speed in full view of every car, coming and going.

Fall #2 was more dramatic and could have ended with far graver consequences. Six bikers were speeding through the New Territories on a night ride and we were moving at high speeds through the hills of Sha-tin. The pace was hot because sparks were shooting wildly from kick stand drags. We were really pushing it that night. I chose to wear my helmet and as we went through one of the corners, I did my John Cooper imitation and hung my body way out of the saddle into the corner.

Many variables lead to a fall from a motorbike. A patch of oil, sudden smooth asphalt, or simply the laws of physics can take over when a two-wheeled machine is pushed to the limit. The Beeza was not built for this level of road handling, and I was not as talented as Mr. Cooper.

The back tire slid away from me (this is the problem with motorcycles: "shit happens") and I was sent flying. I could feel the asphalt tearing into my hands and knees, followed by a resounding whack on the back of my head. My friend Ruuy was riding his Triumph Bonneville behind me and struck me on the head with his front tire and this sent him sprawling across the road. We were very lucky there were no cars traveling that stretch of road since we both rolled into the other lanes. We weren't seriously hurt, just shocked as hell.

We quickly picked ourselves up and surveyed the damage. Ruuy was standing in the middle of the road jumping up and down having a tantrum because the chrome headlight on his Bonneville was damaged. I thought he was lacking good perspective. For cripes sake, his front wheel had whacked me in the head, things could have been a lot worse. When we loaded back on our bikes, caution reared and we headed home at a much slower pace.

Late that night I sneaked into the house careful not to wake my parents, the last thing I wanted was for them to see me scraped and bleeding and my jeans ripped to shreds. I cleaned my asphalt impacted wounds and went to bed, thinking the incident was behind me.

Mum saw me sneak into the house but did not say a word. She hadn't been able to sleep worrying about her son on his motorcycle, but didn't want me to see her staying awake to check on me. The next day I was called for a heart-to-heart talk with my parents and I promised to be more careful. It bothered me to worry them so much, but I never did fall again. I later learned they never slept well until they heard the sound of my bike's exhausts bringing me home safe and sound one more night. If one of my kids asked to have a motorcycle today, without hesitation I would go into an "Absolutely not! Do as I say, not as I did!" stance.

During my bike-riding days two ugly accidents left me with terrible memories. Since age thirteen, I had a friend named Ricky Remedios. He was an only child and the two of us met while riding ten-speed bicycles. Ricky went to LaSalle High School and we often played softball against each other. We rode our ten-speeds through the New Territories, covering about fifty-two miles. We both enjoyed the graduation from bicycles to motorcycles. Soon after I got my motorbike, Ricky phoned and said he was coming to my house on his Honda. We planned to cruise the high school and generally act cool.

I waited an hour for Ricky. Finally I jumped on my bike and headed out to find him. I zoomed to KGV in case he went to the school without me. When I rounded the corner at KGV I saw a huddled group of kids. Something was wrong because they looked very disturbed. They were walking around looking completely despondent with their heads down.

I asked a friend, "Willy, where's Ricky? He told me he was coming over to get me."

Willy answered, "Ricky's dead!"

It was one of those moments when you can't believe what you're hearing and you think it's a sick joke. This was no joke.

"What the hell happened?"

Willy explained that on the way to my house Ricky was overtaking a car. The driver didn't see him and made a turn slamming Ricky's motorcycle hard. Ricky flew across the road into a lamppost and died instantly of massive internal injuries.

It was a devastating moment, the first time a school chum had died. It was truly a tragic loss of a young man, the only son of Mr. and Mrs. Remedios. At the funeral service, I remember Ricky's dad looking at us as we filed by to offer our condolences. As much as he was grieving, I was sure I saw anger flash in his eyes because he associated us with motorcycles and without motorcycles, his son would still be alive. I felt terrible.

The second bad accident did not result in a death, but came very close and was spectacularly awful. Daniel Solabarietta was another bike enthusiast and friend. He had a Norton 650cc Dominator, a fast machine, probably the fastest of all our bikes. While driving one night, Daniel lost control approaching an intersection at high speed. A car apparently ran a red light and Daniel swerved to avoid the car. He wound up crashing into a six-foot brick wall. The bike was traveling at such a high speed when it hit the wall that it somersaulted carrying its rider with it.

Daniel wound up with very serious injuries and was in critical condition. He survived, but limped for a long time after. Daniel went to a rival school and we were both skilled at throwing the javelin, usually winding up in the top two slots for most competitions. Ironically at our last track meet several months later, I was the winner and a limping Daniel came in second.

To this day when I drive a car, I try to be very courteous and mindful of motorcycle drivers. In both accidents the fault lay not with the bike rider, but with a careless car driver. Too often it's not the motorcyclist responsible for an accident; it is the careless driver who is unaware motorcycles share the road.

Jenny's mother wouldn't let her ride on the back of my Beeza and that really pissed me off. What good was it for me to have such a cool bike and not have my pretty girlfriend sitting behind me with her arms wrapped tightly around my waist? Every male would have been insanely jealous.

Thinking back I would have done the same thing and never would have allowed any daughter of mine to ride on the back of a big motorcycle with a testosterone-fueled dude ruling the road. I'd give the third degree to any guy who showed up to collect my daughter and put her on the back of his suicide machine.

Jenny's mother finally relented and I did take her out for a couple rides but had to promise to be extra careful. I respected these conditions and never took Jenny on "fast night rides" with my buddies. It was a great feeling to have Jenny sitting behind me with her arms tightly wrapped around my waist and to hear her squeal with delight as I accelerated the Beeza.

One of the Chinese guys I rode with lived in Aberdeen, a fishing village on the far side of Hong Kong Island. His apartment building was close to the harbor that sheltered fishing junks and sampans that were constantly rowing across the dirty green water. Many people lived all their lives on boats in this water community and only came ashore for supplies.

Fishing folk were said to value their male children more than female offspring because their future work contribution made to the family would be more profitable. The story goes male children would be tied to the boats to ensure they did not fall overboard while females were never tied. Sounds like one hell of a glass ceiling!

Floating restaurants dotted the harbor. They were a big tourist attraction and occasionally frequented by locals. The charm of a floating restaurant was the transportation. Customers were collected at the dock in sampans with the traditional woman or man in a wicker hat rowing with a single oar. Sampan travel was the only way to get to a floating restaurant.

We always had fun checking out the second floor of one of these floating establishments. Down below large cages bobbed in the water. Looking down from the higher vantage point, fish could be seen in the cages, but they were not clearly visible until a shrimp was thrown into the container causing a feeding frenzy. From the swarming mass of sea life, a diner could select the fish, giant shrimp, or lobster to cook for his meal. A Chinese fisherman in a junk stationed next to the floating restaurant would dip a net attached to a long pole into the cage and scoop out the selected fish, then lift it to the second floor balcony for personal inspection. The next time seen the sea morsel would be on a plate smothered with garlic and green onions and covered with a delicious soy sauce. Tourists loved the show, but most locals ate at less ostentatious restaurants where the food was even better and far less expensive since the heavy tourist tax was not added to the bill.

My Aberdeen friend went by the name Ah Ngau. He rode a red BSA Thunderbolt Lightning and was a quiet and pleasant character. I often wondered what he did for a living because he didn't work regular hours, but always had a wad of money and was often surrounded by Chinese friends who seemed to do nothing but sit around and drink Chinese tea.

Riding our bikes in the New Territories, Ah Ngau occasionally stopped at an old walled city where he visited friends. The walled city was as its name implies, an old village completely surrounded by a brick wall fifteen feet high with the makings of a moat surrounding the village.

The moat was bone dry, except for a few swampy sections. Vegetation filled the rest. The village was obviously ancient and had its own local government, customs, and rules of behavior. I walked inside the walls once, but didn't stay long because I felt uncomfortable with the looks I was getting from the inhabitants. They didn't have many *gwai lo* visitors even though I was Eurasian and spoke Cantonese. I thought it best I didn't get too nosy about what Ah Ngau did when he visited this place.

In the U.S. we have the Mafia; in Hong Kong they have the Triads. The gangs or factions are known as *tongs* or by names like 14K (fourteen carat). In Kowloon, there was a notorious section of the city near the Kai Tak airport called "The Walled City." An unusual name given as there wasn't a *physical* wall surrounding this section of Kowloon.

This was not an area frequented by many non-Chinese and even the Hong Kong police were known to stay out of this part of town. They let local leaders handle their own matters. The district was notorious for being under the control of the Triads and there were many stories of murder, vice, and other terrible things occurring within the walled city.

One evening Ah Ngau and I were driving around and I noticed we were approaching the Kowloon Walled City. I thought we were heading past the airport and then up Kowloon Peak, but Ah Ngau turned his bike and headed into the "forbidden section" of town.

It was just the two of us and I felt uncomfortable and motioned him to stop and tell me where he was headed. He laughed and said it was all right, he just wanted to visit his "brothers" to give them *lycee* (money in red paper packets) for the Chinese New Year. Since I was with him, I would be safe. *I would be safe! What authority did Ah Ngau command that he could make such a statement?*

His assurance intrigued me and against my better judgment, we drove side by side deeper into the center of the Forbidden City. It really didn't look a whole lot different from any other Chinese section of town except the streets were narrower and dirtier, but the really big difference – no police presence. We eventually reached our destination, stopping in front of a decrepit apartment building. We parked our bikes and Ah Ngau pulled out a heavy lock and chain from under his saddle to lock our two bikes together.

"Better take precautions, otherwise our bikes might not be here when we return," my friend noted with a false laugh.

I followed Ah Ngau through a series of narrow alleys that eventually led to a restaurant where he was greeted by a number of young men sitting outside drinking Chinese tea. Ah Ngau asked me to wait outside assuring me he would be back in a few minutes.

He walked away and was soon behind the restaurant doors. Through a crack I saw him approach a table where several older Chinese men sat. Ah Ngau greeted them, showing much respect. He did this by bowing repeatedly and wishing them prosperity by intertwining his fingers and shaking his hands in their direction, much like a toast.

As I stood outside I noticed the men drinking tea were watching me intently and didn't seem as friendly as they were a minute earlier when Ah Ngau was standing next to me. I started to fidget, impatiently pacing up and down in front of the restaurant. Wild thoughts ran through my head. I could just see the newspaper headline, **Local athlete disappears in shady part of town**. Then I thought - *That's stupid, if I disappeared nobody would even know I had gone to this God-forsaken place.*

As I paced, I noticed one of the guys was staring more intently than the others. He was making me really uncomfortable. The guy was dressed in traditional black, baggy, Chinese clothing with black kung-fu shoes. There was something about him, but I just couldn't place it. Suddenly he stood up and started walking toward me. Now I was really nervous, what on earth was he up to? Was I in danger? Had I inadvertently insulted him? Should I run to my bike, jump on it and speed off? Hell, it was chained and I didn't have the key. What to do?

The guy walked right up to me, gave a toothy grin, and said "Tong-nay," and gave me a big hug. I finally recognized him! It was Chow-Chai, the street urchin I had befriended and saved from a rooftop fall years before during my kite-flying days. This was the kid who shared my ice cream.

I was happy to see my old friend and even happier I was not about to be stabbed or attacked with a chopper. I asked him how he was doing and we laughed as we reminisced about the old days. After several minutes I asked Chow-Chai what he was doing in the forbidden walled city. He carefully chose his words to let me know he worked for his "older brothers" who had a family business in this part of town.

Older brothers, family business. I may not have been an Einstein, but even I could figure out Chow-Chai was a member of the Triads. I decided to drop this discussion so we once more switched to talking about kite flying, the sport we both abandoned years before. A few minutes later Ah Ngau walked out and was amused to see me talking with Chow Chai.

"How do you two know each other?" He asked with curiosity. We told him our childhood history and once again the incident on the rooftop drew roars of laughter.

"Chow-Chai owes you his life," said Ah Ngau. "It is our custom. It is a debt that he must always seek to repay."

Chow-Chai acknowledged these words and offered us tea, but it was getting late so we politely declined and said our good-byes. Ah Ngau and I wound through the narrow gloomy alleys, unchained our motorcycles and drove off. I never went back to the walled city again and I never asked Ah Ngau what he was doing in that restaurant. I knew when to keep my mouth shut.

Months of motorcycles and late nights ticked by and the day of my departure to Australia was fast approaching. It had been fantastic not to worry about school, have a girlfriend who loved me, and a motorcycle to ride fast. Life could not have been any better.

Before I knew it, I had my airline ticket and reality hit; I was really leaving the nest.

Two weeks before D-Day, I was home watching evening TV with my dad who was complaining about not feeling well. It sounded like his ulcer was acting up. Dad went to bed early that night and I thought nothing further of it.

The next morning I woke up to more noise than usual in the household. The *amahs* were scurrying about and I could hear my mum barking orders with an unusual edge in her voice. I got out of bed and found my mother on the telephone to our family doctor.

Dad had not slept well that night and she was calling Dr. Carey-Hughes to describe his symptoms. I went into my parents' bedroom. Dad was sitting upright in bed looking very pale and sickly. He was breaking out in a cold sweat and clutching his chest in pain. I was scared but had no idea what could be wrong. I had never seen him like this.

Mum and Dad had always been invincible. The only ones in our family who ever got sick or injured were Steve and me. Mum walked into the room with a worried look on her face. As a precaution, the doctor had ordered an ambulance to take my father to the hospital.

I sat with Dad as he groaned in pain and discomfort; it made me very nervous. I felt scared and raw. It seemed like hours before the ambulance arrived and I jumped in the back to accompany Dad because Mum still had to get dressed.

This was my first time in an ambulance. A hollow, sickening feeling filled me as I looked at someone I loved lying on a sterile white draped cot. Sirens blazed as we wound through the heavy morning traffic. We finally stopped at the hospital emergency entrance and nurses quickly wheeled my dad away.

I stayed at the hospital until the doctor told me that I should leave because Dad needed to rest after all the tests he'd gone through. He gently told me there was nothing I could do. I finally left, without a clue what was wrong, but hoping his ulcer was under control.

That night I went to dinner with Jenny's parents at the Kowloon Restaurant. It was a good-bye dinner for me. They knew I was down and were trying their best to cheer me up. Suddenly the waiter announced there was a telephone call for me. I got up shakily and went to the phone. It was my mother on the other end.

In a quivering voice she told me the doctor called with Dad's test results. He had suffered a heart attack. The words hit me like a two by four right between the eyes. A heart attack! It had never occurred to me my dad was suffering from something as serious as a heart attack. People died from heart attacks! How could this happen to my father? He was invincible! This was something I only read about in the newspaper, it couldn't happen to our family!

My knees felt wobbly and the sick feeling intensified in the pit of my stomach. How could I leave for Australia with my dad in the hospital with a heart attack? I wouldn't go!

I wandered back to the table in a daze. Everybody was silent as I told them the news. I couldn't eat a thing. I loved Dad so much and couldn't bear the thought of him being so close to death.

After the initial medical work-up, Dad was transferred to another hospital on Hong Kong Island. For the next two weeks I rode my motorcycle to the hospital as often as they would let me visit my father. I took the vehicular ferry and parked my bike on the bow and sat on my saddle to watch the waves as we crossed the harbor to Hong Kong. It was winter in the Colony; mild by some standards, but cold enough to wear a parka crossing the choppy green-blue water. Looking into the churning harbor, so many things crossed my mind.

Would Dad be all right? How about my mother, would she be alright? And Steve? My wild little brother! How would he function without someone to make sure he didn't step over the edge

This was one of the most worrisome times of my life. It was a good thing sea spray occasionally hit me across the face so people wouldn't know I was crying.

The first time I saw Dad in the hospital bed he looked terribly tired and was hooked up to an IV line. Few things in life are more devastating than seeing your father reduced in stature by relentless pain. I didn't want to leave for Australia with my dad in that condition.

He smiled at me and assured me he would be fine, and then insisted I had to go to Australia. That was the end of the discussion.

As the days passed Dad gained strength and by the time my D-Day approached, he was looking much better and was sitting up in bed most

162

of the time. Reluctantly I accepted the fact I would be going to Australia after all, but I still didn't feel good about the circumstances.

The thought of leaving home for a foreign land was bad enough. To leave home with my father in a poor state of health, coupled with deep concern for my mother and brother made leaving almost impossible. To top it off, I was leaving a girl I loved dearly and who I expected one day to marry. I sure wasn't winning at the challenge life was throwing at me.

CHAPTER ELEVEN
"J'm a Loser"
JOHN LENNON AND PAUL McCARTNEY

The day finally arrived. I was leaving Hong Kong to aspire to a higher education. I would be the first university graduate in the Tebbutt family, a real coup. I was off to Perth, Australia, a location I'd picked on a whim. I can't say I was bursting with excitement for this next adventure to begin. I wasn't brimming with happiness about the whole idea either. I viewed it as a duty I had to perform - get my degree to make my parents happy. This attitude could be interpreted as a bad sign, but I never saw the warnings, and as Peter, Paul and Mary had sung . . . I was leaving on a jet plane and didn't know when I'd be back again.

I was a wreck over the thought of leaving while my dad was still in the hospital recovering from a heart attack. I was torn between guilt for leaving him and even greater guilt if I didn't meet my parents' hopes for my future.

On top of that massive burden, I felt miserable about leaving my sweetheart behind in Hong Kong. I was convinced Jenny was my one true love and ached at the thought of not seeing her for almost a whole year. Jenny had exactly 547 days of high school remaining so it was likely she would still be in Hong Kong when I came back at the end of the school year, but a whole year of separation sounded like such a long time.

I told myself over and over this was only a temporary intrusion in the happiness I shared with Jenny. Believing this was the only way I could deal with the pain of leaving her. Jenny looked really pretty the day I left and even now I can see her perfectly in my mind's eye.

She was wearing her pink suit, a favorite of mine that showed off her fantastic figure. Even though her mascara ran in rivulets down her cheeks, she looked stunningly beautiful. We clung to each other every remaining minute we still had together, the way teenage lovers do. We were both miserable and I was admittedly becoming scared. Not only was I leaving Jenny behind, I was going to a strange place where I knew absolutely no one.

We felt we needed to say goodbye in an intimate way so in the hour before I had to leave for the airport, we asked to be alone. My mum respected our wishes, but I'm sure she never imagined what we planned to do. As soon as we were alone, we locked the doors to the bathroom, undressed, placed several towels on the floor, and quietly made love. Our tender time together would have to last a long, long time. Jenny cried during our lovemaking and held me as tightly as she could. I felt I was lost within her. I was very, very sad as I held her soft young body close to me. I wanted to burn this memory into my mind forever. Thankfully nobody disturbed us; we had been left alone to say a final good-bye.

The hour flashed by and time came to leave for the airport. The drive seemed to go in slow motion. I looked at the passing landmarks, hoping every memory would last while I was in this new, strange place called Perth.

Since Dad was still in hospital and Mum was in no condition to drive, the Kadoories kindly provided their chauffeured Rolls to take us to the airport. Check-in and boarding went much too quickly for my liking. I wanted more time, much more time, before I had to leave. Finally it was time to board the jet.

I said my goodbyes to Mum, Steve, and finally to Jenny. With a lump in my throat I walked down the lonely gangway to the QUANTAS jet that would take me to Perth via Singapore. I sat in a window seat and strained to catch a glimpse of my family and Jenny one more time. I knew they were standing on the veranda waving goodbye, but I couldn't spot them. Before long, we were rushing down the runway and the wheels left the ground. I felt so very lonely leaving my home, my mum, my brother, my dad lying in the hospital, and Jenny.

I also left behind my beloved BSA. We hadn't discussed what was going to happen to the bike, but I assumed it would be there when I returned. The Beeza was greased to prevent it from rusting and covered with a thick plastic sheet. My pride and joy was embalmed until my return.

Leaving home for college is not easy; leaving under these circumstances was gut wrenching. I felt like I was swallowed into an abyss with no clue what my future would be. As the plane left Kai Tak airport behind, I saw thick dark clouds as far as the eye could see, literally and figuratively.

Several hours later we landed in Singapore where I had an overnight layover. Friends of Dad's from British American Tobacco met me and took me out for dinner. They were an extremely nice couple and helped me feel better about my heartbreak as we talked about the good things ahead for me in Australia. We went to a restaurant for *satay*, Asian shish-ka-bob with a pungent Eastern flavor. I checked into the Raffles Hotel, but the charm of the old Colonial hotel was completely lost on me. I cried myself to sleep thinking about everybody back in Hong Kong. I was a very young eighteen year-old who was not ready to face his brave new world.

The next day Dad's friends collected me and we drove to the airport. I walked to check-in, rolled my bag onto the belt, and handed the attendant my ticket. She asked for my passport and flipped through the pages looking agitated and confused. She asked me to wait and walked away with my passport and ticket. She spoke with another woman, probably her supervisor. Plenty of gesticulating was going on, too much I thought, and after five minutes the woman came back to the counter.

"Sir, you do not have a visa to go to Australia." It sounded like she was speaking English, but at the same time her words sounded foreign. From the outset of my expedition I had been in close contact with the Australian consul in Hong Kong, having even played cricket with the guy on several occasions. The senior Australian diplomat helped me with my travel plans and things were supposed to be under control. Now this lady was telling me things were not in order. What was going on?

Dad's friends asked to speak with a supervisor, then a manager, but to no avail. I was told due to the "White Australian Policy" I needed a visa to enter the country. The airline people could tell from my physical features that I was of Asian descent, and said they were very sorry but I could not be allowed on the plane. The Australian government turned back several "non-whites" at the full expense of the airlines.

"Mr. Tebbutt, you will not be allowed to leave for Australia until we hear from the Australian consulate in Hong Kong and they grant you an official visa." Thus sayeth the airline counter personnel.

I remembered reading in the newspaper that the Australian government had imposed stricter immigration rules to maintain the white ethnic majority in the country, but prior to my surprise rejection, the "White Australian Policy" had no meaning for me whatsoever. Not in a million years had I expected to be discriminated against at this time in this manner.

Unbelievable! I was in shock and a complete mess as I watched my plane pull away from the ramp. What the hell to do?

In those days long distance-telephoning was a big deal; calls were very expensive and required a special booth to make a call. There were no fax machines to help me out. In short, I was screwed. We couldn't immediately reach the Australian consulate in Hong Kong to sort out the problem. Over the next few days, my father's friends did everything by telex but Dad wasn't around to help on the other end because he was still in the hospital. Dad's friends tried to console me, but I was seriously shattered, exceptionally lonely, horrifically dejected, and wondering why on earth I was going to University in a country that didn't want me. Dad's friends kindly insisted I stay with them at their home until things were worked out. That was wonderful because I'm sure I would have lost it staying in a hotel.

It took four days of telexes and telephone calls before I was finally allowed to board a plane to Perth. By that time I was absolutely miserable and wished I could just go home. If this country didn't want me, I certainly didn't want them. The irony was the Australian consulate in

Hong Kong was adamant I did not need a visa and was furious about the treatment I received. I eventually boarded the plane carrying no more paperwork than I carried that first day, worrying all the way to Australia I would be turned back at the Perth airport.

When I arrived, I walked through immigration with no issues. The problem had principally existed with the airlines. After being burned by a few returned passengers, airlines had become ultra-cautious with their procedures. An unfortunate happenstance for me!

This unfortunate incident reinforced the feelings of inadequacy I felt about my mixed heritage. For many years after this episode, I harbored bad feelings about the openly racist "White Australian Policy" and the worthless so-called British passport issued to me in Hong Kong. It was the first clue my Hong Kong passport bore little official semblance to an English passport, although outwardly they looked identical. Traveling with a Hong Kong passport was like having a red tattoo on your forehead screaming, *Potential Illegal Immigrant.*

I discovered immigration officials around the world are suspicious of travelers from Hong Kong illegally sneaking into their country. Years later traveling in Europe I found the H.K. British passport no different from passports issued in countries like Pakistan and India. Wherever I went, immigration officials would give me a close look-over before waving me through their country's gates.

Here I was in Australia, in a strange new land. As a little kid, I often felt weird about my Eurasian background and occasionally suffered taunts from English classmates. The cruelest was when they called me "Chink." As I grew older I became less concerned about heckling thrown my way, but my experience in the Singapore airport was a rude wake-up call to a situation I never had confronted before – full-blown racial discrimination. It was confusing to me, especially since I was already in bad shape. I felt hurt, anger, and deep sadness.

Suddenly I heard my name called. A friend of a family friend met me after I left Australian customs, but he was another complete stranger. He drove me to the University of Western Australia and to my place of residence, known as St. George's College. I thanked him for everything and he drove off with a hearty wave. I was once again completely alone.

I stood in front of the massive building and looked around. St. George's College radiated tradition. The red-brick building resembled an English castle and was probably just as old as one. I was introduced to the sub-warden who was a pastor and responsible for students boarding at the venerable institution.

I guess the sub-warden would be known in the States as an assistant dean. I was shown to my room, which resembled a closet with a bed and a desk crammed into it. It was stark and bare. I saw a curved hotdog bun shape by the window and realized it was the mattress on which I was supposed to sleep. My God, this must be the Australian outback! I thought I was in the modern city of Perth.

This was another shock to my psyche, to go from my large, comfortable room at home to roughing it at St. George's. I was probably labeled a whiner because I immediately complained to the household staff about my lumpy mattress and insisted on another. Within a day or so I did get another mattress, but it was only a marginal improvement so I gave up the cause.

It was January, the middle of the Australian summer, and the stone walls kept the rooms nice and cool. I noticed there was no heating system and imagined it would be another story living in these 19th century rooms come winter. By now you'd think shocks and surprises were commonplace, but I had no idea what else was in store for me.

Shortly thereafter I met my roommate. His name was Colin and his family had recently emigrated from England, but lived some distance from the university. We didn't have immediate good chemistry. I didn't dislike him, nor did I like him. Colin seemed to carry a snotty, know-it-all attitude that put me off. Great! Yet another reason to hate being here. I had to live with this self-important jerk for a whole year.

The school year started and I attended classes at the university, which was within walking distance of St. George's residence hall. I knew not a soul and went from being a popular face and top athlete at my Hong Kong high school to being a full-fledged nobody at the University of Western Australia.

Classes were taught in lecture theatres holding a hundred and fifty students and I tried to melt into the crowd. The days and weeks crawled by and I found academics really tough because I had never applied myself at KGV and my high school curriculum had not prepared me for a science degree at university levels. Australian freshmen in the class had studied calculus, organic chemistry, and physics and their high school system prepared them well for university studies.

These were subjects I had heard about, but never studied and I wasn't finding it easy to keep up with the class. A couple other foreign students lived at St. George's - Thai students who were roommates and kept to themselves. They seemed to be doing just fine academically. It was disconcerting to know I was lacking the basics that were apparently a piece of cake for my classmates. Being a competitor, this did not make me feel good. I was angry I was doing poorly and my grades reflected it. Failure was a new feeling for me and I didn't like it; I was not winning at this game! I felt lost, and frustration began to build because I was feeling "so dumb."

The academic side of University was not going well and neither was the social side. Social life revolved around St. George's as the university did not have a strong sense of tradition, history, or team spirit and basically offered only academic classes. There was no attempt to rally the student body to attend sporting events or parties. Freshman orientation and welcoming committees to introduce nervous freshmen to the university were absent.

Several different boarding colleges (dorms) surrounded the university, each with its own tradition and sub-society. St. George's main rival was the Catholic college dorm, St. Thomas Aquinas. Since I had a Roman Catholic upbringing it was strange I found myself at St. George's, a Protestant institution. I don't remember why I applied to St. George's, I think in a fantasy stupor I thought it would be interesting to live in a castle-like building. Another fine example of impulsive behavior that often got me in trouble. As a kid, I didn't look into matters in sufficient depth. The newer dorm rooms at Thomas Aquinas seemed a much better choice, and they didn't feature hotdog shaped beds.

Social life in Western Australia was vastly different from the fast pace in the Hong Kong I left behind. There were no nightclubs, no BSA, no Jenny. It was a shock to decelerate so dramatically; it was as if I was suffering the bends from surfacing from a great depth too quickly.

St. George's evening dinner tradition required wearing a coat and tie and a full black graduation gown over that. Life was very formal and nothing like my Prefect days at KGV. We were required to stand as the warden, sub-warden, and staff walked in to take their places at the head table. This was followed by offering a prayer and eating foul-tasting, even fouler smelling, mystery concoctions. I don't remember a single good evening meal while at St. George's. Hilariously, we were not allowed to go back for seconds, which was a blessing. Seconds were only served at lunchtime to the brave and malnourished. Most evenings I stuffed myself with bread and developed a taste for a unique Australian spread called Vegemite. Vegemite is a brown, salty paste the consistency of butter. The first time I tried it I was unimpressed, but like beer, the taste grows on you. I would spread thick layers of the stuff over my bread so I wouldn't starve.

After dinner it was down to the common room for coffee and billiards or a round of darts in the upstairs hallway. It was all so very British and since the majority of freshmen came from Australian prep schools, they reveled in the pomp and circumstance. I soon learned freshmen were required to serve coffee to the upper classmen and I was not exempt, even though I was a foreign student. Freshmen were not allowed to play billiards if an upperclassman wanted the table during the after-dinner period. I thought this "tradition" was a load of bullshit, but I went along with it since I had no choice. I knew I was the best billiard player in the college and once I was on the table, I would never give it up, freshman or not. These were just a few customs that made life at St. George's unbearable.

To enter my dungeon room, I had to pass through my roommate's living space to reach the door. The second night of school, Colin and I were awakened at one a.m. by twenty plus upperclassmen who forcefully pushed Colin into my room and insisted we stand on the desk in our pajamas while they shined bright flashlights in our eyes. For thirty minutes, Colin and I were heckled, barraged with ridiculous questions, and required to sing songs and do other silly tricks. This was part of hazing that all freshmen at St. George's had to endure in the name of tradition. Those who chose not to participate in the ritual were declared to be unworthy and were carried downstairs into the courtyard and unceremoniously dumped into the central fountain pond which held the dirtiest algae-crusted water possible. The pond was eight feet in diameter with an undetermined sculpture smack in the center. No fish were able to survive in the water; the pond was obviously to be avoided at all costs. When a freshman committed a crime against the unwritten code of St. George's, it was "Off to the pond!"

As time went on I discovered another unwritten rule. Freshmen were required to run errands for the upper class fascists. If a senior had a whim for a hamburger from a grille a mile down the road, he could commandeer a freshman to "Go fetch!"

Coming from the lifestyle I enjoyed in Hong Kong and not being one to put up with this nonsense, it was inevitable a rebellion was brewing. Little did I know one of my fellow Asian freshman classmates was even more upset than I was by these inane antics and would be less tolerant of the jerks that seemingly ruled the roost.

A few months into the term, chatter buzzed in the common room about the upcoming annual St. George's cross-country race through King's Park, an area of public picnic and walking grounds located behind the college. We learned bets were placed on favorites to claim the title of fastest runner. Since one guy in my freshmen class was a cross-country champion, my naive comrades and I thought this would be our opportunity to show up the seniors. Wrong!

As the day of the race approached, betting lines were posted in the common room. We noticed no bets were placed on freshmen, even though it was mandatory we all run the race. Upperclassmen knew there were several top athletes in our neophyte class. Finally, a senior spilled the beans that it was absolutely against tradition to let a freshman win, no matter how fast he ran. There was that ridiculous "tradition" word again. Damn, I was getting sick of hearing it.

Another ridiculous custom practiced by the sophomore class was one in which sophomores would ambush and strip freshmen runners at a determined location in the forest. The stripped freshmen would then have to find creative ways to get back to the college through the public park frequented by picnicking families. *Tradition, my ass!*

This did not sound good to me so I set about organizing my class to rebel against this ridiculous event and show the upperclassmen we would not put up with their crap any longer.

On race day we made yet another discovery - there was a staggered start. Every two minutes a runner would leave the starting line. By doing this, freshmen class runners were stretched out and separated to run alone through the woods. I quickly got the word to my mates that we would meet at a rendezvous point just a few hundred yards into the woods and run the rest of the race as a pack. United we would be able to fend off the sophomore attack, or so I thought.

Things seemed to be going smoothly. We massed at the designated spot and when all twenty of us were together, off we went into the center of King's Park. As we entered the thick wood we came across an ambush scene reminiscent of Robin Hood in Sherwood Forest. The sophomores were hidden high in the trees ready to jump on their prey, the lowly squires of freshman-hood. This was Robin Hood in reverse. My frosh mates were the band of merry men and the Sheriff of Nottingham's bad guys were the sophomores.

Seeing the maniacal sophomores who, along with a few seniors, had numbers greater than our merry band, we stopped to deliberate a plan of action. Two leaders emerged from our small contingency, Ray and me. We decided the best defense was an offense so we planned to charge through the bad guys like human battering rams. Having a plan, we set about implementing our war-inspired maneuver.

Ray and I took the lead and charged . . . the others dispersed into the forest. There was no human battering ram and we were no match for the advancing wall of doom. The two of us were pinned down in seconds flat and stripped naked. As the sophomores left the area, a kind soul threw us each a t-shirt to cover our naked butts.

Ray and I were furious at being deserted by our classmates, but now we had a more pressing challenge, how to make it back to the college with only t-shirts wrapped around our privates. With much ducking behind bushes and skirting public trails, we eventually made it back and were not caught in any further compromising situations. Ray and I were steaming mad and ready to unload on our classmates.

When we finally returned to St. George's, we were surprised and puzzled to find the sophomores were even angrier than we were. What happened to evoke this strange mood in the sophomore crew?

It turned out after we were pinned and unclothed, sophomores cornered a couple freshmen. The meekest looking freshman in the crowd had not taken kindly to the idea of being stripped naked. He was a Thai and could have been mistaken for a science class geek. He was short and slender, had closely cropped hair, and wore thick glasses. Turns out he was anything but a geek.

This kid was a Thai kick boxer and he showed his tormentors a trick or two with flying kicks to the head. For good measure he pulled a six-inch butterfly knife from his shorts and waved it in front of a burly Australian bully who stood eight inches taller and one hundred pounds heavier. The Thai scared the shit out of the Aussie and later back at the college the same bully was protesting the event, complaining the Thai freshman wasn't keeping with "tradition." He wanted to have the kid expelled.

Ray and I missed all this excitement because it took almost an hour to avoid being seen naked by those in the park. Hearing this story later I laughed and didn't feel quite so bad about what had happened to us, especially because the burly Australian was the main guy who relished stripping Ray and me and leaving us to fend for ourselves. Later that evening we had a few beers and Ray had strong words for the freshmen tribe that had deserted us.

Australia is a great country for sports. Cricket and tennis rank high in popularity. Despite my aptitude for these sports, I didn't play either during my nine months in Perth. Instead I played a less popular sport, one without many fans or supporters. I played soccer for the University's varsity team and was the scoring star, but didn't enjoy the game as much as I had in Hong Kong when I played with my old friends.

I was a walk-on during an early practice and stunned the team with my dribbling and the power of my kick. They were delighted to have me as an addition to the team. Unlike the days at KGV and playing in the Hong Kong football stadium, I have no special memories of soccer in Perth, which is unusual given my love of all sports.

The premier sports at the university were rugby, cricket and Aussie Rules Football. Football players were pretty much ignored. I played, but didn't have the same desire to compete that I had shown in Hong Kong. Still, I could not play without doing my best and at my best I was the team's top goal scorer. We ended up doing reasonably well in the local league, finishing the season in third place.

The University of Western Australia's cricket team played in a first division men's league. This was top-class stuff and a much higher caliber game than what I played in the Hong Kong first division. I never went to a tryout nor did I ever see a game. A senior at St. George's played for the university; his name was Magnus, enough said.

After all the tennis I played in Hong Kong, in Perth I only played once and that was when I was fooling around with a couple guys who were novices. It was strange for an ex-jock and all-around good athlete to take so little interest in sports. This was more than likely a reflection of just how unhappy I was.

My passion for my usual sports had diminished, but my interest had been captured by a game I had come to love - Aussie Rules Football. Aussie Rules is unique to the land down under. It is a combination of soccer, rugby, and wrestling played on a large field about the size of two soccer pitches, but is oval in shape. Like American football, the key is to catch the ball, an accomplishment known as a "mark." After that, all similarity to American football ends. Skill is required to make drop kicks and punts, and when catching the ball, it is permissible to run up your opponent's back and onto his shoulders to make the catch. I've seen the better professional players jump off the ground, plant one foot on the hip of an unsuspecting player while the other foot is placed on his shoulders or small of the back. The attacker then catches the ball with outstretched hands twelve feet above the ground. When a catch is made in this dramatic fashion, it's an awesome sight. We played Aussie Rules on the college grounds every evening before dark. We played on an elevated grassy section surrounded by fencing that had been the site of tennis courts at one time. I was captivated by this game and I found it to be a great diversion.

The ball was a hybrid of a rugby ball and an American football. Accurate passing by drop-licking the ball was essential, as was catching the ball. An inter-college tournament was scheduled and I wanted desperately to make the team so I put in long hours of practice. I managed to make the cut and my moment of glory came when I actually scored points on a mark to help St. George's win the championship. I also managed to screw up a couple times but that was all a part of learning the game. The rules state the ball has to be bounced every ten yards, alternatively the ball can be lightly touched to the ground. I thought it looked better to touch the ball to the ground and I attempted this on a run, but lost the ball as I touched the grass and went running down the field empty-handed. There was much laughter at my expense over this mishap, especially that evening over coffee. Occasionally I'd see professionals play and was blown away by how they owned the game and how rough the sport was on a body. As much as I enjoyed the sports I played in Hong Kong, I found this game unique and wished I'd been introduced to this physical form of "aerial ping-pong" earlier.

A couple of months after arriving in Australia, Mum and Dad wrote they were coming for a brief visit. This was part of Dad's recuperative process as well as a scouting expedition to check the country for possible immigration. I eagerly looked forward to seeing my parents. The day they arrived I took a bus downtown to their hotel; I couldn't wait to see my dad out of his hospital bed. When the hotel door opened we hugged and I saw Dad had lost some weight, but all in all he looked pretty healthy. This was a huge relief for me.

We went to dinner that night where I enjoyed a thick, juicy steak, the first decent meal I savored since arriving in Australia. Over dinner I convinced my parents I was in withdrawal because I didn't have my own transportation and was confined to the college every weekend. Mum and Dad agreed it would be okay with them if I bought an old car, but a motorcycle was definitely out of the question. This seemed reasonable to me and truth be told I would prefer to have a car anyway. Early the next day we went to look for a used car. I don't remember why or how, (probably price) but we settled on an old grey Morris Minor 1000.

The Morris Minor is a classically revolting English car produced in the fifties and sixties. It is best described as an exceptionally ugly British version of the Volkswagen Beetle. Still it was a car; it was transportation offering newfound freedom and I was very happy to have the wheels. Mum, Dad and I explored much of Perth and the surrounding area during their brief visit and I took every opportunity to gorge myself on decent food.

Soon it was time for them to leave and this goodbye was said with more happiness than when I left Hong Kong because Dad was now on the mend. I asked my parents to give my love to Jenny and Steve, and tell them I looked forward to seeing them at the end of the school year. When I said good-bye, homesickness for Hong Kong hit me again and I was reminded how little I was enjoying my Australian adventure.

British cars of this era were notoriously unreliable, and unfortunately the Morris Minor was a true-blooded British automobile. The car cruised zero to sixty in twenty seconds and top speed was no more than sixty miles per hour with the engine screaming in pain as the rpm skyrocketed. The gearshift was a stick two feet in length and had the terrible habit of popping out of gear and sticking in first.

The first time this happened I had to drive twenty miles in first gear to reach the garage where I bought the car. Good thing they were able to show me how to fix the problem because it would happen at least once a week thereafter. This was not a "little Deuce Coupe" or anything remotely resembling that beauty, but once again it was a set of wheels and it was better transport than what most freshmen had. Actually freshmen were not supposed to own cars so I had to hide my buggy on a side road behind the college. When the weekend rolled around, my mates and I would jump into the Morris and go to a local dance or to the beach. The car made my life a lot more fun, but my existence was still a far cry from what I had known in Hong Kong.

I missed Hong Kong entertainment and I missed female companionship so I persuaded a few guys to go with me to an advertised dance in the seaside town of Fremantle. We drove down on a Saturday night looking forward to having a good time and a little lady action. After paying a small cover charge, I scouted around the hall, working my way through the shoulder-to-shoulder crowd of gyrating students. I noticed the music was different. They were playing the sounds of Australian bands and I recognized a group called the Easybeats and Men at Work. Another difference in this club scene was beer was ubiquitous and everyone drank the local brew, Swan Lager. I was hoping to meet a nice young thing, but struck out completely. I didn't even get a second look from one girl. I quickly discovered I was the only person in the room with Asian features. All others in the dance hall were definitely Caucasian. I wondered how much my looks were a factor in my inability to meet women. We left after a few hours and very little excitement. After that I never went to another dance. This place sucked.

One thing I did enjoy was the beach. Australia is blessed with some of the most beautiful beaches in the world, populated by some of the prettiest women. The beaches at Scarboro were much wider than those in Hong Kong and the waves gave a better ride, but were far more dangerous. Waves in Hong Kong were never tall enough to bodysurf, but Australian waves gave me the opportunity to learn this sport. Powerful waves can certainly be fun, but they can also be frightening if they catch you unaware and you aren't a strong swimmer.

One afternoon while learning to surf, the waves were huge and a riptide was often pulling swimmers out to sea. I kept getting dumped by the breaking waves and then forcefully pulled deeper, only to be dumped again. This situation was scary because it taught lessons about how powerful the ocean can be.

I was repeatedly dragged into deeper waters and gasped to catch my breath as I tried to return to shore. Choking on seawater is not pleasant. In the back of my mind I knew when a rip current caught an unsuspecting swimmer, stroking parallel to the shore is the only way to break its grip. This is an unnatural choice to make because when frightened, most swimmers instinctively swim for shore. The effort to swim parallel to the shore is easier said than done!

I was panicking as the powerful waves started to own me, but I learned a funny lesson while battling the sea. Most young Turks would almost rather drown than be embarrassed by shouting to the beach patrol for help. This is nuts. As scared and tired as I was, the thought of being dragged onto the beach by a lifeguard and given mouth-to-mouth in front of everybody (especially girls in bikinis) was a fate looming larger than drowning.

Somehow I mustered enough strength for one last Herculean effort to save myself. After an eternity ingesting gallons of seawater, I made it back to the beach. I was completely exhausted. But of greatest importance at the time, I reached the warm and welcoming sands with my pride intact. No way was I going to be rescued like a beached whale with young Aussie babes as my audience!

Other friendly visitors to Australian beaches were the omnipresent sharks. The sounding of the shark siren always freaked me out. It demanded swimmers leave the water immediately and I was always one of the first to head to shore; no way was I going to be fish food. I had enough problems.

And then there were the surfers who paddled out to sea on their boards. For them, warning sirens were a dare and as a sign of manhood they defiantly faced Jaws. I thought those guys were crazy. The closest I ever got to shark jaws was the set I bought at a local flea market and hung on the wall in my room. I once scratched myself badly on this fixed set of teeth and shudder to think what could happen if they chomped shut! It was eerie and surreal to stand on the beach and see grey fins cutting through the water so near.

One night I was with friends at a restaurant escaping dinner served from the St. George's kitchen. The St. George's matron was the cook, a scary woman reminiscent of Dickensian times and whose best meal was still slop. We had to find our way to a restaurant to re-charge our bodies at least once each week.

During dinner I noticed a guy looking at me and thought he looked vaguely familiar. Toward the end of the meal the guy came over and it immediately clicked - this was Les' older brother, a flight officer with QUANTAS airlines! Les was my old gambling friend and partner in crime on our many trips to Macau.

"Tony, what the hell are you doing here?" exclaimed big brother Cecil. I was really surprised to see him and remembered him well for teaching me tricks with a soccer ball when I lived next to the China Light and Power Company. Cecil was friends with Cheryl Hart-Baker who lived in the same apartment building and was one of my close childhood friends.

"Cecil, what a surprise to meet you in this Aussie restaurant, great to see you!"

Ces gave me his phone number and told me his apartment was down by the Scarboro beach and I was welcome to visit anytime. He had been living in Australia for several years and had a promising career with QUANTAS.

Ces told me he was making good money and loved the Aussie life-style although frequently had the opportunity to get back to Hong Kong. We both loved cars and when I was a kid would talk about them for hours; he was quite proud of his green Sunbeam Tiger. The Tiger was a souped-up V-8 version of the sedate Sunbeam Alpine.

I can't tell you how great it was to see somebody from home, and for his offer to get away from St. George's occasionally. I took Ces up on this kindness and would frequently drive to Scarboro and stay at his apartment for the weekend. It felt fantastic to have a friend from home and this connection saved my sanity and made my year bearable. I will always be grateful to Cecil for the friendship he showed me at a time when I really needed it. We have remained good friends ever since, even though we live continents apart.

As the year marched on, I made several friends with seniors at St. George's which was considered quite unusual. A lowly freshman cavorting with seniors upset the social norm at St. George's College. My best friend was Rob, an all-Australian athlete and a professional Aussie Rules player.

Rob was a big man on campus, but also one of the nicest guys around. He was studying for his master's degree in computer technology and was a great guy, lots of fun, and had a terrific personality.

My other close friend, Horace, was going for his Ph.D. Biology and was about as nerdy as they come. Horace (Horrie, as he was known) was doing postgraduate work on the metabolism of alcohol in white rats. I only know this because I saw him performing experiments with drunken rats. He was measuring the amount of urine output relative to alcohol ingestion. Let me tell you, drunken rats lose control at both ends, it was messy!

In contrast to Rob, Horace was a recluse and stayed away from most other students. I don't know why he took a liking to me; maybe he pitied the dumb Hong Kong kid who always looked lost. During one of the semester holidays Horrie and I drove to the Australian outback to visit friends. We piled into his new Morris 1100 since it was considerably nicer than my old Morris and headed for our first stop on the map, the old gold mining town of Kalgoorlie.

Nothing left a lasting impression on me. I did see native aborigines wandering around with little evidence their lives had changed much over the last 100 years. Of course this wasn't true, it just seemed that way. The aborigines were treated as lesser persons, given the degrading name "abbo." Like many native Indians in the United States, many had drinking problems. Perhaps it was my own experience with the "White Australian Policy" that alerted me to the excessive racism that existed in Australia during the mid-sixties; I was unimpressed by the country's social conscience. Time and again the terms "abbo" and "half-caste" were inserted into general conversation.

After Kalgoorlie we headed south to the coastal town of Esperance where freshman twin brothers by the name of Keith and Alan Longbottom had a family "station," or ranch. I genuinely liked Keith and Alan. The pair was always smiling, showed great humor, and both were excellent athletes. When they extended the invite for us to come to visit, we gladly took them up on the offer.

In the mid-sixties, Southwestern Australia was fairly undeveloped. Along the drive we saw little evidence of civilization, outback and wildlife spanned the miles. Kangaroos and emus occasionally ran by the side of the road and I found the big ugly birds particularly captivating. They reminded me of ostriches but boy, could they get high speed out of their long legs.

The Longbottom's station was a humble farm with few livestock but many acres of farmland. There was nothing exotic about the house and surroundings, the Longbottoms were true salt of the earth people, a genuine family that lived off the land.

It was in Esperance that I had my first and last gun hunting experience. I hadn't been hunting before and the twins said kangaroos and rabbits were considered vermin because they ran wild and would eat crops wantonly and voraciously. I accepted this as a reasonable cause why they should be killed so I agreed to go on a hunt one night. It was quite an expedition. A few neighbors came over and we set out in two Chevy El Caminos with frames built on the back so riders could stand up, hold on, and try to keep from tumbling out of the fast moving car.

We were armed with every kind of gun imaginable, from .22 rifles and shotguns to 303s. Eight of us piled into the Chevys with hunting dogs packed in for the ride. Bouncing like balls, we raced whooping and hollering like a bunch of maniacs. In the passenger seat of each car a man sat holding a powerful searchlight panning the fields for 'roos and rabbits. It didn't take long before the spotlights focused on a couple 'roos feeding nonchalantly on almost-mature crops. The light dazed the animals, but they could hear the cars and picked up our scent so it was difficult to get close to them.

We parked as close as possible, about fifty to seventy yards away, and took aim. *Bang!* Once the first shot was fired, the animals were spooked and raced off with our Chevys hot on their tails. It was sheer madness! Those packed in the rear were hanging onto the frames for dear life. Guns were firing (and missing by substantial margins) and hunters were yelling, just having a grand old time.

I wondered if this was the Australian version of a foxhunt. The men didn't wear red coats or hats, carried no horns, and pomp and circumstance was in short supply. I surmised this hunt must be the "convict" version.

We didn't shoot many 'roos; it was almost impossible to get off a good shot on such rough terrain unless the shot was taken at point blank range. However, we bagged a few with lucky shots. The third 'roo was one I shot, my first kill. Until this point I had never shot a gun at anything alive. The guys urged, "Go ahead, Tony. You take a shot with this .22 rifle, there's a real big one out there with your name on it."

I took the rifle and lined up my sights at a huge kangaroo a long way away, but sitting nicely in the spotlight. I squeezed the trigger. *Bang!* A second or two passed and I thought I missed but slowly the kangaroo dropped flat to the ground. My hunting party was stunned. Nobody expected me to hit the animal from that distance with such a small-bore bullet, much less kill it.

Laughter filled the night and the twins claimed the 'roo was so old that it had died of fright; no way I could have shot it. When we piled the animal on the Chevy rack we couldn't find the bullet hole so I claimed I must have shot it through the mouth. There was no doubt we had bagged a big one.

The only other animal hunted in this fashion was rabbit and they seemed to be everywhere. Once again the method was to catch the little critters in the light so they would freeze, becoming a sitting target. With rabbits hunters could get much closer, just ten to twenty yards away. We'd aim and shoot, but once the gun fired, the dogs would leap out of the truck in a flash and no more shots were fired for fear of hitting the dogs. If the bullet didn't hit the rabbit, it was still a goner. The dogs probably claimed more rabbits than we did. They'd bring the rabbits proudly back to the hunters and that's when I learned the origin of the term "rabbit punch."

To quickly kill the animals, hunters would grab the rabbits by their hind legs and give a sharp blow to the back of the neck with the edge of their hand. When done properly, the maneuver would snap the rabbit's neck.

At the end of the evening we turned for home and counted our bounty. In a couple hours we'd killed three kangaroos and thirty-eight rabbits. I was wondering what would be done with the carcasses because we had accumulated a slug of meat. The brothers assured me the meat would be used to feed the dogs and not go to waste.

I thought a lot about what we had done, and I didn't feel good about it. Even though hunting was justified, there was something about the experience that just didn't feel right. There was no sport in the activity, it was pure killing to provide crop protection and dog food, but I sensed the thrill of the kill was what it was really all about. After that night I knew I would never go hunting again.

Before Horrie and I headed back to St. George's, we took a short hop to the Esperance coast, which turned out to be a good decision. The combination of the rugged beauty of the barren coastline, azure blue water, and clear skies was truly one of the most memorable images I have of Australia. It wasn't a swimmer's coastline, the choppy water looked menacing and the water was very cold. We camped on the beach for several days and I'd sit for hours staring at the breakers, admiring the sheer beauty and power of the land and sea. The long drive home was mile after mile of dull roadway and thoughts of returning to my small bedroom and the tedious studies waiting for me back in Perth was depressing as hell.

As always, time passed and I started to settle into life at St. George's and the University of Western Australia. Weekdays were a grind of classes and mounting frustration at my inability to master my studies. I was losing the academic battle and it was discouraging. Calculus and organic chemistry were light years beyond my comprehension and I saw no way out of my spiraling downward dilemma. My classmates were up to the academic challenge and this led to further feelings of inadequacy on my part.

Soccer matches scattered across the city suburbs followed by beer drinking at the college typically occupied my weekends. I developed quite a taste for Swan Lager brew. Unlike Hong Kong, there were no discos or clubs to visit and a trip to Perth was necessary to catch a movie. I did hear of a new club and gave it a chance one Saturday night. I wanted to see what a "hot spot" in Perth looked like compared to the discos in Hong Kong.

The club was a big disappointment. It had absolutely no character and was a shell of what a bar should be. A local band played on one side of the room with a few tables dotting the center. The bar was ordinary and plastic with few young women perched on barstools. A couple aborigines hung around the entrance pandering for a drink. It was definitely not my gig so after a couple minutes I headed back to the college and never hit the bar scene again.

I was beginning to adjust to the social structure at the college, so naturally it was time for something to go wrong. I was about to experience a character forming, conscience jolting event that called upon my sense of right and wrong.

For the most part, seniors treated freshmen like dung, but I had formed solid friendships with several upperclassmen so I was often given a pass. Perhaps my athletic ability appealed to the sports-loving Australians. Or perhaps my stories about Hong Kong and daring escapades involving gambling, nightclubs, and wild women fascinated these guys who had been raised so conservatively. Racy times in far-off Hong Kong had to be captivating.

Senior class leader and awesome athlete Rob MacMillan soon became my unlikely best friend. His classmates couldn't understand why he would spend time with a lowly freshman and many in my class thought I was sucking up to the seniors.

One Saturday evening after juicing a keg of beer, Rob stood on wobbly legs in the common room. A couple freshmen decided to take advantage of his inebriated state and throw him into the dreaded murky pond. Rob was quickly overpowered by a half dozen rowdies, and big as he was, didn't stand a chance in his drunken state. As he was being dragged to the pond, Rob's close friend, Peter Rock, ran to his aid. Peter shouted at me "Aren't you going to help your mate?"

In the Australian code of honor, a mate, or buddy, held a revered special place. Rob was indeed my friend, but I was torn between helping him or standing united with my fellow freshmen. Which side to take?

If I helped Rob, my class would think I wasn't supporting them. If I joined their ranks, I would be letting my friend down.

Pressed to make a choice, I decided there was no reason Rob should be thrown into the pond, he had done nothing to deserve it. I made my decision - I would throw my lot with Peter and help Rob.

We elbowed into the throng and together were able to peel the freshmen mob off Rob and saved him from a soaking. We took Rob back to his room to sleep it off while Peter and I headed to the common room for a game of billiards. I think I impressed Peter with my decision and our friendship was strengthened. As billiards became my focus, out of the corner of my eye I noticed freshmen guys congregating in the corner with serious scheming going on. Sure enough, I was suddenly tackled from behind. My arms and legs were tightly gripped and I was carried toward the courtyard and the pond. I squirmed and struggled to free myself since I had no desire to bathe in the scum.

In the struggle I hit a guy. He swore up a storm and hit me in the face while my arms were held. This really pissed me off and while spread-eagled, I managed to free an arm and punched the guy on the chin. He dropped like a rock! Hands released me and I fell to the ground like a discarded rag. I scrambled to my feet on full alert.

The mob was staring at the guy I had punched; he was on the ground and appeared unconscious. In a minute or two he came around, got to his feet, rubbed his chin, and scowled at me. I was screwed. What was next? If I had been close to my classmates, I would have taken my medicine and let them drop me in the pond. But I didn't feel that way about these guys or the college.

I was apprehensive over the next few days. But the freshmen I battled that night had written off the whole experience as the consequence of a rollicking beer bash. Being good Aussies, they acknowledged I had gone to the assistance of my mate and respected me for that. Swan Lager was declared the instigator that evening. The difficult decision I made to support my friend would shape my strong values of loyalty, friendship, and integrity for years. Only the guy I decked wasn't so friendly after that night.

My college social life was extremely limited compared to the hotspots of Hong Kong, and I was feeling the lack of excitement. I felt I was living a monastic life in a city where the most exciting nightlife happened in a bar that looked like something from *Crocodile Dundee*. In the whole nine months I went on exactly one date and even that was a disaster. Failure at academics was frustrating, but social failure was catastrophic and threw me into a deeper depression.

I can't remember the name of the only woman I dated in Perth. We met when I drove by a bus stop in Crawley, a suburb of Perth. She was a pretty blonde standing alone, and since buses stopped infrequently, I offered her a ride into town. We struck up an interesting conversation and when I dropped her off I thought, *Why not?*

We made a date for the following weekend and I was looking forward to spending time with someone of the opposite sex. I was tired of hanging out with the guys. All week I fantasized over the date as if it was my first ever; it had been so long that I forgot what dating was like. My expectations ran high as I looked forward to a great evening.

The following Saturday I drove to the address she'd given me and walked to the front door with a spring in my step. I rang the doorbell and the door opened wide. Before me stood a six-foot one-inch Amazon! I stretched at five-foot ten, so the monstrous woman towered over me. When I found this woman at the bus stop, I realized she'd been sitting down the whole time and I never noticed how tall she was. I'd dated girls my height, but never an Amazon.

I was determined to make the best of it, even with this shaky surprise. Embarrassment, enough to crush my male ego, was yet to come.

We went to a restaurant recommended by Rob and after a reasonably pleasant dinner I was beginning to get over the height issue. Without nightclubs to visit and too late to catch a movie, I drove to King's Park and we parked on a cliff to talk and admire the view. Of course I had other ideas too.

Perth with its fabled lights was beautiful. There was the usual small talk and we had a few laughs. Talking led to kissing. Things were looking up! Maybe my luck was turning and I was headed out of the long, dry spell.

Then I heard ZZZZZZZZZZ . . . my date was asleep and snoring! I was so stunned I didn't know how to react. I was in complete and utter shock - was I really *that* boring?

Finally I regained my composure, gently nudged her awake, and mumbled something about starting the long drive home. The miles could not pass fast enough as she quietly sat next to me saying nothing, I thought maybe she had fallen asleep again. Being the gentleman my mother raised, I walked her to the door and said a platonic goodbye. My ego had been severely gouged.

Growing up in Hong Kong I had great times with the fairer sex. In Perth I wondered if I had contracted leprosy. I couldn't seem to get anywhere. Once again I started to feel self conscious about my heritage. Western Australian girls were not accustomed to a Heinz 57 variety like me who spoke not with an Aussie drawl, but with a very proper British accent. I repeatedly struck out with women. There seemed so little opportunity to socialize with females when 80 percent of the time passed within the walls of an all-male college. This sterile life was not what I had expected for my Perth adventure. I was feeling absolutely rotten.

For nine months I struggled through life at the University of Western Australia. I never felt comfortable scholastically and this left me with feelings of inadequacy and frustration. I was a competitor, a winner, but this was not a life event I was winning. I didn't even feel I was in the race. I hated the hazing thrown at freshmen, knowing relief would only come as we turned into sophomores. Perhaps accepting this tradition allowed my Aussie classmates to endure the constant torment, but nothing in my upbringing prepared me for this puerile treatment

As the school year drew to a close, it was time to sit for the annual exams. By that time I'd made up my mind I was not returning so I really didn't care how I did on the tests and didn't even study. I just went through the motions. The sub-warden and several upperclassmen got wind of my intent and tried to persuade me from my perverse course of action.

Rob and Horrie pleaded with me to make a go of it and offered to help me study. They were wasting their time because I just didn't care. My high school years at KGV had not prepared me for the math and science classes I was forced to take, nor did I know how to study since I'd always survived on native intelligence. Here at University I had to apply myself and study hard to pass exams, a concept alien to me.

I sat for the obligatory exams but walked out an hour before deadline. Truth be told, I should have walked out right after writing my name on the test booklet.

I'd chosen my course and was determined I would not return to Australia. The end of the school year came and it was time to fly home in defeat. Mum and Dad asked if I wanted to fly back via Sydney to visit

Melbourne and Sydney. The side trip held zero interest; I just wanted to get back to Hong Kong ASAP.

I said goodbye to my Aussie mates, invited them to visit me in Hong Kong, and was once again on a QUANTAS jet. This time there would be no problem with immigration or "White Australian Policies." I was going home. I didn't once look back.

CHAPTER TWELVE
"I'll be Back"
JOHN LENNON AND PAUL MCCARTNEY

When I arrived at Kai Tak airport after the long flight, Mum, Dad, Steve, and Jenny were there to give me a big welcome home. They held a banner reading "Welcome back, Tony!" They treated me like a returning hero instead of a university dropout. I had failed, and I knew it. I lost my bid for academic greatness, and the feeling of failure would haunt me for many years to come. But for now it felt great to be back with the people I loved and cocooned in familiar surroundings.

In my nine months away, little had changed in Hong Kong. I slipped back into my old ways in no time flat. Parties, nightclubs, and of course, life with sweet Jenny consumed my days and nights.

As much as I enjoyed cavorting with my old crowd, a little voice told me this life could not last. I was no longer in high school and now was facing adult decisions. I couldn't be a bum living off my parents; I had to do something worthwhile to earn a living, but what?

There isn't much work a young "local" in a place like Hong Kong would find interesting, especially without a university degree. I searched employment ads in the papers daily but wasn't qualified for most positions, nor was I interested in what I did find offered.

A couple friends went into the aviation field and suggested I apply for a job as an air-traffic controller so I went for an interview. At the time I really wanted the job and thought it would be a respectable way to make a living. This was one of my first job interviews and I bombed royally. Looking back, I thank God I didn't get the job. I might have burned my brain staring at radar screens every day trying to keep planes from crashing into each other. I kept looking and interviewing, but jobs were scarce.

As is often the case, I finally found a job through a contact. My mother's boss Lord Kadoorie partnered in a joint venture between the China Light and Power Company (he was board chairman) and Esso Standard Oil. Lord Kadoorie placed me in position as an office clerk at Esso, a job which gave absolutely no chance for me to burn my brain. It was a menial job in the office services department, which is another way of saying I was a gopher and mailroom clerk. But I was happy to be back home with my friends and family and enjoyed the opportunity to make spending money, even though it was a pittance. I found it amusing my entry level job was arranged at the highest levels of Esso, requiring interviews with the Vice President of Finance, an American expatriate who was feared by the locals.

Lord Kadoorie knew the chairman of Esso and must have asked he hire me as a favor. I had actually met the chairman years before at Boulder Lodge while visiting the Kadoories, but it never entered my mind one day I would be working for his company. The people in my department wondered about the strange relationship I had with executive management. I'm sure it was whispered I was there only because of contacts, and of course that was absolutely true.

My job at Esso was uneventful, but a couple interesting encounters helped pass the time. One involved a reasonably attractive woman who sat at the front desk. Cassy was the receptionist and was a former "Miss Legs of Hong Kong." She wasn't the most pleasant person and seemed to take her former title more seriously than the rest of us did. Her legs were fabulous, but her looks above the hip weren't of the same caliber and besides that, Cassy had a rotten personality. We called her the Queen of Hong Kong.

One day I was sitting at Miss Legs' desk providing her relief for a pee break. I was looking for a pencil and paper to take messages. As I scavenged through the drawers I came across photographs of her, face up for all to see. Naturally I looked at them and discovered Miss Legs posed in scanty lace underwear in diminishing stages of undress. My guess was she had them taken hoping to sell them to a men's magazine. The photos were tantalizingly provocative and I had wicked thoughts of what I could do with these pictures of our young receptionist.

What if they mysteriously appeared on the message board in the break room or inserted in the company newsletter?

I heard Miss Legs coming back from the john so I quickly tucked the photos back into the drawer. The usual frown covered her face as she walked back to her desk

"Did anything interesting happen while I was away?"

Perhaps I should have been a gentleman and said nothing about my find. But since Miss Legs usually carried an ugly attitude, I decided I would play things a little differently.

"Well, I was looking for a pen and paper and found interesting photographs of you. You looked pretty hot and I'm guessing everybody in the office will rush to the newsstand to buy any magazine that publishes them." Game, set, the match over!

"Tony, if you liked the pictures, maybe we could get together tonight and take pictures of the two of us."

I couldn't believe what I was hearing! An office scandal in the making! But no photos would be taken with this walking keg of dynamite, especially when I worked at a company where my mother's boss got me the job. As curious as I was about Cassy's ideas for an evening's frolic, I knew it would be a bad idea, a very bad idea.

"Cassy, I appreciate the offer but I'm dating another girl and I'll have to pass."

With that I got up and went back to my office. I wondered what might have happened if I'd said yes. The evening could have been interesting, but also big trouble and assuredly messy.

I may have handled the Cassy incident well, but failed miserably when it came to the next challenge that presented itself at Esso.

I pride myself on being an ethical person and as a kid never stole candy bars from stores, even though a few pals thought shoplifting was great sport. An incident during my tenure as an Esso office clerk bothered me over the years and the memory still haunts me today.

My job included negotiating with printing companies to purchase invoices, requisition forms, and stationery supplies for the office. Only two printers competed for the business, and I had no strong preference for either of them. I chose to give business on the basis of quality and pricing. Discussions with the printers had to be conducted entirely in Cantonese because they didn't speak a lick of English. This could be challenging for me. It was one thing to engage in social, conversational Chinese and quite another to negotiate business transactions.

Late one afternoon I concluded a business meeting with one of the printers to get a bid for a new line of invoices. As he got up to leave, he matter-of-factly handed me an envelope. I was caught off-guard by his action, but had a funny feeling about it so I decided not to open the envelope immediately. I put it aside for later reading.

At the end of the workday when I was alone in the office, I opened the thick white parchment envelope. Inside was a Chinese red paper packet. Aha! A clue!

Opening the red packet, a cashier's check for several hundred dollars fell out. What should I do?

The next morning I asked several friends in the office if they had ever been given an envelope and the answer came back, "Certainly." Apparently giving such "gifts," which today I would call outright bribery, was a common business practice in Hong Kong. I wanted to give the money back, but my colleagues convinced me I had to accept the check. If I returned it to the businessman he would lose face because it would be assumed the amount wasn't high enough, meaning I was essentially closing him out of the bidding war.

If I kept the check there would be no loss of face and business would go on as usual. Not having much disposable income, I pocketed the cash but felt guilty and soiled by my action. After that, I couldn't bring myself to give this particular printing company any special consideration beyond choosing them if, and only if, they offered the best bid and service.

I knew what I had done was morally wrong, despite what my friends had to say about it. To this day I regret accepting that money. It wasn't a winning move. The only good coming from the incident was I learned from my mistake with relatively little collateral damage associated with my action.

I vowed I would never come close to doing anything like it again, and I haven't.

CHAPTER THIRTEEN
"Drive My Car"
JOHN LENNON AND PAUL MCCARTNEY

When I left for Australia I said goodbye to my blue and chrome BSA 650cc Thunderbolt Rocket. I wasn't sure when, if ever, I would see that incredible machine again. I spent hours tenderly greasing her down so rust wouldn't mottle her beauty while I was gone. It was almost like caressing a woman as I slowly spread the brown, greasy concoction over her long, shiny tailpipes and sensuous chassis.

After finishing, I wrapped her in plastic as a shroud. I had a suspicion as soon as my plane left the ground, my parents would sell the bike and I'd never see my love again. Truthfully, I wasn't that concerned. It knew it was time to get rid of the "hot throbbing thing between my legs" before a serious accident claimed me.

Now back in town, it was confirmed my parents had sold the motorcycle to a lucky young man living in Mongkok. I needed to find wheels to get around and though I briefly considered another motorcycle, I decided on a car. In Perth I'd driven only cars so I set my sights on four wheels. Fate smiled in another lucky moment when the stars were aligned just right. Lord Kadoorie's daughter Rita had just bought a new car. She could have traded her old car, but instead she very kindly offered to give it to me. What a wonderful gift! It wasn't just any car. This car was my introduction to a special breed of legendary English rally cars known as Mini-Coopers.

Mini-Coopers were a road rally phenomenon in the '60s. They were small, matchbox-shaped, front-wheel drive vehicles made by BMC and brought a new dimension to road handling and rallying.

A world of difference separated this Mini and the Morris Minor I owned in Aussie. The Morris Minor was a granny's car while the Mini was the coolest thing on wheels for those who couldn't afford a Lotus or Porsche. Thanks to Lord Kadoorie's family, I took proud ownership of a 997cc red Mini, license plate AA7711. The Mini had its engine mounted transversely creating a tiny hood or "bonnet" as the English call it. The windows did not roll down, they simply slid partially open. The instrument panel was Spartan at best. A long gearshift led to a manual gearbox. Four could be seated not-so-comfortably, but the car maneuvered best with only the driver as ballast.

The Chinese are believers in numerology and are very superstitious about license plates. The right numbers will bring the owner good luck and keep away bad spirits that might cause misfortune. I soon learned AA7711 was unanimously declared to be an excellent and desirable license number and enjoyed that unexpected bonus that brought my car even greater notoriety. I really loved that red Mini and drove it proudly around the New Territories with a new crowd of road racing friends. Two-wheel motorcycle racing was replaced by four small wheels and I felt like I owned the road. Life with number 7711 was going well, until the night my brother Steve surprised me.

Steve was right out of the Steppenwolf song, "Born to be Wild." While I was the jock in high school, Steve was the rebellious rock star. At school he soon grew tired of walking in my shadow and feeling the constant comparison to my accomplishments. People expected Steve to compete in sports like his older brother did and I'm sure the expectation made him want to scream. Steve was born with a congenital defect in his left arm, which hampered his ability to use full range of motion. Although he was reasonably proficient in some sports, he was never motivated to pursue them aggressively. Steve had to find his own outlet, his own "thing" as it were.

Music, particularly the drums, became Steve's thing, and the kid could really beat those skins.

I've always been envious of the attention rock stars get from women and my kid brother Steve epitomized this phenomenon. As a rock drummer Steve found his niche and women found Steve! In our family apartment, Steve and I lived in one wing of a sprawling 3,000 square foot space with adjoining bedrooms and a common bathroom. This led to some interesting run-ins.

When Steve was fourteen, I woke up one night to take a leak but the bathroom door on my side was locked. I cursed, thinking Steve had gotten up, used the toilet and forgot to unlock the door to my room. I walked into the adjoining hallway and marched into his room. I was certainly not prepared for what met my eyes.

My fourteen-year-old brother was in bed with a damn good-looking blond who looked about the same age. I must have made a noise or bumped the door because they both woke up and found me staring at them. My reaction was almost comical; I felt like a pervert staring at the kids and I think I said something inane like, "Do her parents know she's here?"

I can't remember Steve's response, but I decided the best thing to do was take my pee and go back to bed. My fourteen year-old brother was getting it on while his "cool, athletic brother" was wondering, what gives?

Once Steve discovered sex, there was no stopping him and there were many nights I cursed at the locked door and walked down the hallway through his room to get to the bathroom. By this time, a female body in Steve's bed didn't startle me. Steve started early, and girls lined up to be with him. During those days of safer sex, the biggest problems were a severe case of blue balls or a drippy case of the clap, which could be easily cured by a shot of penicillin.

All this sex was happening without Mum and Dad's knowledge, so sneaking in and out of the apartment during the early hours of the morning happened regularly. Steve would sneak his girlfriend in through a back window to bypass my parents whose bedroom was at the other end of the apartment, close to the front door. To be fair, Steve did not have a new girl in bed with him every night. Like me, he pretty much stuck to one girl at a time for months before a new one came along. I never thought the girls he chose were good enough for him, even though they were darned attractive. I wonder if that's a natural reaction among siblings. Do we ever think any girl or guy is good enough for our brothers or sisters?

Steve's social life was great, but he was bombing badly in school. All his time and effort was spent on music with zero on studies. The inevitable result was at fifteen Steve dropped out of high school and joined the ranks of professional musicians touring Southeast Asian hotels and clubs. The name of his band was "Peter Nelson and the Renaissance." They were a fabulous group comprised of mostly New Zealanders playing contemporary rock music kids loved. Peter was the leader and had an incredible voice; it was a cross between Tom Jones and a bawdy New Orleans blues singer. For a white guy, he had a lot of soul! One of their trademarks was a rendition of the song "Vehicle" by the Ides of March. When they played that number they really rocked it and brought the house down. With Peter's voice and young drummer Steve creating havoc on the drums, how could the group not succeed? Steve's musical success was inversely proportional to his academic success, but he didn't care, he had the world by the tail.

Steve and I were close, but we were not inseparable brothers. We had different interests and we pursued them vigorously. Occasionally our paths would cross in a nightclub or disco but we didn't hang out regularly. Despite our differences, we were always there for each other when needed and our blood connection ran strong. Like most brothers, we fought, but I can only remember one time we got physical - a wrestling match with no punches thrown.

On one occasion my little brother pushed me to the limit and I could have killed him, but he almost saved me the effort.

It was a Friday night and Steve shook me from a deep sleep. He was standing over my bed and speaking in a low, but urgent voice.

"Tony, get up, come on, get up." It was dark; I glanced at the clock and it reported four a.m.

"Damn, it's late," I mumbled. "Go back to bed and leave me alone." I turned over and pulled the sheets over my head.

"Wake-up, Tony, I had an accident in your car." I was nineteen and Steve was fifteen. A driver couldn't apply for a license until eighteen, so what Steve was saying wasn't making a lot of sense. He must have been having a nightmare and sleepwalking to boot.

"Go back to sleep, you're dreaming and not making any damned sense." Steve stubbornly stood above me insisting I get up. By now I was slowly rallying as the early hour haze lifted and the reality of what he was saying settled in. *He wasn't kidding!*

I quickly pulled the sheet away from my head and demanded, "Okay, what the fuck happened?"

Staying remarkably calm, Steve told me he'd lifted my keys from my bedside table and took a drive around town. *This kid who never had a driving lesson in his life had been tearing around town in the early hours of the morning in my car!* A terrible feeling settled over me, my stomach churning as things started to register.

With hope in my voice, I asked, "It isn't a bad accident, is it?" Steve's body language told me what I didn't want to hear.

"It's bad, Tony, the car is smashed and I think I broke my nose." For the first time I noticed Steve's nose was swollen, but at that moment if it hadn't been broken, I might have been tempted to break it for him. Then my dear young brother told me he'd been racing with a motorcycle. *Shit!* Not satisfied to steal his brother's car and drive it without a license or insurance, this maniac was racing a motorcycle! Steve admitted he lost control of the car going around a corner at high speed and ran head-first into a wall.

"Who was riding the bike you were racing?" I asked. A stupid question, since what did it matter?

Steve mumbled, "I was racing Kwan, the guy with the MV Augusta and he's waiting downstairs to take you to the accident. Will you go with him?" Steve was begging me now.

"Is there anything else wrong with you besides your nose being broken? Did you break anything else?"

Steve sunk into a chair and said, "My knees hurt where I banged them on the dash, but other than my nose, nothing too bad." I told him to wait at home; I would try to take care of things.

Even in my foggy state of mind I realized there was the potential for big trouble and I had better scout out the situation. I was angry with Steve, but that didn't mean I wanted him in trouble with the authorities. Family anger can be controlled, but when you piss off the law, it's another story.

I quickly pulled on my jeans and t-shirt, rushed down the back stairs and jumped on the back of the waiting bike. I knew Kwan from my motorcycle days and he nodded at me but didn't say a word. Hopefully he felt plenty bad and guilty. Fortunately the accident site was only five minutes away and at this time of the morning nobody was on the road.

I groaned when I saw the wreck. The Mini didn't look good and neither did the wall. But who cared about the wall? I surveyed the damage - the entire front end was caved in and both front tires angled in weird positions. A lamppost had taken the brunt of the hit and red paint smeared over ten feet of the wall. No way could the car be driven; it would have to be towed to a body shop and might possibly be totaled.

A few minutes later the police arrived on a routine patrol and asked what happened. I made my choice unhesitatingly. Speaking in Cantonese, I told the young police inspector I had lost control going around the corner. He looked at me suspiciously and asked if I was hurt and if I had been drinking.

I assured him I was fine, but he said I would have to go to the station to file a report. After a few minutes walking around the accident site, off we went in the police car. Sitting in the back of a cop car at four thirty a.m. is not my idea of fun. I had a gnawing feeling growing in the pit of my stomach. I was worried about the accident and busy fabricating a story to tell the police, but I was also really upset about my AA7711. Where was the good luck that plate was supposed to bring? My car was in terrible shape and I doubted it could be resurrected. The inspector arranged for a tow truck to take the Mini to a body shop; it would be hours before I got the diagnosis, and worse, the prognosis.

We arrived at the police station and I was placed in a small room and given an accident report form to complete. There were the usual questions and I filled in my answers in a few minutes, giving a short and simple description of what I *thought* probably happened. The young inspector came into the detention room and read my report with a serious look on his face. He turned to me and said in very good English, "This is not a believable story. It was a clear night, nothing on the road, and plenty of light. How could you crash the car? You must have been going very fast in a 30 mph zone."

A chill ran down my spine. Where was this heading? Visions of jail and money pouring out of my parents' pockets flashed before my eyes. The policeman looked me in the eye. I didn't blink and held his stare. Finally I said, "I lost control while changing gears. I went into neutral by mistake and the car lost traction and swerved into the wall. That's it."

He slowly shook his head in disbelief and announced emphatically, "That is a terrible story," and walked out the door. *Holy shit, what next? Was I going to be strip-searched for drugs and beaten with a hose?*

Less than a minute later he returned and handed me another blank accident report form and pen. He firmly instructed, "You write down what I tell you to write." I thought he was going to dictate a confession and I would surely end up shit creek without a paddle.

But the words coming from his mouth were those I certainly didn't expect to hear.

His story went something like this . . . I was driving around the corner of the overpass when an illegal taxi, called a *pak pai*, cut me off. The taxi supposedly forced me into the wall and then drove away leaving me at the accident site, unable to jot down the license number.

When he finished dictating, the policeman took the form, read it over and pronounced, "This is a much better accident report."

I wholeheartedly agreed with my newfound savior, signed the report, and thanked the young inspector for his help. I was out of the station within five minutes. My motorcycle ride was outside waiting for me. We drove back to my house and I walked upstairs absolutely exhausted. It was now seven a.m., and my parents were drinking coffee with serious expressions on their faces. Steve was slumped over the table holding an ice pack to his nose. It was early, I had little sleep, and it had been a stressful time at the station. I was beat and didn't want to face an inquisition.

Mum started in on me. "Your brother told us what happened to the car. Is everything all right? Where have you been?"

I told them about the police, the accident report, and my good luck finding a friendly inspector. As tired as I was, I momentarily contemplated punching Steve's lights out but decided against it, instead I joined the chattering consensus that Steve was a total idiot. *No more wake-up surprises, please!*

Later that day I inspected the damage to my car and discovered an interesting arrangement between the police and body shops was in place. Apparently accident tows were hauled to favored shops whose owners undoubtedly greased a few palms. My car had been towed to a small, unknown garage far away from the accident scene; it was not the type of place I would have chosen to do delicate frame-straightening work.

But I was at their mercy and had to take them at their word when I reviewed the long list of repairs to be done. My red Mini was in the body shop for weeks. The car was in bad shape - the front end had been shattered resulting in extensive damage to the suspension system. When I eventually got the car back, it looked fine cosmetically, but simply did not drive the same. The accident severely bent the chassis affecting road handling and the great Mini performance just wasn't there anymore. I was incredibly disappointed. I was driving a different car.

Not all stories involving my red Mini had an unhappy ending. One story brings a smile to my face every time I think about it.

Jenny and I never knew if her mother and my parents were aware we were sexually active. They probably would have been furious and we'd have hell to pay. One Saturday night we thought the jig was up and expected to find ourselves caught in the act. My red Mini-Cooper had been stolen a few nights earlier after I left it parked at a movie theater. I reported the theft to the police, but hadn't heard back from them.

On Saturday nights, Jenny and I liked to catch a movie, grab a quick meal of Korean barbeque, and follow our night out with a trip to my house to listen to music. My parents were out for the night so we thought we'd be left undisturbed in my room. Our lovemaking was about to reach crescendo level when loud knocking interrupted our coupled beat.

"Tony," my mother called, "it's the telephone for you. The police are calling; they found your car!"

Crap! My parents had come home early! Jenny and I freaked out but somehow we both did see the perverse humor in our panic. We probably looked like the Keystone cops in action.

"I'll be right there, Mum."

We untangled ourselves as hysterical laughter took over. Jenny yelled for me to get dressed fast and answer the phone which was in another room (in those days telephone extensions were rare). I pulled on my pants and was throwing on a shirt when my mother pounded on the door again.

"Tony, what's the matter with you? Hurry-up, the police can't be kept waiting!"

I finished speed dressing, unlocked the door, and ran to the telephone. The telephone was in the entrance hallway, directly across from the TV room where Mum and Dad sat patiently waiting to hear what the police had discovered.

I picked up the receiver said "Hello." The police found the car in good condition, luckily it hadn't been vandalized and they wanted me to come down and claim it right away. I thanked them, hung up and told my parents I was going into town to get the car. They were happy to hear the good news, but I noticed they were looking at me like I should be saying something more. I made a quick exit to my bedroom. By then Jenny was dressed and when I walked in her hand flew to her mouth and she gave an anguished howl.

"Look at you! Did your parents see you?"

I looked in the mirror. My hair was tousled, my untucked shirt was partially buttoned, but fortunately my fly was up. I was wearing my shoes with mismatched socks, and they were inside-out. I looked a complete mess! My parents never said anything, but I'm guessing they knew damn well something was going on.

When I re-took possession of the Mini, I instantly discovered major problems. Along with impaired maneuverability, a weird smell permeated the Mini; it just wouldn't go away. I couldn't tell if the thieves had puked in the car or if something ghastly had been spilled. It was a horrible smell and I had to get rid of it or get rid of the car.

During my time at Esso, I'd befriended a guy in the propane gas division. His name was John Tse and he was quite a celebrity around Hong Kong known for driving production cars in the Macau Grand Prix. The Portuguese province was well known for this annual race. John won his category several times and was known locally as the Mini-Cooper King. He raced a highly modified version of a Mini-Cooper S that was street legal, but had been raced "as is" in Macau. John heard about the accident and my disappointment over the rebuilt car. He called me and said we should talk.

John talked about selling his car to upgrade to a different class car for racing. He offered to trade my recently repaired car along with cash for his street racer.

On the surface this sounded like a pretty interesting proposition, but I had yet to see his famous Mini-Cooper S or drive it. My best friend Norman and I met John the next evening to check out the car. We really wanted to see how the S performed in the hands of an expert.

We met on a road leading to Hong Kong Peak, a curvy, challenging route that would make a great test run. I walked around John's car and ran my hands over the body to check it out. I sure liked the way it looked. The car was painted British racing green capped with a white top. It hung low to the ground sitting on fat Bridgestone racing tires accented by wheel spacers. The fenders were flared to cover the extra wheel width and the bonnet (hood) had rubber straps to prevent it from flying off at high speed.

This was a wicked looking machine and when John started the engine, the deep throaty sound of a racing Abarth exhaust assaulted the ears. The 1275cc engine was bored out, and the racing cam and pistons combined with a Weber carburetor to replace twin SUV carbs. My adrenaline was pumping! I folded my seat back so Norman could climb into the rear and I buckled up in the front passenger's seat.

John asked, "Are you ready? Hold on!" For the next fifteen minutes Norman and I alternated between sheer joy pumped by the need for speed and sheer horror experienced on a roller coaster ride from hell. We'd never driven in a car with a professional race driver and drifting around corners at such speed with nothing but cliffs leading to the harbor below was terrifying. The performance level of that car was unbelievable; John was definitely a pro and the sounds heard at high rev were pure *"Testosterroar."* It was exhilarating!

I knew John was doing me a favor selling the car at a reasonable price, but then I wondered why? Turned out my friend had an ace up his sleeve. Remember the Chinese love for lucky license plates, especially AA7711? John removed the license plate and sold it to a Chinese gentleman for a good sum of money. This helped to make the S more affordable for me. I could care less about license plates and the less valuable AH3277 on the S would suit me just fine.

For a year Norman and I ruled the streets of Kowloon and Hong Kong with one of the fastest street cars made, not counting the pure-bred exotics we could never afford. There were a few Jag E-types and Porsches around, but they were rare and night racers certainly didn't drive them.

Norman was my constant co-pilot and we drove at night on the country roads of Clearwater Bay or on Hong Kong Island near Deep Water Bay. On those roads traffic was less congested and cops were few and far between. These were the same roads I'd programmed into my memory flying on my BSA so I felt comfortable snaking through the corners at high speed. What I lacked in ability, the car more than made up with exquisite handling. Its brute power allowed me to overtake other cars effortlessly. On straight roads we'd often race in caravans of a dozen cars of all makes, shapes, and sizes – of course I was always leader of the pack.

Mini Coopers, Ford Cortinas, Alfa-Romeo GTVs, and a myriad of lame excuses for sports coupes trailed behind me. Traditional sports cars like MGs and TRs could not compete in our impromptu races. Japanese cars like Mazdas hadn't made their mark yet; they were thought to be clumsy and clunky although they were better appointed when it came to options and interiors. Large American V-8s were never seen, partially because they would not be suited to the smaller, tighter Hong Kong roads and also because they would have required an expensive conversion to right-hand-drive. Yes, we drove on the "wrong side of the road." Exotic European cars did exist, but were very rarely seen.

Then entered one of the first truly sensational exotic sports cars.

Mum came home from work one day and announced Michael Kadoorie had taken delivery of a new toy, and this one was really special. She told me to head downstairs as he would be coming to show it to me in a few minutes.

His first sports car was a real classic, a Jaguar E-type, but today Michael was coming to take me for a drive in his latest Italian dream machine. Our apartment was at the top of a hill, named Kadoorie Avenue (yes, the same Kadoorie), and I was anxiously waiting downstairs. Soon I heard a roar that increased in volume. Louder and louder, it honestly sounded like a jet coming up the hill, the decibels were outrageous! I saw the crest of the car peeking over the hill and in less than a second, Michael whipped into my driveway. I was looking at a custom-built Lamborghini Miura P400S, a world-class exotic supercar. It was metallic blue, housing a V-12 that sat just inches above the ground.

The Lamborghini was so sleek it looked like it could cut through the air like a rocket. The Lambo had gull-wing doors, reminiscent of the famous Mercedes 300SL. I opened the passenger side and the door swung up to face me. I climbed in and off we went. It felt like we were busting Gs. The acceleration was phenomenal as I was pinned to my seat. At the time this was the fastest production car in the world and it carried the absolutely outrageously expensive price tag of approximately twenty thousand U.S. dollars. Nobody paid that much for a car except the super, super rich and Michael fell into that category. As we drove through town, everybody turned to stare at the beast. Most turned before they could see it, unsettled by the terrific roar.

We drove to Shatin in the New Territories where there was less traffic and long stretches allowed the Lambo to be put through its paces, absolutely astounding! This car was a young man's wet dream. But the best was yet to come.

We reached a long, straight stretch and Michael stopped the car.

"Want to try?" My mouth hung open, but it didn't take me long to jump into the driver's seat. I practiced shifting through the chrome Italian gate and then took off. It was an incredible thrill to drive the Miura, a memory that still makes me hot. The acceleration was as fast as my BSA 650cc cycle, and for a car to match a big bike, well, that was phenomenal. Running through the Lambo's gears was not an easy feat and I knew it would take time to master the gearbox. I drove a couple miles, thrilled by every inch.

I was so grateful to Michael for letting me drive his supercar, and all he asked was I reciprocate by letting him drive my Mini-Cooper S sometime. *It's a deal!* Michael was gracious with his comments about my pride and joy, but somehow it didn't seem a fair trade. I got to drive an exotic, Italian V-12 supercar and in return Michael was handed the keys to a four-cylinder, matchbox type English sedan. But, hey, I wasn't complaining!

As was the case when I had a motorcycle, there was a cadre of car drivers who would enjoy spirited excursions on the roads in the New Territories. Again there would be the occasional fender-bender, but nothing that resulted in loss of life or limb. I don't think Mum and Dad worried about me when I drove cars. Their cabin cocoons and strong seat belts gave my parents a false sense of security. The only *really* close call I experienced came as a passenger in a friend's car.

Every group of friends has one nerd who wants to be one of the guys, but never quite makes the cut. In our group the wannabe's name was Raymond Kwan. He was one of the nicest, gentlest guys, but I really had little time for him as a driver.

Raymond wanted to show Norman and me he deserved our respect. His big opportunity came when he bought a new car. Even before we climbed into the car, Raymond's nerdiness rang the bell because his new pride and joy was a sedate Volvo with a couple token racing elements bolted in place. Still Raymond begged to take us for a ride. *Hey, why the hell not?*

We drove up Kowloon Tong, through the tunnel to Shatin, and then headed back to town for a noodle supper. As we drove down Waterloo Road, Raymond was itching to impress us with his Volvo's top speed.

I was sitting in the front passenger seat, Norman in the back when we started to accelerate down the road. The Volvo didn't pack much horsepower, but Raymond was determined to break 100 mph. I could see this wasn't going to happen because an intersection with a traffic light was coming up fast. I told him to back off. My words had exactly the opposite effect. Raymond gripped the steering wheel and went pedal to the metal.

As we approached the busy intersection at high speed, cars were lined up right and left. The traffic light turned yellow as we rushed toward it.

If we'd been in my Mini Cooper S, the intersection would have been in my rear view mirror, but the truck-like, clumsy Volvo was struggling. The light turned red, cars started to move and we were still roaring toward the intersection, too late to stop.

I closed my eyes and braced for the inevitable sound of metal impacting metal. Red light, twenty yards to the intersection, and ninety miles per hour. What a bad combination! How we ever made it through that intersection remains a mystery to this day. I was furious and screamed at Raymond to pull over and made him get out of the car so I could take the wheel. We were lucky to escape with our lives that awful night.

There were few cars in Hong Kong as fast as my Mini Cooper S; I could blow away just about anything on the streets, Lamborghinis excluded. But there were a few exceptions - the Lotus Elan was a great car as it was super light and had an excellent racing engine. The Elan was a true sports car and featured a 1600cc overhead cam Colin Chapman engine. The downside was this car afforded little protection in case of accident. Other than the Elan, there were no "common" cars on the road that could give me a challenge, until I found a wolf in sheep's clothing.

Norman and I were idling at a traffic light when a gun metal blue Ford Cortina pulled next to us, engine revving. I glanced over and thought the guy was kidding since Cortinas were no match for a Mini-Cooper S, let alone my highly modified version. Cortinas were generally heavy family sedans, but there was something about the way the car sat on the pavement. Hmmm.

Nah, I'll show this pretender what my S can do. The light changed and we shot away.

First gear, second, third, hell, we were neck to neck at sixty! Something strange was happening here.

Jonathan Wong was the guy behind the wheel of the Lotus Cortina, another car destined to develop a great reputation in road rally circles. Ford had come up with the brilliant idea of dropping a Lotus engine into its respectable Cortina sedan, toughen the suspension, and tweak what was already there to make it a genuine contender. The Lotus Cortina was no slouch and became popular among those with spare change to throw at automobiles. It was not an inexpensive car, far costlier than the Mini.

After our sprint at the traffic light, we pulled into a deserted parking lot and began swapping stories. We were equally surprised. Jonathan had never seen a Mini Cooper as fast as mine and I had never seen a Cortina like his. From that evening on, Jonathan, Norman, and I were great buddies and spent a lot of time together. My newfound friend was quite a character.

Jonathan Wong was the son of a wealthy businessman who owned the largest funeral home business in Hong Kong. I liked to kid Jonathan that he was inheriting a "dying business." His father was a Chinese patriarch of the old style who kept a wife and three concubines. Until I met Jonathan I didn't know concubines still existed in Hong Kong. I'd heard of the custom, but never knew a man who practiced it. Jonathan was born of Mother #3 and we later met his brother Richard who sprang from Mother #2. Dad and his many children lived a great lifestyle, all supported by the thriving funeral business.

It turned out Jonathan was a sports celebrity as one of the best ten-pin bowlers in the Colony. In those days ten-pin bowling was hot. Its popularity in Hong Kong exploded and the game became a fashionable pastime receiving much ink in the local sport pages. Anybody who was anybody often frequented the new bowling alleys built in the Colony. I'd taken up the game and true to form I was a decent bowler with an average in the 180 range. My high series was a respectable 677 with a high game of 247. Jonathan, on the other hand, was one of the top ten bowlers in the Colony, won numerous tournaments, and had his picture slapped on the front pages of the paper. The inscrutable Mr. Chan was one of Jonathan's best bowling buddies.

The first time I learned of Mr. Chan was a situation I won't ever forget. Norman and I drove to the Brunswick bowling alley in Tsimshatsui and noticed an abnormal number of cars circling the alley, each car loaded with tough-looking guys. This was not the normal "let's have a good time" crowd.

Inside we found most Formica coffee tables were occupied by two or three similar looking guys sipping drinks and smoking. They looked like they were waiting for someone, but we had no idea who the poor bastard could be. These guys looked awfully mean, nasty, and rough around the edges. We found Jonathan commanding a far lane and asked if he knew what was going on. He whispered his friend Mr. Chan was behind all the cloak and dagger stuff.

Apparently this Mr. Chan was enjoying dinner with friends in a popular restaurant when a contender from the bowling alley walked by his table. This man had recently lost a closely contested, high stakes bowling match to Mr. Chan and continued his displeasure by spitting in Mr. Chan's general direction as he sauntered by, thereby showing great disrespect.

The two argued earlier and the loser's behavior sprung from impulse, but was still very stupid. One thing you never do in the Chinese culture is cause someone to lose face. Spitting was a capital sin. Unfortunately for the spitter, Mr. Chan was boss of 14K, the notorious Hong Kong Triad. The unfortunate loser should have known better.

A Triad boss rules largely through his reputation and will take any action necessary to ensure he retains the fear and respect required to rule his territory. This particular evening the evil-looking guys were patrolling the bowling alley waiting for the offender to appear. Once captured, they would take him away to a remote place and he'd never be seen again.

I was dumbstruck. A murder in the making at a public bowling alley and the whole damn thing was unfolding before me! Norman and I were morbidly fascinated and waited at the alley for several hours to see what would happen. Fortunately for the offender he never showed and the Chinese equivalent of wise guys eventually left around midnight. Later I learned the foolish offender who had insulted Mr. Chan had wisely groveled enough to claim his life back.

A couple months later I ran into Jonathan at the bowling alley again. I walked in for a friendly game and saw him sitting at the bar. He motioned me over, grabbed me by the arm and said, "Tony, come along. We have a match against two guys for big money."

It wasn't uncommon for us to bowl for ten or twenty bucks, but this night I answered, "Sorry, Jonathan, I don't have any money to gamble tonight."

"Don't worry!" Jonathan insisted. "It's for two hundred dollars and we have a financial backer to sponsor us."

I had no idea what he was talking about…financial backer? I grabbed my shoes and ball from my locker and headed off to the lane where our opponents were warming up. Sitting on the back bench was Mr. Chan and a few rough companions. I respectfully said hello in Cantonese and bowed politely. Then I grabbed Jonathan and whispered frantically, "What the hell is Mr. Chan doing here?"

Jonathan's words caused the blood to drain from my face.

"Mr. Chan is our financial sponsor, he's betting on us to win."

Gulp! It was too late for me, the bet had been made and it would be bad form to try to get out of it. I wondered if I refused, would Mr. Chan lose face? I remembered what happened the last time Mr. Chan lost face. *Shit, I was screwed!* I unhappily accepted my fate and hoped Jonathan was as good as he said he was. Jonathan assured me all I had to do was to bowl my average score and he would do the rest. He seemed confident we would win.

"Don't worry, we can beat them. The guy we're playing thinks he's better than he is and unless we fall apart, it will be a good win."

The match was sealed and the balls rolled. Jonathan bowled first and calmly walked to the line, took a few steps, and let loose. *Pow!* He rolled a strike and now it was my turn. I felt uncomfortable edging the line as I started my take-away. I released the ball and sent it flying at the pins. It curved into the pocket, but at the last minute dipped a little too far left. *Kerplunk!* I had a seven-ten split. What an inglorious way to start my game. Jonathan told me not to worry, there were another nine frames to go.

Our opponents took their turns and both managed to spare the first frame. Ball after ball was hurled down the alley. Apart from the clatter of the balls rolling and hitting the pins, no sounds could be heard. Heavy concentration leaves no room for small talk.

Three of the four bowlers did very well that night. Unfortunately the fourth bowler should have stayed home. I was that fourth bowler. I bowled every type of split formation that existed in the sport. To make a long story short, I bowled one of the worst games of my life and barely broke 100. Jonathan scored 220, but it was not good enough to cover my ineptness. Our opponents averaged over 200 and we lost . . . badly.

I sat down and unlaced my shoes, not quite sure what to do next. I was upset with my performance and apologized profusely to Jonathan who was disappointed, but shook off the loss with a shrug. I watched Mr. Chan pay out the bet and quietly leave with his friends. He never said one word to me.

For days I had visions of tough guys driving outside the alley just waiting for me to appear. They were probably armed with choppers searching for my right hand since it had been so useless during the match. But fortunately Mr. Chan was a good loser and Jonathan was a friend of his so I was safe. I'd conjured far more awful things in my head than the night deserved, and I never saw Mr. Chan again. I was going to live! This was one time I lost, but won.

I discovered I didn't have to go to Macau to gamble, there were other avenues available provided you knew the right people. Casinos existed in Hong Kong but they were illegal and run "underground." Mr. Chan owned many of these fine establishments.

Norman wasn't much of a gambler but I was a bad influence on him. I persuaded Norman to visit a couple casinos, and we always had an interesting experience. First we had to find out where the gambling was located. The *dai dong,* or casino, moved around to reduce the likelihood of a police raid, even though most cops were on the take.

Jonathan was a frequent co-investor with Mr. Chan in Kowloon casinos and could readily provide whereabouts of a *dai dong*. Norman and I were enticed by these risky adventures and were excited when Jonathan gave us an address to check out in a shaky part of town. We made our way up the stairs of a rundown apartment building in Tsimshatsui and came to a nondescript door with the lucky number 7 plastered on it.

We knocked and a peephole opened. Norman gave the password in Cantonese and we were ushered to a second door a few feet down a small corridor. The second door was obviously built for the occasion. Door one closed, and we knocked on door two. Norman gave the password a second time, but there was an extended delay while we were checked out through the peephole. Finally door two opened and we were quickly ushered into a smoky, neon-lit apartment full of people gathered around three gaming tables; it was standing room only. The scene was classic - smoke, noise, sweat, and masses of people waving large bills while shouting and cursing in Cantonese.

The shout *dew nei lo-mo* rang out. This is a vulgar Chinese swear phrase concerning someone's mother. A hundred people filled the room and the crowd was 98 percent Chinese. It was strange being there since we represented only two percent of the population. Undoubtedly some thought we were inspectors with the Royal Hong Kong Police, renowned for being on the take. Every so often the *South China Morning Post* or *Sing Tao* newspaper would report of yet another high ranking police inspector caught accepting graft from a gangster.

Steve once played in a band with an English kid whose father was the Chief of Police and the top man ended up being tried and convicted for accepting bribes. Corrupt cops often visited illegal gambling dens, brothels, or whatever else they were being paid to stay away from. When they did show up, they expected special monetary favors.

We made our way to a blackjack table and eventually got close enough to place bets. We played several hands, but the climate just didn't feel right to me, I was not enjoying myself. I lost about fifty dollars and stopped playing and watched Norman work his cards. I've always found that to gamble successfully, I have to feel comfortable in the surroundings so this time I was content to play spectator. As I watched gamblers and gangsters "policing" the operation, I sensed Norman and I were being watched. It wasn't a friendly watch either. Norman was oblivious because he was on a winning streak, but I could sense we were unwelcome outsiders. When whispering started behind our backs, I knew it was time to leave.

I grabbed Norman by the shoulder and urged, "Let's get out of here now, Grup!"

"No way," he argued, "I'm on a winning streak, Tony. You always do this to me when I'm winning. How about another thirty minutes?"

"Norman, we may not have another thirty minutes. There are remarkably unfriendly looks being shot our way and we could be rolled." I discreetly nodded in the direction of the thugs and Norman got the message.

He picked up his money from the table, chips weren't used in a place like this, and within seconds we were out of there. We ran down the stairs but waiting at the bottom were six ugly SOBs. The ugliest of the group pulled a butterfly knife from his pocket and with a flick of his wrist the blade gleamed in his hand. For the uninitiated, a butterfly knife has a two-piece handle that opens and flips out a blade. In the hands of an expert, it has the same effect as a switch blade, perhaps even more so because the sudden wrist flip is so menacing.

"Give us your money and your watches! Now!" We hesitated, not knowing what to do. Should we try to fight? Run? Neither of us wanted to give up our wallets or watches. *Damnit!* There were six of them. Our chances of getting away without being knifed were not good. My initial thought was to turn around and head back to the *dai dong* until a better exit could be arranged.

Suddenly another thug walked down the stairs and I knew we were in really big trouble - our escape route was now cut off. The guy coming behind us was young and wiry, but muscular as hell. Norman and I were up the proverbial shit creek. Another three hulky guys appeared out of nowhere and stood behind Wiry.

I started to worry less about my watch and money and more about my life! What happened next caught us entirely off guard. The wiry fellow started shouting threats at the gang gathered at the bottom of the

216

stairs. We were now really confused. Were two gangs out to take our money? The wiry fellow was obviously the leader of the three big guys who stood quietly, but menacingly behind him. He screamed in Chinese, "*Dew nei lo mo!* What do you think you are doing in my territory? Get out of here before me and my brothers cut off your dicks."

What? Apparently this guy carried high status because the thugs at the bottom of the stairs backed off. Even the ugly one carrying the butterfly knife meekly folded the blade and walked away. Wiry and his henchmen were obviously part of the Triad running the casino upstairs and the other characters were just regular bad-asses infringing on 14K territory.

When Wiry swore, I thought I recognized the voice, but it didn't fit the body I was remembering. The light wasn't good in the hallway, but it was enough for me to see the scar on the back of his hand. The scar was shaped like a shining sun. It was Chow-Chai!

"Once again, it is good to see you, old friend," I said with a grin. Chow-Chai smiled and said, "Yes, Tong-nay, but I think this will be the last time I see you in our establishment. The customers think you *gwai-los* bring them bad luck and asked you not return."

I got the message. My old friend was telling me our lives had grown too much apart and it was better we not see each other again. With that, I thanked him for his help and we shook hands firmly and said good-bye. I whistled down a cab and Norman and I jumped in and sped into the night. We wasted no time putting distance between us and the thugs at the casino. They might be around the corner waiting for Chow-Chai's gang to leave so they could hassle us again.

Jonathan later told me Mr. Chan owned several gambling establishments and each one was well known to the Hong Kong Police. The good old constabulary was paid more than a few dollars to turn their attention to more serious crimes than simple wagering. Because of graft, *gwai-lo* European police inspectors were neither liked nor welcome. I could see how we might have been taken for cops. Some things don't change, no matter which side of the world you live in.

CHAPTER FOURTEEN
"She Said, She Said"
JOHN LENNON AND PAUL McCARTNEY

As reported, my experience "down under" was a whopping failure, but I was back in Hong Kong with Jenny and having loads of fun at discos and playing sports. It wasn't too long after I returned that Jenny graduated from high school so it was now her time to move on. However, her parents had a slightly different plan for furthering her education and it bugged me Jenny was excited by the prospect.

Jenny's parents enrolled her in finishing school in Switzerland. Finishing school! I couldn't believe it when she told me. It sounded so ridiculously artificial and pompous. Normal people didn't go to finishing school. Finishing school was the path taken by a girl born with a silver spoon in her mouth and Jenny's family was far from being aristocratic. Why would they take her away from me like this? Worse, why would Jenny want to go? There was nothing I could do; everything was set in place and the days were ticking away. I still had crazy ideas about marriage, but soon dismissed them because that idea was even more harebrained than finishing school was. We were both far too young.

The day of separation came and we found ourselves at the airport once again, only this time it was Jenny leaving on a jet plane. I was sad and heartbroken because I didn't know how or when I would see her again. When I went to Australia I knew I'd be back at the end of the school year, but Jenny's family had been talking about moving to the States so our future was up for grabs. We said goodbye once again with tears, hugs, and kisses. In a blink, my beautiful first love was gone, and I had a feeling this time I would lose her forever.

When Jenny left for Switzerland, I assumed she would miss me and would be writing letters expressing her pain at being apart. I was expecting she would write every three days following the pattern I established when I was in Australia. The first week passed. No letter. The second week passed. No letter. Surely there must be a postal strike or Jenny's letters were lost in the bowels of the post office.

I phoned Jenny's family and asked if everything was all right. They said Jenny was fine. They had evidently heard from her. After twenty six long days, I received a short note telling me what a great time she was having with all her new European friends.

Well, bowl me over! I was so thrilled to hear this good news!

Obviously, this was not what I wanted to hear. Why wasn't my girlfriend pining for me? The outcome was predictable; I reacted in an immature way and mailed Jenny a nasty letter telling her where to go and letting her know we had reached the end of our wonderful love affair. I didn't hear back and news of Jenny became scarce. I was terribly upset; someone for whom I held very strong feelings had hurt me deeply and I was not handling it well at all.

Time passed and I began to heal . . . but with bitterness as my constant companion. One night friends and I were having drinks at The Scene, the local disco in the basement of the Peninsula Hotel. I saw a friend of mine from several years back. It was Rob, the guy who had suckered me into covering his back in the parking lot while he made a drug buy. After a round of back slapping and trash talk, we sat down to reminisce over a drink or two. Coincidentally my friend's sister happened to be Jenny's roommate at the finishing school. Quickly I learned what I had suspected for some time. Jenny had hooked up with an Italian guy and was dating him regularly. Supposedly he was a really good guy and I would certainly like him except for the circumstances. With that news flash, I closed the chapter in the book titled *Jenny*.

We had enjoyed a wonderful relationship filled with happiness, fun, and love, but now it was over and I needed to move on. I played the field in Hong Kong and conquered dozens of gorgeous women. This was definitely the sowing wild oats period in my life.

When I was thirteen, I disliked my looks intensely. The mirror reflected a funny looking guy. A big head sat on my body and my hair never looked cool, it hung straight with no style. As I grew into my late teens and my large head and smaller body called a truce, my looks developed into what some might describe as exotically intriguing.

Western girls thought I looked slightly Asian while Chinese girls thought I looked Western. I never thought I was good-looking, but I did think I had become dangerously mysterious looking and I liked the change. During my post-Jenny period I had no serious relationships; most affairs were short, hot, and sweet. I was probably trying to get back at Jenny for leaving me.

I was mostly dating Chinese girls I met at parties, bowling alleys or nightclubs. Some dates were ballroom groupies and they were rougher around the edges than the girls I'd known in high school.

One of the prettiest girls I came across was Leticia. She was drop-dead gorgeous but had a mouth like a sailor and a vicious mean streak. Leticia and I were introduced by a mutual friend, Jonathan Wong of Lotus Cortina fame. Jonathan and I had been bowling and were slurping it up at a Chinese noodle shop when we decided to end the evening at an after-hours club. While jostling for a table, the most gorgeous creature walked up to Jonathan, put her arm on his shoulder, looked right at me and asked Jonathan who the *gwei-lo* was.

When I responded for him in Cantonese, she laughed and asked if she could join us to buy her a drink. Leticia stood five feet four inches tall, with a cascade of beautiful long black hair falling below her shoulders. Her figure was stunning and she had an angelic face. We flirted, we talked, we danced, and pretty much forgot about Jonathan.

Leticia said she noticed me years before when I was dating Cerena and had wanted to meet me. At one time she too had been a ballroom hostess but now was freelance modeling with an occasional gig as a hostess for product displays. The night was getting late and neither of us was sleepy, but both wanted to go to bed. We found a room in a small Chinese hotel that catered to lusty lovers looking for a passion pit.

Ah, ah, ah! Leticia could fulfill every young man's fantasy. Not only was she a beautiful woman, she was a *horny*, beautiful woman. That evening was unbelievably sexy and pleasurable, and surprising in ways I never experienced. Leticia was not one for staying in the standard missionary position. No, she was not. I learned a lot from her about lovemaking acrobatics. Sweating and panting after an intense session, I asked my bedmate where she had learned her incredible moves. She explained she had a very good teacher when she turned sweet sixteen; her lover was a Filipino sax player with a local band. *Note to self: If you ever met this guy, buy him a few rounds in appreciation for building the local talent pool.*

Leticia and I ran hot and heavy for about a month, doing the night-club scene, dinners, movies, the whole nine yards. Men and women stared at us because she was so stunning and damn if she didn't know and enjoy it.

I thought my arm candy looked her best wearing the traditional Chinese *cheongsam* dress with a high collar and deep slit along the side teasing her thigh.

One night we were closing the evening's entertainment at an after-hours club. It was late and Leticia was sitting on my lap, arms around my neck. For the hour, quite a few people were still living it up, particularly a bevy of pretty Chinese women. Ballroom and bar girls often visited this club after they were off the clock. Caucasians rarely frequented this nightspot; it was a hangout for the local working crowd. Before long girls started flirting with me, smiling and giggling from several tables away. I was eating it up since usually Leticia was the one getting the attention. My girlfriend didn't like the smiles thrown my way and started to sulk. Sulking turned to pouting, and then she whispered in my ear, "You know Tony, if I ever catch a girl touching you, I will cut her face with a razor and then you won't want to look at her any more. And if I'm mad enough, I might slice you!"

I almost laughed, but her eyes penetrated mine and I suddenly realized she was not kidding. It hit me - *Leticia was capable of doing some-*

thing like that! Maybe it was time to move on while I still retained my male anatomy. A woman as hot-blooded as she was in bed could well prove to be hot-blooded in other ways. As beautiful and sexy as Leticia was, self-preservation won out and I moored in other harbors. We remained friends so her pride was left intact and later she would tell her Hong Kong friends that she had dumped me.

After Leticia, I went through a series of relationship disasters as I searched for the right woman. This was is not an easy proposition when the primary criterion on the list was sex. Plenty of the female persuasion met my initial criterion, but after the excitement of the act was past tense, other qualities I wanted in a woman dropped off sharply.

There was Melissa, a cute thing I met at the bowling alley. Guys lined up behind her lane because when she bowled, her tiny mini-skirt inched up to display a remarkable ass. Melissa's heritage was a blend of Chinese and Thai. She had huge beautiful cat-like eyes that were mesmerizing. She couldn't speak a word of English but there were other ways to communicate. I spoke Cantonese well enough to get my message across.

It didn't take long before I knew something was missing in the relationship - no chemistry. We went on a few dates, never went to bed, and I wasn't having much fun so I decided to break things off. My mistake was delivering the message in a nice way; I wanted to let her down easy. I had the feeling she liked me, a lot.

After a night at the movies, we parked at a Kowloon reservoir where I planned to make my announcement. The location was out of the way and peaceful, but there had been reported muggings of people walking around the reservoir. As long as we stayed in the car with the doors locked and behaved sensibly, I figured we would be relatively safe.

After parking, an awkward silence filled the car. Melissa suddenly turned to me and cried, "Tony, I lup you!" *Note: I made the big mistake of telling my friend Norman about this romantic interlude and for years he went around saying 'I lup you' every chance he got.*

Hell, Melissa had misread me completely! I wasn't taking her out here to tell her I was head over heels in love; I was here to tell her just the opposite. I didn't feel too good about what I was about to say. In the kindest way I could, I explained I didn't "lup" her and we would not be seeing each other any longer.

At first she seemed to take my edict well. I was about to congratulate myself on the successful handling of the matter when Melissa started acting crazy. She opened the car door and bolted into the dark night. I had no idea where she had gone or what I should do. Thoughts of swarthy muggers throttled my brain. *This was not a good thing.*

I contemplated driving away, but that would be really low. Melissa could run into trouble and even though I wasn't crazy about her, I certainly didn't want anything bad to happen. I jumped out of the car and ran around like an idiot shouting her name as I bumped into trees and bushes, occasionally tripping over gnarly roots. Bugs winged in the hot summer air and dive bombed my sweaty body as if on a search and destroy mission.

I called in Cantonese, "Melissa, please come back," but no response. I was starting to get really nervous. I couldn't just leave the woman out here, but I couldn't search all night either. I might fall into a hole or get bitten by a snake. Scenes from an apocalypse attacked my senses.

Wiping sweat from my body with my shirt, I walked to the water's edge and surveyed the scene for thrashing movement. I was stuck how peaceful and beautiful the reservoir appeared with the full moon shining on the water. *What the hell was I doing appreciating nature at a time like this?*

Hey, what was that? A crash sounded in the bushes behind me and I expected a wild animal to pounce and rip me to shreds. I grabbed a rock and braced myself for the assault. Next thing I knew Melissa ran out of the bush like a Tasmanian devil! I was paralyzed at the sight of her, naked as a jaybird and showing a killer body.

She jumped on me as I struggled to get free. We fell backward and rolled into the reservoir, a pile of arms and legs. *Splash!* Hitting the cool water was a shock, but an even greater shock hit when we surfaced. Melissa's arms and legs were wrapped around me in an Anaconda-like grip, her hands grasping at my pants. I staggered through the shallow water as Melissa sexually attacked me with frenzy. I didn't know whether to be angry or laugh, but I did know I was becoming aroused as my belt buckle released. The reason I brought Melissa to this secluded spot floated through my mind, but a perpetually horny young man can resist only so long when a pretty, naked girl is begging you to make love to her.

Abbreviated version of this tale: I didn't leave Melissa that night. I'm no fool! Thoughts of muggings were forgotten as the water around us rushed with pleasure, our bodies tossing in the torrid whirlpool of desire. I had to drive home wearing soggy underwear and damp jeans, but wearing a sunny smile on my face. We laughed all the way home at her crazy behavior and when I gently scolded her she confidently answered, "It worked, I did what I wanted to do and I know you enjoyed it too." I shook my head in disbelief and admitted, "You certainly know how to get a guy's attention."

Back at my apartment, I snuck into my room and hung my clothes in the bathroom to dry. I didn't want to explain what I was doing swimming fully clothed. Melissa and I went out a few weeks more, but the relationship didn't have lasting power. It was purely sexual and high octane, nothing wrong with that. With this little honey I wasn't afraid of razor slicing as I had been with Leticia, but I did have recurring nightmares of drowning in my bathtub.

Next came Mabel, but her story is relatively short. Mabel was a club go-go dancer and once again had a body built to kill. Unlike my other conquests that were thin and petite, Mabel had a full woman's body. She also had one of the deepest, huskiest voices I'd ever heard. As pretty as she was, Mabel wasn't a main attraction for me. My buddy Robert was interested in her so I introduced them and told him to give it his best shot. They seemed to be hitting it off just fine after saying timid "Hellos" and the next thing I knew Mabel and Robert disappeared somewhere private for the evening.

Several weeks passed and I thought nothing further of the evening. Then one day I saw Mabel walking down the street while Rob and I were driving in his car.

"Hey, there's Mabel, want to call her over?"

"No way," Robert answered with venom. "I'm not going anywhere near that bitch."

I was surprised by his words because Robert had been so infatuated with Mabel.

"What happened? I thought you were going to have a great time with that hot number."

Rob looked at me with a disgusted expression on his face.

"The hot number gave me a dose of the clap and I had to get shot up with penicillin." Of course this wasn't funny, but I laughed anyway. In fact I doubled over and couldn't stop laughing. A dose of the clap wasn't really that serious and could be easily cured. But Rob was not amused. I guess I was lucky the chemistry wasn't right with this one, otherwise I would have been her victim, no doubt about it.

I had a good laugh at Robert's expense, but life's jokes even out and we would have many chortles in the future about the date I had with a girl named Sue.

This isn't a sordid story with sexual overtones, it's quite PG. I got a telephone call from a friend of the family who was a few years older than I was. He told me a business acquaintance was in Hong Kong and his sixteen-year-old daughter Sue was traveling with him. He was wondering if I would take her on a date, he would cover all expenses. I wasn't too keen about a blind date, but my friend assured me the girl was very good looking so I agreed. What the hell, it was only one night.

I went to pick up Sue at the Peninsula Hotel and knocked on the door. I was feeling nervous expecting the bride of Frankenstein to appear at any moment. The door opened and I was relieved when an all-American pretty girl met me with a smile. She had blue eyes and blond hair done up in a Sandra Dee ponytail. I met her dad, told him where we were going, what time I would have his daughter back, and off we went. We started out at The Scene since it was located in her hotel. We sipped drinks and danced for several hours.

The night was still young so we crossed the harbor on the Star Ferry to a club called The Den at the Hilton. We danced another couple hours before crossing the harbor for home.

Back at the Peninsula we went to her room, sat on the couch and watched TV. Her dad was still out with his business associates. This girl was all over me in a flash and obviously in heat. After all, I was the "older man" at the ripe age of twenty.

This was tricky. I decided it would be a bad scene if Sue's dad found me fornicating with his daughter. I may have had raging hormones, but self-preservation was my stronger instinct. Reluctantly I tore myself away to say goodnight, but it really took a lot of willpower. Sue gave me a warm, wet goodnight kiss and asked if she could see me again.

Hmmm, this might be a good idea, if we could find a discreet lust lair someplace far away from the Peninsula so I wouldn't risk good ol' Dad killing me for fooling around with his young daughter. I left the hotel feeling pretty good, thinking this relationship might have possibilities.

I went to an after-hours club for a nightcap and found my friend Norman in a booth. I told him about my American sweetie and my plan for the next night. My friend gave me heat for dating a sixteen-year-old and warned me to be careful. I didn't treat his words lightly.

The next evening I collected Sue and we took the short walk from the Peninsula to Jimmy's Kitchen, a popular gourmet restaurant. Since my friend was paying full fare, I thought a lights-out dinner was in order. We started with a drink - I had a gin and tonic and Sue had a Singapore Sling, complete with a paper umbrella. The menu offered quite a selection of fine dining. I thought a trendy Hong Kong establishment would be a good way to impress the sweet young thing, which could play to my advantage later.

Sue selected the specially prepared roast chicken and I decided on the pepper steak. When the waiter took our order he asked how I wanted my steak prepared and I replied with my usual, "Medium-rare."

Then Sue surprised both of us when she said, "I'll have mine medium-rare too."

The waiter looked at me and winked. It was obvious the young lass hadn't been to dinner in a fine restaurant too often, especially with a date. Asking for chicken to be prepared "medium-rare" was a first in my book.

As cute and hot as she was, I knew serious involvement wasn't going to happen. Hit by her comment, I was reminded how young and innocent this girl was and I knew I better be a good boy and not do anything stupid I would undoubtedly regret later.

Sue probably didn't even know the meaning of birth control and was quite possibly still a virgin, although I somewhat doubted that. We had another fun evening of dancing but didn't beat the bed and I took her straight home.

Later that evening I bumped into Norman and made the mistake of telling him about the humorous restaurant snafu.

I heard about "I lup you" and "medium-rare chicken" for years and years to come. Isn't that what friends are for?

CHAPTER FIFTEEN
"Doctor Robert"
JOHN LENNON AND PAUL MCCARTNEY

Over the years I became close friends with Robert Alvares, aka Mabel's penicillin date. Robert came into town with a bang! He was of Portuguese descent, but was born and raised in Hong Kong. He'd spent the previous few years in Vietnam where he made a small fortune, just how he made his money he was never willing to discuss. I had a suspicion Robert's business ventures weren't completely on the up and up.

Like most of the in-crowd, Robert was a keen bowler and drove a BMW modified for improved performance. With a noisy Abarth muffler, Robert had a distinctive calling card as he rolled the roads. His Beamer was no match for my Cooper S, but it was a decent set of wheels. Since we both liked bowling, fast cars, and spins with the gang in the New Territories, it was inevitable our paths would cross. Robert was several years older than I was and he treated me like a kid brother. He was generous and liked to buy his friends lunch and dinner followed by bowling, gambling or other vices. His wallet was always the first out of the pocket. After returning from Vietnam, Robert didn't work, but seemed to have an endless supply of money. I figured Robert must have made quite a killing in the war-torn country.

One night after bowling we went to a Chinese restaurant for noodles. It was late, almost two-thirty in the morning, but Robert urged Norman and me to go with him to an after-hours club owned by an American buddy he had befriended in 'Nam.

"Come on guys, it's my treat and besides, you'll enjoy meeting Trapper, he's a friend from another time in my life."

Norman and I thought this might be fun so off we went. After-hours clubs opened at two a.m. and were frequented by nightclub entertainers, night owls, and insomniacs. We got the royal red carpet treatment from Robert's friend Trapper and were invited to sit in the special plush arm-chair section of the club reserved for VIPs. Everybody else was scattered throughout the club in far less ornate seating. Robert leaned over and said to his old friend with a wink, "Why don't you call over your pretty girlfriends?"

Trapper smiled, looked around for his stash of girls and beckoned a couple women to join us. Two women in expensive cocktail dresses walked over and sat down on either side of Trapper. My first thought was they were call or ballroom girls, but they didn't look the type. Neither woman was Chinese, but one was drop-dead gorgeous. She was the spitting image of Raquel Welch and had a silky voice to match. She crossed her legs slowly and seductively and smiled at me. I had to catch my breath, she was that awesome.

My reaction was substantially different when I glanced at the second woman. She was very tall, well over six feet, but what really caught my attention was the breadth of her shoulders and her meaty muscular arms. One woman looked like Raquel's twin; the other looked like Charlton Heston in drag, but admittedly with a nice smile. I put two and two together and realized they were part of the female impersonator troupe from Australia performing at the Miramar, a Kowloon nightclub. *Whoops! Hands off this pair.*

We had a great time talking with the "girls" and they were extremely open about their sexuality and extensive cosmetic surgery. The pair considered themselves women born into male bodies. Raquel had completed her surgical procedures and was now 100 percent female and looked wonderful.

Heidi, the more masculine of the two, was fun and a real character. Heidi presented over-the-top feminine mannerisms, using humor to play her chosen role well. She confided she still had surgery to undergo "down below" and then laughingly pointed to colleagues from the nightclub act. They were seriously necking with guys at a nearby table.

"If only those guys knew, I wonder how they would react?" she mused. As I watched several Caucasian guys sucking tongue with the "girls," I wondered what would happen later that night when they discovered unmistakable male anatomy tucked in silk underwear. There could be two outcomes: instant throw-up or extreme anger. For the sake of the "girls," I hoped they could handle either outcome. We talked for hours and drinks warmed our conversation. Norman and I made nice friends that night, I thought. I was very comfortable talking with the manly women or womanly men, whatever. Little did I realize the embarrassment I would suffer later.

Two weeks passed since our evening at Trapper's place, and I was once again sitting with friends at The Scene trying to impress the women at our table. Suddenly in walks my "girlfriend" Heidi with her "date." Heidi can't be missed, six foot-two plus heels, lineman's shoulders, and an exaggerated, oh so exaggerated, feminine sway. Her baritone voice boomed across the disco floor, "Hi, Tony, how have you been? I've missed you." She growled her greeting while blowing me a kiss and giving a hearty wave.

Action in the disco stopped mid-stream as everybody turned to see who was catching this man/woman's blown kisses. Eyes rested on me. The Singapore Sling sitting on the table and my face were the same shade of magenta! I had a lot of 'splaining to do to the gang at the table that night, frantically trying to assure them I was not engaged in kinky sexual activities. I could tell from the skeptical looks around me that a couple of the guys weren't buying my story. *Oh, well!*

My friends and I became regulars at Trapper's place most weekends. Trapper turned out to be one of the most interesting people I'd ever met. He was another driver of fast cars and owned a green Lotus Elan, a hot set of wheels in those days. The Elan was an ultra-light sport convertible powered by a highly tuned 1600-cc overhead cam engine and truth be known, it was faster than my Cooper S.

He was another one of those guys from Vietnam who was loaded with money but nobody knew how he made his fortune. He had certainly done well because he had enough to buy an after-hours club, a fast car, and plenty of fast women. Trapper was a guy you suspect has a dark side and I knew to be wary in case his switch flipped.

I was killing time one night, alone with nothing to do. My friends had disappeared someplace so I dropped in Trapper's club for a nightcap. I ended up hanging around until the club closed, watching people do strange things in the early morning hours when several drinks filled their veins. I found it amusing to watch the Australian impersonators work the club and pick up unsuspecting "dates." Good-looking straight women circulated the club's parameters too. It was obvious which girls were "working women" setting themselves up for a little moneymaking at another location.

Sometime later I found out that my brother Steve and his co-conspirator/brother-in-arms buddy Hans Ebert had also met the boys from Oz. I had never seen Steve or Hans at Trapper's place but I knew that they were out there exploring Hong Kong's nightlife. They were two peas in a pod, rebels, musicians and high school was not in their list of priorities. They even went on to cut a record together in a band called "The Sons of Han."

As he closed the place, Trapper invited me to go for a late night/early morning spin in his Elan. Always one to enjoy fine cars and speed, I readily agreed. Within half an hour we were taking the hills around Kowloon Peak with the Elan's top down and thoroughly enjoying the deserted, twisting roads.

When we reached the summit, Trapper pulled the car over for a smoke. He offered me a cigarette but I told him I'd never taken up the habit. Looking over the city airport from Kowloon Peak in the early hours of the morning is one of the most beautiful sights you will ever see. We enjoyed the view and to break the silence, I asked a question.

"Hey, Trapper, how did you and Robert meet in Vietnam?" I was always curious about these two very different characters and wondered how they had hooked up. As it turned out, Trapper had quite a story.

"We had a scam in Saigon operating around the black market for U.S. currency. To keep too many American dollars from circulating in Vietnam, Military Payment Currency (MPC) had been introduced. The MPCs were equivalent to a dollar, but only the American military could convert them to actual U.S. greenbacks and only GIs could use them in the PX to purchase items.

"The result was MPCs were heavily discounted in the free market operating outside the base because they had limited purchasing power and could not be used as freely as cash.

"The scam involved convincing GIs to convert MPCs to U.S. dollars at par, and then use American dollars to buy larger quantities of heavily discounted MPCs on the black market. This process was repeated over and over with much money made, all of it illegal of course."

So now I knew how Trapper and Robert amassed their small fortunes. They had been in the business of recruiting young, naive GIs to help with their laundering scam.

"And how did the two of you become such close friends?" I continued. "It seems you have a special bond." Trapper smiled and nodded affirmatively.

He continued his story. While in Vietnam, he fell hook, line, and sinker for Asian women. He eventually hooked up with a crazy Vietnamese gal who was a real party girl. She took him to her bed and introduced him to all manner of pleasure and became important in his life. The problem was she introduced him to the particular pleasure of snorting heroin before sex.

As money started to flow into Trapper's pocket, the amount of heroin increased and pretty soon Trapper and his girlfriend were shooting needles. He was sinking into the abyss, becoming a recluse rarely leaving his darkened room.

Robert worried about his friend and tried to reach out to him. He knocked on Trapper's apartment door many times, but Trapper and his girlfriend were too far gone to answer. Robert wasn't sure they were actually in the room. Eventually Robert became very concerned and smashed down the front door of the apartment. Inside he found Trapper and the girl lying on the bed with needles haphazardly sticking out of their arms.

It didn't take Robert long to realize the girl was dead and his friend was barely alive, soon to join his girlfriend in Never-Never Land if something wasn't done fast. Rob grabbed his friend, took him to his home, and stayed by his side until he pulled through withdrawal, undoubtedly saving his life in the process.

After he recovered from this near-death experience, Trapper went cold turkey with Robert steadfastly at his side until he was free from the white powder's tentacles. This was so typical of Robert, a true humanitarian, yet with a criminal background. Trapper knew full well that if it wasn't for Robert, he wouldn't be here today so tremendous loyalty and friendship developed between the two rogues.

Trapper talked about other criminal activities he had been involved with in Vietnam, usually involving fraud and theft. Some theft involved heavy armament, most likely lifted from a military base. By this time I was pretty wide-eyed and wondered just what this guy hadn't done in Vietnam.

I had to ask one more question.

"Trapper, this is pretty interesting stuff and it leads me to wonder, what would you say was the 'baddest' thing you've ever done?"

Dawn was creeping over the horizon when he finally answered my question. He took a long drag from his cigarette and slowly o-ringed the smoke into the night sky. Shades of Casablanca filtered through my head. Trapper seemed to take forever to answer the question. Was there so much to catalog, or was he debating how much he should reveal?

Finally he turned, looked me in the eye and said coolly, "Well, Tony, let's put it this way. If someone convinced me there was no need for a certain person to be around any longer and there was enough money to make him disappear, I would give that proposition an awful lot of consideration."

I just about crapped in my pants! Trapper was telling me he would consider being a paid assassin and here I was alone with him on a deserted road in the Kowloon hills at dawn. Not that I thought he was going to whack me, I had no money and he had no reason to think I shouldn't be around. Still, it was a strange feeling to be sitting next to someone after this revelation. Trapper always seemed to be a real nice guy, but now I wondered what could make him snap and change his mind about our friendship. *Damn!* I had never met a potential assassin before. Truth be told, I was a pretty happy camper when he finished his smoke and we set back for the city. The ride back was quiet; neither of us too chatty at the time. We were getting tired and the sun was about to rise over the horizon. Then again, I was still shook up about what I had learned about Trapper's past and didn't feel much like forcing the conversation. He dropped me at my car parked outside his club and I jumped behind the wheel and headed for home. When I was once again safe in my own bed, I let out a big sigh.

Whew! That was interesting, but I don't think Trapper and I will grow our friendship much deeper.

Those were my thoughts as I nodded off to hours of restless dreams.

Robert, Jonathan, Norman and I became great friends, speeding around Kowloon in our souped-up cars, meeting lots of pretty girls, and eating at many of the great Chinese restaurants.

We met Peter, Jonathan's brother, and his wife Mandy after they moved back to Hong Kong from London. Peter and his brother enjoyed the benefits of having wealthy Chinese parents. Peter attended English public school (which is what Brits call their private schools) and then lived in England for a few years before marrying an attractive Irish girl who surprisingly spoke Cantonese fluently. I marveled at how this woman could come from an Irish Catholic background and live in a house with a family that included Jonathan and Peter's father, his number one wife, and rooms of concubines. What a culture clash!

Mandy gave Peter two beautiful children and was one of the sweetest women I'd ever met. But once Peter came back to Hong Kong he morphed into his dad and reverted to the supposition that one woman was not sufficient to meet his needs. In other words, Peter liked to play around. Like his brother Jonathan, Peter owned a Lotus Cortina but it was painted metallic silver. We frequently found him driving around town with a different girl sharing his snazzy wheels in the late hours of the night.

Peter was becoming more brazen with his debauchery as he showed up at the local haunts with a honey in plain view for all to see.

One evening, Jonathan, Norman, and I found Peter parked right outside the bowling alley with a pretty young Chinese thing sitting by his side. He proudly introduced us to his latest squeeze.

Right after, all hell broke loose. Mandy appeared from nowhere and furiously starting slamming her purse on the back of Peter's head. She called him every name in the book as Peter tried to protect himself.

The screaming, crying, and head bashing ended almost as quickly as it started. Mandy took off down Nathan Road, sobbing hysterically. As she ran away she yelled back at Peter telling him she was going to sleep with the first man she found.

Peter was embarrassed, but decided the smartest thing he could do was let his hot-tempered Irish wife cool off before explaining his actions. Peter laughed and said Mandy would get over it, and then drove off with his girlfriend.

Jonathan, Norman, and I felt awful. We really liked Mandy and worried about her, even though we didn't really believe she'd carry out her threat. We climbed into Jonathan's Lotus Cortina and combed the streets hoping we would find her. Finally we spotted her walking down a side road, eyes spilling tears as she walked blindly past the shops. Those on the sidewalk probably thought we were trying to pick her up. After all, three guys in a car trying to carry on a conversation with a pretty woman walking down the street as she completely ignored them was a classic scene.

We finally talked Mandy into the car. I was driving and Mandy sat next to me with Jonathan and Norman in the back. We drove the quiet roads of the New Territories and circled around for hours without saying a word. The entire time Mandy was curled up in the seat whimpering and crying like a hurt puppy. My heart really went out to her.

Finally she announced she was hungry enough to eat and noodles sounded like good idea. The closest noodle shop was one of our favorites in the village of Shatin and we made quick work of bowls of steaming thin noodles layered with shrimp. We all felt a little better after eating, especially Mandy.

The conversation picked up and we talked about mundane topics like the latest James Bond movie and the new nightclub opening in the Ocean Terminal. Mandy talked about her kids and their adventures in school. You could tell she loved them dearly.

We drove Mandy home and she hugged each of us, but it seemed my hug lasted a little longer as she nuzzled my throat. A tingle ripped down my spine, but I caught myself. *Don't be stupid! This is a dead-end street with danger lurking everywhere.*

Mandy and Peter settled their differences and life was soon back to normal, whatever that was. Peter still played around but his behavior wasn't as blatant. Often in the early hours of the morning we'd go to Peter's house to bring a close to the evening. We'd often play cards, usually blackjack. Stakes weren't high; we played for the company, fun, and conversation. Sometimes Mandy would play with us, occasionally in her nightgown. I realized I had developed a crush on this older, unavailable, married woman and I knew she was sending me subtle signs, and some not so subtle signs, like brushing her breasts against my shoulder. My crush never went away, but I congratulated myself on being smart enough to know getting involved with a married woman, especially the wife of a friend's brother, (undeserving as he was), would not be my best move. I had a strong suspicion if I had ever made a move on this lady, something would ignite between us. In the end there was nothing to tell. I think I did the right thing.

A few months later Robert told us Trapper had disappeared. Like Robert, Trapper was not one to put his money into a savings account. Apparently he'd spent his 'Nam stash and decided to go back and replenish the supply. I suppose Trapper didn't have many "honest" work options since he didn't have marketable skills that I knew of. He was damn lucky to get away with what he did the first time around, and testing his luck again wouldn't be the smartest thing to do.

When guys returned from Vietnam, Robert would try to get news about his old buddy. Rumor had it he was last seen heading down the Mekong River with a boatload of contraband just before the Tet Offensive. None of us ever heard from Trapper again and we could only assume this time his luck had run out.

While it was sad to hear of Trapper's misfortune, what became of Robert was even more heartbreaking. I was much closer to him and felt Robert could have been my big brother. Eventually and inevitably Robert had also blown his wad of bills. All he did was spend money, usually on his friends. He never thought about investing or saving a cache for a rainy day.

Unlike Trapper, Robert was smart enough not to take the chance of a second run in Vietnam. But like Trapper, Robert had few skills he could fall back on. Robert decided to test his luck against the law.

In Hong Kong there was a lot you could get away with, and God knows the police were known to pocket a bribe or two to keep their eyes focused away from any action. But there were two things you just didn't mess with – running guns and selling drugs. Either offense brought harsh consequences. Robert never told us of his plans; if he had, I think we would have been able to talk him out of putting them into action.

Unknown to us, Robert foolishly decided to take a shot at smuggling marijuana into Hong Kong to supply the U.S. armed forces enjoying R&R leave in the Colony. Marijuana was not harvested in Hong Kong and had to be smuggled in from Bangkok. None of my friends smoked the stuff so I had very little knowledge about the distribution chain.

One morning I opened the paper to read Robert had been caught on a junk in the harbor with a cargo of grass. Sentencing came fast and after spending time in the Stanley jail, Robert was deported to Macau because he held a Portuguese passport.

Exiled from Hong Kong, Robert had to leave his wife and child and was dead broke. I saw him several years later when I visited Macau with Norman for a short gambling excursion. He was a shell of his former self, had little money, and no steady work.

Robert had a big, big heart and had been good to Norman and me for many years so we tried to help him as much as we could. After the fast life of nightclubs, restaurants, girls, and BMWs, Robert's new life-style in sleepy Macau was vastly different. He had no money to gamble or wine and dine. His favorite pastime became piecing jigsaw puzzles together. For years Norman and I sent him puzzles with cash tucked in the box. Ironic that someone with such a checkered past would grow to enjoy something as mundane as a jigsaw puzzle.

Eventually we lost contact with Robert, but wherever he is today, I hope he is well. He was always a very kind friend to me and I loved him dearly.

CHAPTER SIXTEEN
"Tomorrow Never Knows"

JOHN LENNON AND PAUL McCARTNEY

Jhad been back from Australia for fifteen months. While I was having a great social life, my business life was not challenging. I was still working in junior clerical capacity, making very little money with my prospects dim and fading. Managers I had befriended at Esso told me I was wasting my time doing menial work and encouraged me to return to college and earn a degree.

My original thought of moving from "office boy to president" was starting to look unrealistic so I began investigating the possibility of enrolling at the University of Hong Kong. As desperate as I was for a change in career, the thought of studying in Hong Kong was not appealing and I had continuing doubts about the value of such a degree. I also investigated several Canadian universities, but couldn't warm up to the idea of going to another country I knew very little about, only knowing I would freeze my ass off come winter.

Uncle Joe flew into town from the Philippines and phoned me from his room at the Peninsula Hotel. Uncle Joe was the guy I had to thank for getting me a Hong Kong driver's license. I was able to transfer my Manila license for a Hong Kong document with little wait and no red tape. Joe was a real character; he always had a deal in the works and would have been a great candidate for the Mafia. Joe looked the part of a Mafioso with his dark Spanish features. Steve and I really liked our uncle, and not just because he was generous and fun to be around.

When a deal was hot, Joe would blow into town and give my brother and me a couple hundred dollars or a valuable gift. Once he gave us solid gold bracelets with our names engraved on them. The hefty, thick-linked chain ID bracelets were popular with guys at the time, but most were made of silver. Uncle Joe knew how to do things right!

Joe's call summoned me to his hotel right away. I was hoping to get a nice surprise, perhaps extra cash. I wasn't expecting what happened once the hotel door closed. Joe lit into me with an unexpected tongue lashing.

"What's the matter with you, Tony? You're wasting your time working in the mail room of Esso, You gotta get out of there and make something of yourself. You're too smart to be stuck in a place like that; you have to get a higher education. I'll fix it so you can go back to college."

I listened in shock. This lecture was coming out of left field and totally unexpected. Joe had never been to college and I was surprised at the value he was placing on higher education.

"Uncle Joe, I tried University and I screwed it up. I've been thinking of going to the University of Hong Kong, but honestly, I can't get too excited about the idea. Tell me what you are thinking?" I hesitantly questioned.

"My friend's son went to Santa Clara University in California and I'm sure we can get you accepted there. It's a good Jesuit University, you're a smart kid, and a Catholic so it's a good fit. I'll make a donation to God and the Jesuits will smile and accept you.

"Tony, you know you're wasting your time in Hong Kong and I'm disappointed to see you like this. You have to go!"

I knew my surprisingly caring uncle was right. I *was* wasting my time. The more I thought about Uncle Joe's suggestion, the more exciting it seemed. My immediate concern was I would have to face my parents because I certainly could not go to college without their financial help. I knew I was in a rut and the thought of going to California loomed attractive. Hey, the number one song on the hit parade was Scott McKenzie's

"If You're Going to San Francisco, Wear Flowers in Your Hair." Hippies, California girls, sunshine - this was sounding better and better!

"What do I have to do? Where do I sign up?"

All I had to do was manage a decent score on the SAT exam and Uncle Joe would do the rest. It was a lock according to him, and he had never let me down before so I had utmost faith his proposal was entirely possible.

As I walked out of the Peninsula, I thought about our impromptu meeting and how the least likely of my relatives had pushed so hard to help me. Still, he was absolutely right. I was at the point I was no longer winning in my life and I needed new tools and an attitude adjustment to make the next step.

But, the next step was a big one. I had to approach my parents and this was done with much trepidation. That evening I asked Mum and Dad if I could have a few minutes to talk with them about my future. As always, they were very willing. I think I surprised them with my request for an audience. Maybe they thought I had bad news to share, like getting a girl in trouble. They were probably as nervous as I was.

Mum and Dad had been patient with me; they never chided me for my failure in Australia and continued to be supportive and understanding. But this was something different. California would be more expensive than my jaunt to Australia. My parents were earning local Hong Kong dollars and this venture would make a big hit in the family pocketbook. As I explained my plan, I could tell they were warming up to the idea. My parents knew I was going nowhere fast, but still believed in their dream that one of their children would be the first in the family to get a university degree.

Dad finally questioned, "Are you really serious? We can't afford to keep sending you away." This was the first time my dad verbalized disappointment at my Australian expedition and I felt a shot of embarrassment. No, not just embarrassment, I felt like crap.

"Dad, I promise you I won't let you down this time. I'll work hard and I will be successful, I promise that." My commitment to them was all they needed to hear, and I knew this was a promise I would absolutely see through to the end.

They agreed to let me take the SAT and apply to Santa Clara. Hugs followed the decision. I was so grateful to Mum and Dad, they had come through for me again and I swore they would never, ever regret their decision to give me another chance. This was a promise I would keep no matter what.

I had not studied in over a year so preparing for the SAT was a challenge. I hit the books hard and took practice tests with a vengeance. Unlike the last time I sat exams in Australia, I had to score well.

The day came. I sat the two parts of the SAT, did fairly well, and combined with my GCE A level high school performance, along with help from Uncle Joe, I soon received acceptance from the University of Santa Clara.

Travel documents weren't really a problem this go-around. I had to obtain a student visa to enter the United States and that was an eye-opening experience. American foreign consulates have to be the busiest places on earth since so many people abroad want to enter the land of milk and honey. After hours of waiting and filling out forms, I finally said goodbye to the madhouse. My visa soon arrived in the mail and there was nothing left to do but wait for the day of departure. During the interview and student visa processes I was once again reminded how worthless a Hong Kong British passport could be.

The summer of '68 passed quickly and before I knew it I was once again at Kai Tak airport saying goodbye to my family. This time my heart was light since my family was healthy, happy, and thrilled I was heading to capture a university degree. Still, I was sad to leave my family and the hugs we exchanged had to last a long time.

I asked Steve to watch out for our parents while I was gone. With his blond Afro, dark Roger McGuinn glasses, and ragged jeans, Steve assured me he would make sure everything stayed fine at home. As I walked to the big 747, a dark thought struck me. In the crazy world of rock music, who would look out for Steve while I was gone?

A chill of trepidation enveloped me, but soon the excitement of my adventure extinguished any worries. For the second time I was leaving Hong Kong for college in a foreign country. What would be waiting for me? Would I endure freshman hazing I found at St. George's? Would I enjoy living in California? Would I miss Hong Kong? Would I win, or would I lose?

Hey, the girl sitting next to me is kinda cute, I wonder…

Epilogue

I went to university in California with a more mature approach than I took with me to Perth. Most importantly, I made a promise to do well in my studies given this second chance. I enjoyed some of the best fun-filled years of my life in my chosen American university and still earned scholastic honors that led to a graduate degree from a top West Coast institution. I re-kindled my love for soccer and co-captained the college team in my senior year, establishing goal scoring records along the way. This led to playing semi-pro soccer for two years.

I became a nomad with a career that took my family on moves to Canada, England, California, New Jersey, Georgia, California and finally to the mountains of North Georgia where my wife and I built our dream house. I am happily retired and focus my competitive nature on golf, pool, and poker. In my spare time I am working on a novel about the pharmaceutical industry in which I spent over 30 years. This Eurasian kid even managed to become the president of a drug company. I'm still married to the same pretty girl who gave me the two best children a father could ever ask for.

Sad to say, many of the people I spoke of in my book are no longer with us. Dad died of a second coronary while I was a junior in college. Soon afterward, Steve died too young from an unfortunate, accidental combination of alcohol and barbiturates. I lost Norman to blood cancer; this was like losing a second brother. Les Harvey was the sad victim of early onset Alzheimer's. I've kept in touch with many of the friends

I grew up with in Hong Kong through the Internet and the occasional reunion. Mum and I have grieved our losses, but we have also been blessed with very special lives shared with many special people.

One other motivating factor for writing this book was a diagnosis I received, that of Parkinson's disease. I am managing well aided by pharmaceuticals and exercise, but the specter of a chronic, progressive disease is always there. Every day is important for me to live to the fullest and to document and celebrate the wonderful life which has blessed me.

How many yo-yo champions do you know?

Hongkong Bottlers

FEDERAL INC. U.S.A.
N.K.M.L.& BUILDING NO. 8
LAICHTKOK, HONG KONG.
(THE LIABILITY OF THE MEMBERS OF THE COMPANY IS LIMITED)

Authorized Bottler of Coca-Cola

MAILING ADDRESS
P. O. BOX 1.
CABLE ADDRESS
"REFRESHMENT"
TELEPHONE
71851

香港汽水廠
美國註冊有限公司

IN REPLYING PLEASE REFER TO

25th July, 1960

No. 2848

Master Anthony Tebbutt,
5 St. George Mansion,
141 Argyle Street,
KOWLOON.

Dear Master Tebbutt,

We are writing to congratulate you on winning 1st position in the Yo-Yo Championship of Hong Kong and to confirm that this means you have won a Scholarship Grant from us to the value of HK$7,500.00.

Would you be good enough to write and give us your Father's full name, address and occupation so that we can have legal documents drawn up appointing your Father as trustee of the amount you have won.

Yours sincerely,

Hongkong Bottlers Federal Inc. U.S.A.

Peter W. D. Fairbairs,
Assistant General-Manager

PWDF/JAB
c.c. Education Dept.

Yo-Yo competition award letter from Coca-Cola

Final Of Yo-Yo Contest

The final of the Yo-Yo contest, sponsored by Hongkong Bottlers, Inc., was held yesterday at Princess Theatre. Twenty-seven boys took part. Picture shows Anthony Tebbutt (centre), who won the contest and a $7,500 scholarship grant. Second and third were Choi Bor-yee (left), who won a scholarship grant of $5,000 and Americo Diogo, the Macao champion, who was awarded a scholarship grant of $2,500.—(Staff Photographer).

South China Morning Post announces my 1st Position win

Mum and Dad, simply the best.

KGV Friends L-R Me, Frank Drake, Alex Wernberg, David DeVelder, Les Harvey

KGV Friends L-R, Nand Wadhwani, Jose Barros, Me, Norman Hope,
Ramesh Assomull, Kip Kirpalani at a party

A canon well placed to protect Boulder Lodge

The Hon. Sir Michael Kadoorie's Lamborghini Muira P400

My brother Steve, always the best on the drums

Manila Cola advertisement starring yours truly

My BSA Thunderbolt Lightning 650cc – what a ride!

A sad ferry ride across the Hong Kong harbor after visiting Dad in the hospital

Roo hunting in Esperance, Australia

My first Mini-Cooper

Fastest Mini-Cooper S in Hong Kong

Made in the USA
Charleston, SC
02 April 2014